Greenhill Books

'A FACE LIKE A CHICKEN'S BACKSIDE'

If sweat be the price of captaincy,
Lord God, we ha' paid in full!

With apologies to Rudyard Kipling

And should you ask, where do they live
These men with skill superlative
Who showed superb initiative
Enhanced their name, achieved success
And gave the 'baddies' no redress?
— The Jungle is their home address.

Anon.

To sing by a hill river,
To work in the dark.

Nepalese proverb

My clothes get wet as I wear them,
They dry on me as I wear them:
That is why I grow old so quickly

Gurkha soldiers' saying

'A FACE LIKE A CHICKEN'S BACKSIDE'

An Unconventional Soldier in South East Asia, 1948–1971

J. P. CROSS

GREENHILL BOOKS, LONDON
STACKPOLE BOOKS, PENNSYLVANIA

Greenhill Books

'A Face Like A Chicken's Backside'
First published 1996 by Greenhill Books, Lionel Leventhal Limited,
Park House, 1 Russell Gardens, London NW11 9NN
and
Stackpole Books, 5067 Ritter Road, Mechanicsburg, PA 17055, USA

British Library Cataloguing in Publication Data
Cross, J.P. (John P.), 1925–
A face like a chicken's backside: an unconventional soldier in
south east Asia, 1948–1971
1. Cross, J.P. (John P.), 1925–   2. Commando troops – Great Britain –
Biography   3. Jungle warfare
I. Title
356.1′67′092
ISBN 1–85367–239–4

Library of Congress Cataloging-in-Publication Data
Cross, J.P.
A face like a chicken's backside: an unconventional soldier in
South East Asia, 1948–1971/by J.P. Cross
240 pp.   24 cm.
Includes index.
ISBN 1–85367–239–4
1. Asia, Southeastern—History, Military.   2. Asia, Southeastern—History—
1945–   3. Counterinsurgency—Asia, Southeastern.   4. Cross, J.P.   I. Title.
DS526.7.C76   1996
959.05′3—dc 20   95-51990
                                                  CIP

Typeset by DP Photosetting, Aylesbury, Bucks
Printed and bound in Great Britain
by Bookcraft (Bath) Limited, Midsomer Norton

Contents

List of Illustrations

List of Maps

List of Abbreviations

ANZUK	Australia, New Zealand, United Kingdom Brigade
ARVN	Army of the Republic of [South] Vietnam
CINCPAC	Commander-in-Chief Pacific [US]
CJWC	Commonwealth Jungle Warfare Centre
CRW	Communist Revolutionary Warfare
DOBOPS	Director of (Borneo) Operations
FARELF	Far East Land Force
FCO	Foreign and Commonwealth Office [UK]
GR	Gurkha Rifles
HBMG	Her Britannic Majesty's Government
IGP	Inspector General, Royal Malayan/Malaysia Police
JCLO	Junior Civil Liaison Officer
JUSMAG	Joint United States Military Assistance Group
JWS	Jungle Warfare School
POLAD	Political Adviser
RBMR	Royal Brunei Malay Regiment
REME	Royal Electrical and Mechanical Engineers
RPKAD	Indonesian Para Commandos
SAS	Special Air Service Regiment
SEATO	South East Asia Treaty Organisation
SEP	Surrendered Enemy Personnel
STAP	Services Training Assistance Programme

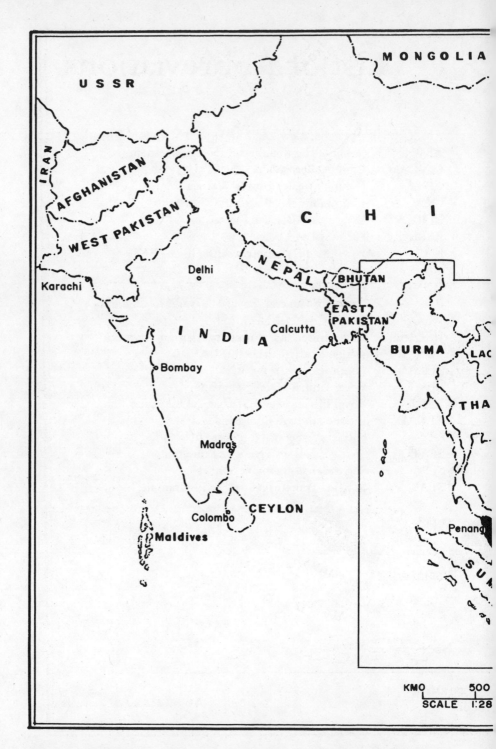

MAP 1: **MALAYSIA**. The boxed area shows the limit of the South East
Asian rain forest terrain.

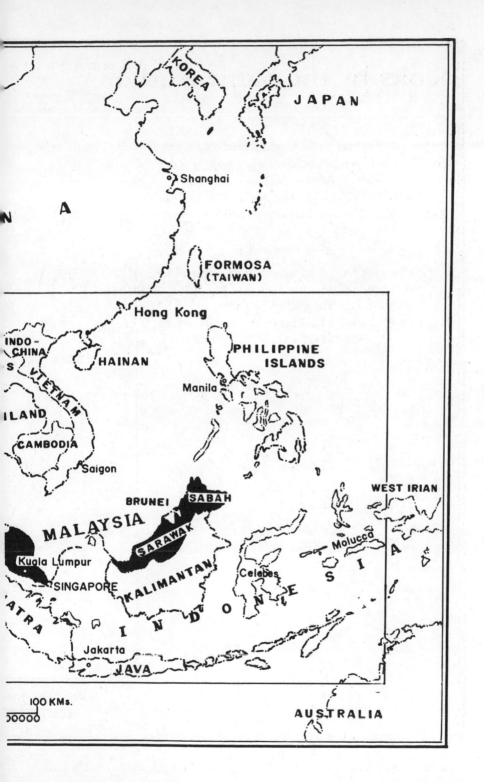

KOREA

JAPAN

Shanghai

FORMOSA
(TAIWAN)

Hong Kong

INDO-
CHINA

HAINAN

PHILIPPINE
ISLANDS

Manila

VIETNAM

ILAND

CAMBODIA

Saigon

WEST IRIAN

BRUNEI

SABAH

MALAYSIA

SARAWAK

Molucca

Kuala Lumpur

KALIMANTAN

Celebes

SINGAPORE

I N D O N E S I A

ATRA

Jakarta

JAVA

100 KMs.

00000

AUSTRALIA

Books by the Same Author

English for Gurkha Soldiers
Gurkha – The Legendary Soldier *(photographs by Robin Adshead)*
Gurkhas *(photographs by Sandro Tucci)*
In Gurkha Company: The British Army Gurkhas
Jungle Warfare: Experiences and Encounters

Autobiography

First In, Last Out: An Unconventional British Officer
in Indo-China (1945–46 and 1972–76)
The Call of Nepal
'A Face Like A Chicken's Backside': An Unconventional Soldier in
South-East Asia, 1948–1971

Part One

MALAYA, 1948–56
Gurkhas and Guerrillas

CHAPTER 1

In Gurkha Company
1948–54

Corporal Balbahadur Rai, a veteran with three bravery awards from the Burma war and Malayan Emergency of the 1950s, lay dying in his mountain village in Nepal. I found him on a hard wooden frame in the porch of his small house, 5000 feet up in the foothills of the Himalayas, a week's walk from the Kathmandu road. His face was puffy, his breathing laboured and, when I unexpectedly called in to see him the day after the severe earthquake of 21 August 1988, he only managed to sit up by clutching at a stool put between his legs by his wife.

We had not met for thirty-five years since we had been together in A Company, 1/7 Gurkha Rifles (GR), operating in the jungles of Malaya – I commanding the company and he the section. 'Saheb,' he wheezed at me after he had recovered from his surprise, 'never did I think we would meet again or that you'd come and see me. This is wonderful.' He looked at me steadfastly and said, 'I do not have long to live but, from today, because you have bothered to come and meet me, I can now die happily.' He paused, looked pensive, then, shaking his head as he recalled the distant past, said, 'Looking back on my life, the happiest times were when you and I were in the jungle together. We showed them, didn't we?'

He broke off, eyes moist but whether from coughing or nostalgia I could not tell. He did not complain about his illness but spoke about his impending death with the usual stolid indifference of a Nepalese hill farmer, never far from the destructive whims of nature.

He looked hard at me. 'You don't look much different from when we first met forty years ago. I keep my ears open for news of you. I heard you had stayed on in Nepal after leaving the army, working at the university. What brings you here?'

I told him I was passing by and thought I'd drop in on him. I did not say that meant three days' hard walking off my route. He bade me sit beside him and, after a few minutes, I started to talk about some of our earlier exploits together in the jungle, so many years before. That, in turn, set him talking and chuckling with glee as he recalled those days. He grew visibly stronger. He picked up a sickle and, twisting it in his hands as he remembered contacts and clashes with the guerrillas, his voice strengthened, his eyes sparkled and, transformed by the

15

magic of memory, I listened to him, encouraging him and prompting him when necessary, while his wife gazed on him open-eyed with wonder.

An hour later he came back to the present. He slumped back, exhausted.

With death so near, he saw it as his duty to sum me up, which he did with sincerity, clarity and deep conviction in familiar terms, as an elder brother would his younger. 'You know your greatest mistake?' I kept quiet. 'It was that you never cared what your superiors, your own countrymen, thought of you. You never toadied to them to steal their minds for your own enhancement, nor did you change the course of your ways if it were to be to our disadvantage. They knew that you loved us as you loved the jungle, that you would do for us what you would not do for them. It was your own people who stopped you from going much higher in the army as you should have done. That was your own mistake.'

A rude man would have said I was unconventional, if not eccentric!

*   *   *

Balbahadur was referring to the Malayan Emergency and the eleven-year struggle against the guerrillas of the Malayan Communist Party. Much of it took place in dense tropical jungle and we had to learn how to live in it, move through it and fight in it. Living was how to make oneself as comfortable and keep as healthy and alert as circumstances allowed without prejudicing security, surprise or secrecy — making an overnight camp, cooking, sleeping, remaining healthy, keeping weapons spick-and-span, staying alert, all as silently and surreptitiously as possible. Moving was more than leaving as few traces as possible, although, for the hunted, a single trace could mean life or death, whereas for the hunter, it might only mean a missed contact. Moving entailed formations, crossing obstacles, reading a map and compass, not getting lost, not losing contact with the man in front or behind and always being ready to fight. Fighting involved every hostile and protective act from ambushing, patrolling and assaulting a camp to avoiding an enemy ambush, defending one's own camp and performing sentry duty.

From the air the jungle looks like a sea of cabbages and a novice might be forgiven for thinking that underneath it is impenetrable. It is not. Under the treetop canopy nature jostles to find a space to catch the sun's rays, producing a litany of sounds and a library of sights. Myriads of insects help to propagate new growth as well as slowly, slowly working to eradicate the old. Damp soil and a mulch of fallen leaves cushion noise but retain tracks for those who know how to read them. Birds and animals are heard rather than seen. Navigation is a skill that anyone can learn: map, compass and a retentive memory, along with a cool head, are the main requisites. The direction of stream flow, a rise or fall in contours, are normally the only aids in featureless terrain. A Sherlock Holmes-type of reasoning is needed when lost: 'If I can't be in those two, or three, places

MAP 2: **MALAYA**. Scene of the Emergency in the 1950s, the only campaign where the Communists were defeated on land of their own choosing.

then, however improbable it seems, I must be here,' with a dubious prod of a finger on the map. But the depth of a stream, the thickness of bush, the flight of the birds, the age of a track and many other signs are always there to be read like a book by the initiated and turned to advantage when, to others with senses deadened and mind dulled by a depressing and endless similarity, the jungle imposes itself as an environment which cannot be mastered. Spencer Chapman has said that the jungle is neutral: indeed so, but it is an armed neutrality that can never be taken for granted.

Tactical movement through the jungle is normally restricted to about a thousand yards an hour, while in swamp it can be as little as a hundred. Under the canopy of tall trees visibility is also heavily restricted, often being no more than a few yards in any one direction, so the ears take over from the eyes. Jungle fighting assumes the characteristics of night work.

The lower lying the area, the nastier it is. Swamp, and particularly when bombed, is the worst. There a hundred yards' progress an hour is good going. Also, the lower the ground, the hotter, sweatier, damper and more insect-worried does a man become. The converse is true: above 1000 feet the stream water is cool and sweet, a crisper air restores vitality and sometimes, through a break in the trees, a distant view delights. But always there is a load to be carried, a weapon ready to be fired and an enemy who may be quicker than you – 'There are only two sorts of gunmen – the quick and the dead'. This is when high morale is of paramount importance. I define this as 'giving of one's best when the spectators are of the fewest'. In other words, it is the soldier's determination 'to go those last few yards' when he finds himself tired, cold, hungry, frightened, lonely, possibly outnumbered, perhaps wounded and far from base.

Those whose task it was to operate in the jungle knew what it meant to be afraid, exhausted, wet through, freezing, hungry and lost. They knew the effects of sweat and thirst, aching limbs, a heavy pack and chafing equipment, taut nerves and a fleeting enemy. They knew success sometimes, failure often, effort ever: and they were on familiar terms with the all-pervading, close-horizoned, never-ending green of trees, bushes, shrubs, swamps, grasses, creepers and yet more trees which surrounded them as they endeavoured to dominate the jungle – a major undertaking that so often lacked any visible result. In addition, leeches, mosquitoes, hairy caterpillars, ticks, wasps, hornets, along with the occasional scorpion and snake, all added to the hazards, not to mention misery, which induced an enervating and body-racking weariness.

Victory over Japan brought little peace or stability to many parts of Asia. The inability of the colonial powers to defend what they had looked on as theirs, and the turbulence, disruptions and depravities of war, had stirred up a new political atmosphere in the whole region. The Japanese had shown that Asians were more than a match for Europeans; Asian nationalists and communists took full advantage of the new situation. Malaya was no exception.

The first post-war government in Britain, facing enormous problems at home, had little interest in sustaining an empire. Disengagement in Asia began with cataclysmic events in the Indian subcontinent that resulted in the jewel in the crown of the British Empire being fragmented and handed over to two sets of home-grown masters. I fretted that this would spell the end of soldiering but, to the surprise and delight of many, and the annoyance of some, the British Army's Gurkhas – soldiers from a non-Commonwealth, mountainous, Third World country who habitually produce results out of proportion to their numbers – were sent, in the nick of time, to save Malaya in a war of entirely new dimensions: Communist Revolutionary Warfare (CRW), mainly in the jungle. It was still tying down some security forces over thirty years later.

Had the Gurkhas who were sent to Malaya on joining the British Army on 1 January 1948 not been there at that critical moment when trouble broke out, it would have taken far longer than it did to have beaten the communists. It is even possible that they would have won. Lucky for us that the guerrillas were as inexperienced as were we!

*　　*　　*

Broadly speaking, CRW is fought in three stages. The first is the Passive Phase: penetration of such organisations as trades union movements, local governments, student unions and touring repertory companies. Police, not the army, have to be on the alert. In post-war Malaya this stage lasted for twelve years. Previously, during the 1930s, the main form of action was the attempted disruption of the two major industries of rubber and tin.

The Chinese communist guerrillas who had sided with the Allies for the war years started the second phase of their struggle, the Active Phase, in June 1948. This entailed small-scale military actions, coercion, intimidation, acts of banditry and sabotage. The response involved soldiers, often in conjunction with the police. The security forces proved insufficient to wrest the initiative from the guerrillas, let alone protect civilians.

This Active Phase was aimed at extending communist influence to a degree that more and more swathes of territory became 'liberated zones' in which the government lost its influence except when it sent in large numbers of troops. As these zones were increased in size and number, so the third phase of CRW, the Counter-Offensive Phase, would emerge. This envisaged the communists using regular troops rather than guerrillas to topple the government and take over responsibility of running the country. Under such a scheme, people had to be won over before territory was taken. This was the opposite of conventional operations in the Second World War when, initially, territory was captured and then, willy-nilly, the population was governed by the new rulers – or handed back to the old ones, as in Burma in 1945. Sadly, it took a long time, first for British, then for Malayan, rulers to grasp the difference – fundamental and vital for ultimate victory.

This third phase never occurred in Malaya; the second phase, conducted as an Emergency from 1948 to 1960, revealed not only that the communists over-estimated themselves, but also that their political base was never as strong as that of the government. The main communist political plank was removed when Britain promised Malaya its independence. Thus they failed in their objective and the movement petered out.

What was a 'cause' for the guerrillas was 'just another job' or 'regimental pride' for the security forces. The overwhelming power of the one against the comparative impotence of the other is shown in the maximum strengths of the Emergency: 40,000 regular troops with aircraft, artillery and naval craft, 70,000 police and 25,000 Home Guards, against 8000 guerrillas.

Only the British, in Malaya, were successful in imposing a military and political defeat on Asian communists in terrain of the latter's choosing, even though it took all of eleven years. The twofold strategy was offensively to dominate the jungle and defensively to keep the civilian population on the side of the government in order to neutralise the guerrillas' potential – always much easier said than done.

In addition to that ever essential commodity – luck – information was of cardinal and constant importance. Chance contacts were rare and fleeting, nor were they ever enough to neutralise the guerrillas, much less eliminate them. Something else was needed.

In conventional war the military pundits see a three-to-one superiority as essential for success. How was it then, that even with the overriding numerical superiority in numbers, it took so long to win in Malaya? The same question can be asked, in quite another setting, of police and criminals: a minority with the initiative has many advantages over the majority that so often merely reacts to that initiative.

Apart from always adhering to proven operating techniques, laced with jungle lore, the one tactic we practised assiduously but seldom achieved was to surround an occupied enemy camp in the jungle and then to eliminate, by kill or capture, its inmates. Capture was preferable – dead men don't talk. An alternative to surrounding guerrillas in their camp was eliminating them by ambush. Alas, the success rate of this play was equally elusive. Chance encounters did, nevertheless, result in a steady but often unspectacular erosion of guerrilla strengths.

To coordinate all security force efforts, joint military, police and civilian committees were formed. These were variously responsible for overseeing, promulgating and regulating other ploys to help defeat the guerrillas. They included such measures as resettling outlying Chinese families without title to their dwellings; moving the 'squatters' into New Villages (the Briggs Plan); and imposing food denial and curfews. Meanwhile Special Branch played its own clandestine, sometimes clever, sometimes clumsy, game behind the scenes.

Rifle companies, too, worked within the framework of joint plans in their own designated areas. These 'Framework Operations' were our staple.

*   *   *

By mid-1948, when this story starts, I had been in the army five years. I was twenty-three. I had already trained, served and campaigned with Gurkhas in India in 1944, in Burma in 1945 and then in Cochin-China, before returning to India – for more action on the North-West Frontier prior to the horrors of partition – again on to Burma, and finally joining the British Army Gurkhas in Malaya. I found that I had a strong empathy with these men from the mountains of Nepal.* Apart from an obvious love of serving with them, I had absorbed sufficient of their skills and tenacity to be branded even then as an eccentric by my British lords and masters. They never quite knew how to treat me, unlike Asians who, regarding eccentricity as an inner strength, found it no problem. Yet although I was not an easy person to fit into the modern army as far as promotion and postings were concerned, I was nevertheless given opportunities to work under circumstances always demanding, often positive and sometimes rewarding, alongside many fascinating people.

As the years rolled by I found myself drawn, irresistibly, unwittingly and unpredictably, almost always with Gurkhas, into jungle situations, as an operator and a trainer against an Asian enemy. Later, maturer and more wily, I was a defence attaché, still in Asia. By the time I realised that I was painting myself into an Asian corner, I had long passed the crossroads of destiny that fortune so often hides from our gaze, and the idea of even trying to retrace my steps never entered my head. The British Army which, like the Royal Academy, requires conformity in her children, and where any hint of originality still has to be stereotyped, had by then recognised I had my uses even if I was eccentric. Eventually, strangely and against all the laws of averages, it allowed me to have very nearly thirty-eight years' unbroken service in Asia, ten of them in the jungle.

Having opted out of the military 'rat race' and undertaken tasks which, albeit important, did not count towards high-ranking enhancement, I was in a strong position to do what my military instincts told me were right, without worrying too much about any future stigma, whereas others, with stars in the eyes but not yet in their rank, preferred to shy away, taking refuge in platitudes, prevarication or the purely pedestrian.

Although I sometimes felt the pull of my native England – four seasons, a

---

* For a full account see my *In Gurkha Company*, Arms and Armour Press, 1986.

pastel-shaded countryside, drinkable tap water, the supposed fulfilment of married life (fireside, slippers and a growing family) I still experienced the stronger urge to go a little farther, to stay put a little longer, to learn a few more words in yet another language, to answer another challenge. Consequently I found myself still in Asia with Gurkhas in 1982, at the end of my army service.

Over the years personalities have often played too big a part for comfort or even success. I found myself in situations unfamiliar to my mentors (or tormentors), for which their remedies were as inapposite as their experience was limited. This some of them seemed to resent, so it seemed better I kept silent until the principal actors were off the stage. They are now all dead or have been 'put out to grass'. Certain of them, probably rightly, regarded me as 'knocking the nail out of sight' and were disruptive in their attitudes; others, bless them, accepted me as they found me, trusted me and even liked me – without them and without the support of the Gurkhas and what they taught me, I could never have done what I did.

My Gurkhas fitted into the scheme of things as we tackled the problems of operating in the tropical rain-forest jungle of South-east Asia, seldom with a set 'school solution' and more often than not defying the views of those who, because they were senior, thought they knew better. It is not a heroic tale, but the incidents related, although seldom meriting inclusion in regimental history, and often going unreported, are a true record of endeavours at ground level. In other words, the antithesis of normal military history, one definition of which is 'bullshit and quick-drying ink'.

*   *   *

Until 1952 there was little or no direction from the top. In 1948 the senior general promised that the Emergency would be over by Christmas. 'What do you do when you get a report of guerrillas from the planting community?' he was asked. His answer was, 'Take off the last nought then decide.' Before I went on my overdue home leave I 'thrashed around' in the jungle for a month or so, as did many others. I remember how ill-equipped we were: we carried our water in bamboo containers; we were ordered to shoot rubber-estate dogs to prevent them from barking a warning of our presence; we had neither canvas jungle boots nor waterproof capes, so we slept on and under leaves; our 'wireless sets' were so heavy we had to carry them on stretchers; and on one occasion the police ordered me out on a job to contact guerrillas, then wanted me arraigned for murder when we killed one.

Even our jungle lore was rudimentary. I scared away some guerrillas by making cuckoo noises with my hands to keep in touch with a group of soldiers to my flank – there are no cuckoos in Malaya!

When I returned from leave in 1949 I was appointed chief instructor of the

Gurkha education school and did not get back to the jungle until late 1951. By then conditions had improved immeasurably, and the standard of soldiering was also very much higher. Guerrilla policy was intimidation – buses burned, rubber trees slashed, suspected informers assassinated – and disruption of the rubber production that was so essential for the country's economy. Soldiers were tied down by having to escort and guard the rubber tappers from harassment as they worked their way around the estates. Only occasionally did we get accurate forewarning of a guerrilla presence. One example was in early 1952, when we were led by the tapper himself to within a few yards of a 'red cell' lying up in a remote rubber estate. All were eliminated. By that time there had been a change at the top. General Sir Gerald Templer was High Commissioner and Director of Operations. He introduced an analysis of every occasion that troops went on an operation. One of the questions on the Form ZZ that we had to fill in was, 'Could you have done [it] any better?' This time I boastfully wrote, 'No'.

From then on the initiative slowly turned in our favour.

*   *   *

While on home leave in 1953 I became engaged to Jane who agreed to marry me in Malaya in March 1954. On my return to the battalion I was again given command of A Company and spent most of the next three years in the jungle on operations against the guerrillas. Although I still have the record of them, not many remain in my memory. In retrospect, much merges into a vague, tangled, confused recollection: the weight of the pack, the heat, the damp, the difficulties of navigation, the discomfort, the frustrations, the failures of communication, the occasional adrenalin-heavy pounding of the heart and – on the positive side – the staunch comradeship of the Gurkha soldiers.

By 1953 the first flush of guerrilla aggressiveness had subsided. They now had a policy of consolidation in deep jungle, growing their own food and waiting for an opportune moment to upgrade their activities. In order to disrupt such attempts to become self-sufficient, we now undertook massive and often cumbersome food-denial operations deep in the jungle rather than on the rubber estates. The aim was to find and destroy the many cultivations, previously spotted from the air, that the guerrillas had been forced to make. There was a surprising diversity of produce in these 'gardens': beans, rice, egg plant, tapioca, chillies, sweet potatoes, maize, pumpkins, mustard, pulse, bananas, nuts and spring onions. In flat, featureless country, it should have been easy enough to go on a compass bearing from one cultivation to another, but a number of inaccuracies both in plotting and navigation inevitably meant that cultivations took more time to find than had been planned for and some were overlooked. Even having spotted them, it was quite a problem to know how to despoil them without the use of chemicals. Burning the undergrowth merely produced wood ash which acted as a fertiliser, and uprooting crops – tedious and effective in the short term – helped keep the place weeded.

We were sent back to the same area for another three weeks to gain information about the enemy, and this we hoped to do by kills and captures, and by finding camps, tracks and documents.

Within a couple of days we killed a Chinese guerrilla. I searched him, photographed him, took his fingerprints and then had him buried. Gurkhas, however, are much more prone to 'atmosphere' than are British soldiers and believe in the progress of the soul. That night one radio operator refused to sleep in camp because he said that the dead man would try to recover his clothes. He spent the night by himself in the jungle. Something must have been in the air because the man who shot the guerrilla, Dharmajit Rai, experienced unaccountable movements in his stomach that felt like the writhing of snakes, so much so that two hapless men were detailed, unbeknown to me, to sit on him all night. Whatever madness was in the air communicated itself to Special Branch in far-off Seremban, whose boss next morning sent a radio message angrily asking why he had not yet been sent a copy of the dead guerrilla's photo.

Our first air-drop contained bully beef – anathema to Hindus – and replacement rations were mistakenly dropped on a guerrilla camp five miles to our south. After another resupply we captured a guerrilla and sent him out by helicopter. On our week's walk out we came across one guerrilla camp and a two-foot mound of porcupine quills. But we found no running water and only just managed to survive by filtering the stuff from animal wallows. And when we did get back to base, stinking, there was no water until the next day.

*   *   *

I was beset, at irregular intervals, by a nightmare. Around me darkness, above me light, in front of me a guerrilla and I was lying down, taking aim at him with my carbine. I squeezed the trigger, hoping to kill him, but no bullet would be fired and the guerrilla would turn round and shoot me instead. Sometimes I would awaken from that dream into another which was nearly always a hospital with someone bending down and telling me not to be afraid nor impatient: I only had twenty years to wait until I could leave. I would awaken in a muck sweat, wondering why I should have such a dream.

One day on the range I stupidly forgot to release the safety catch of my weapon; I suddenly remembered my dream and was thankful for the warning. But even after that I was still haunted by the guerrilla's evil grin as he turned and shot me, nor could I understand the darkness around me and the light above. I tried to shrug it off but was sensitive enough to believe it presaged something unpleasant and probably dangerous.

*   *   *

Jane arrived two weeks before we were due to get married, during the battalion's retraining period and soon after that the CO, Lieutenant Colonel Alan Forestier-Walker, was wretchedly killed in a guerrilla ambush on his way back to base after visiting us all in our new locations. A large operation was mounted in deep jungle to try to find the gang responsible.

I had to take my company back to the area of our previous contacts and, on the third day out, it was time for midday halt and brew. I now had a golden rule that, when there was a halt, no one would be allowed to smoke for five minutes in case any guerrillas were in the immediate vicinity and would otherwise be alerted to our presence by cigarette smoke if not by noise. It had paid off in the past and it paid off now. An armed and uniformed Chinese youth walked straight into us and was shot. He fell to the ground. I went over to him to give succour and he died as I touched him; the death rattle, convulsing his throat, spent itself in the silence of the jungle.

I searched his belongings and found a new shirt and trousers, fifty-two new exercise books, a saw, nine maps, five letters and many diaries. While a grave was being dug, I stripped him, searching for any tell-tale tattoos or birthmarks, the better to recognise him. I also photographed him and took his fingerprints. I told headquarters what had happened.

That evening I was astonished to get a message telling me to take the body back to the nearest rubber estate, six hours' walk away, whence the guerrilla had come. In vain did I remonstrate, saying that he was obviously a courier moving the same way as ourselves, towards the central gang which we were looking for. To alert the rubber estate's population that their contact had been killed could easily nullify much of the information waiting to be culled from the papers I had found. The soldiers, too, were unhappy with this task, for although the body had only been buried a few hours, it would be an unpleasant and exhausting task: it had to be exhumed and carried back through the jungle, a path being hacked out.

Higher formation, in the person of Brigadier Howard, was adamant, so I detached a platoon and sent it back with the corpse. When the soldiers eventually arrived at the estate boundary it was as I had gloomily prophesied: the news spread like wildfire so everybody knew that troops were operating in the area, a secret until then.

During the next few days I found my strength and appetite waning. By the time we were out of the jungle I felt weak. I went back to Seremban, thirty winding hill miles away, by scout car. That type of vehicle held three people, a driver and two Bren gunners. The arrangement for the gunners was simple: twin-mounted light machine guns were fixed onto a metal stalk outside on the roof and operated by remote-control handlebars from inside. The first gunner's seat could be elevated, so that when the sliding lid-like roof was open, the whole was raised sufficiently for his head to protrude. This was cooler than being cooped up inside. The second gunner sat right down in the front of the scout car, next to the driver, at the feet of the first gunner.

Soon after we started I began to feel uncomfortable. By the time we were winding over the top of a mountain pass I felt I had to vomit. I stopped the driver, jumped out and retched emptily. I sat gloomily by the side of the road while the two Gurkhas waited patiently. Presently they suggested we move on. Once again in the scout car I felt we were moving with incredible speed. 'Slow down, slow down!' I begged the driver. Apparently we were moving very slowly. I felt fish-belly cold and lowered my seat to get warm. A dizziness assailed me and I must have started behaving queerly. The driver turned to the other man and said something I could not fully catch, '. . . has affected him'. An uncontrollable impulse made me bend forward and embrace the gunner for warmth. I dimly heard the answer, 'But he is a Christian. His church will protect him.'

Any effect my religion might have had must quickly have worn off so I was told to sit up and, shakily, I did. Because I needed to be smart in Seremban I wore polished shoes but they had become muddy when I had left the vehicle earlier. The driver, Kalibahadur Limbu, a shaman in his own right, snicked some earth from my shoes onto his finger, then scratched some polish off both toecaps.

Kalibahadur spat on the mixture, making a paste of it. He began to mutter but I was too uninterested and remote to care how he was driving or to listen to his words. He dabbed the paste on my forearms, my forehead and the tip of my tongue. 'That should do it,' he told his companion.

Almost immediately I felt a ball inside the pit of my stomach pushing up and up. I gasped as it struggled against my throat, choking me. As it burst through I started sobbing out loud. I pulled myself together and, feeling warmer, told the driver to drive on normally. This he did, saying nothing.

Within ten minutes I was very much better, although I felt utterly worn out. I was informed later that the guerrilla's soul had entered into mine when I was touching him as he died. I have since learned that Christian exorcism has the same effect as Kalibahadur's had on me.

As we drove into the camp, the two Gurkhas saw Jane and waved to her. I was so slow in reacting that I failed to wave and saw a shadow cross her face. She scolded me when we met later on that evening, and I apologised. During the next few days, we completed the arrangements for our accommodation and, finally, bought the ring and a wedding veil. However, with only a few days to go, Brigadier Howard himself ordered me back into the jungle. Information from the dead man's diaries and my personal knowledge of the area meant I had to be there to take advantage of the situation.

It was too much for Jane. She wrote me a letter, unsigned, to be airdropped to me, telling me she would have left Malaya by the time I received it. I was flown unexpectedly out of the jungle; we had a torrid meeting, and she left the next day. A woman, speaking in English, telephoned me from Singapore but I was not there to answer. 'When love is over, what of love does even the lover understand?'

Around then one of our British officers decided to join the guerrillas and disappeared into the jungle. After some days, hunger forced him out, looking dreadful, not having contacted any enemy to surrender to. At least, being alone and keeping quiet, he saw a lot of wildlife. We were very glad to see the back of him. Always an oddball, he told us he would have joined the Nazi army had he been a few years older.

After the brigadier had intervened in my marriage plans, bad luck had it that he came to see me one afternoon. 'John, I'm browned off,' was his opening remark. Without a second thought I forgot my military manners and very rudely said, 'That's because you're a brigadier and a brigadier is the most useless rank in the army.' I could have bitten my tongue off as I heard myself yapping away.

'Why?' he asked, glacially.

Inspiration! 'Because, sir, you are not near enough ground level to influence the fighting nor are you near enough the top to influence planning.' I was pleased to learn that after he had retired the brigadier said that if only he could have his time again he would have been more than happy to have listened to company commanders' advice from the very beginning.

*   *   *

I was walking down the aisle in full ceremonial uniform, not wanting to go through the bother of it all but faced with the inevitability of the foredoomed. The best man, whom I could not recognise, whispered to me that my laces were undone. I bent down to tie them up and saw that I was barefooted. I turned back to look for them and, to my dismay, found that they were jungle boots. Then I discovered I had no coat. 'Here, take mine,' someone said and gave his to me with a slight shove. I woke up sweating, aware of the night noises of the Malayan jungle, the sighs, chirrupings and rustles, and the smell of my clothes after some time on operations. A hand gently shook me again. I turned over on the leaf 'mattress' and sat up. 'Are you all right, Saheb?'

'What is it, Balbahadur?' It was my batman, a cheerful, strong lad, hard-working and very keen. 'What are you doing here? What do you want? It's not morning yet, surely? What's the time?'

It was around 1 o'clock. The jungle had had its nightly wash of rain. Moonbeams danced on the floor, mixing with the phosphorus of decaying undergrowth.

'No, I'm not the sentry. I came to see how you are. You were in trouble and I had to save you from it.' He spoke softly, out of habit when in the jungle, and partly so that the tired, sleeping men would not be disturbed.

'Yes, I again had the bad dream that has been haunting me.' Bits of similar recurring themes cluttered my mind: walking up the aisle, wrong or missing clothing; preparations that never properly materialised; subterfuges to which others resorted in order that I should not escape again. 'Sit down and have a chat,' I said.

He did. It was several weeks since that telephone call had been made to me, three days after Jane had gone, and my company, which had returned to base on the eve of my planned wedding day, was preparing to go into the jungle again. From the time Jane left me, I started going on double the number of patrols that I assigned to my junior commanders, believing that physical exhaustion and a good night's sleep were therapeutic and banished other worries. It also allowed the whole company to reach as high a standard as any, so I believed, in all the requirements of countering CRW at company level: patrolling, ambushing, watermanship, surrounding enemy camps or whatever the need was. It was not easy, as a company commander, always to find the type of target or terrain to deploy a company of between sixty to eighty men but I generally managed as, even had I not wanted to work Jane out of my system, I quailed at the idea of commanding some of the world's finest soldiers from an office chair.

I now learned that every night between midnight and three Balbahadur would visit my room, or stay beside my bed, to stop me doing myself a damage during that loneliest part of the night. I was immensely touched and told him that I was burning my anger out by hard physical work in the day and as good sleep as possible at night; he should not worry about me any more and should try to get enough sleep himself from now onwards. (Five years later he came to me and said: 'I'm going on home leave and I won't be coming back. Please look after my sons.' I repaid my debt by educating both of them to university level as Balbahadur did indeed die within ten days of getting home.)

*   *   *

Brigade decided to put me under command of 2/7 GR for the next phase of its six-month-long food-denial operation, another month in deep jungle, when we tried to prevent the guerrillas getting food from the villages. I had been briefed, along with the other company commanders of my sister battalion, to take particular care, with so many troops milling around, as to the whereabouts of contiguous companies' operational boundaries. Many fatal accidents had occurred by this basic requirement not being fully understood by each and every soldier. My company stayed a night with 2/7 GR, noting that their recognition sign, worn on their jungle hats, was crossed large yellow kukris. Ours was a small white square.

My operational boundary was extended north, from a well-defined river to a line on the map indicating a state boundary that had last been cleared and used as a path before the war, and therefore unrecognisable on the ground. I was deeply worried, as I knew that the 2/7 GR operational commander back in camp had been a prisoner-of-war in Japanese hands; lacking jungle experience, his judgements were often faulty. Operational boundaries had to be inviolate: there could be no doubt in anyone's mind when split-second decisions had to be taken whether or not to open fire on a fleeting target.

I queried it and got a shirty reply which did not make sense. So, for absolute peace of mind, I checked once more. This, with the radio operator's confirmation of the original message, made three checks. I had it confirmed that indeed my tactical boundary was as stated and also that my northern neighbours, A Company, 2/7 GR, knew about it, having had their own boundary shortened. So I accepted it and went patrolling, as far as necessary, even up to the new boundary – anyone we met was 'them', not 'us'.

Unfortunately, the change in boundary had not been advised to the others and we only prevented a dreadful accident because one of my Gurkhas recognised his brother when we met face to face in a swamp. But at least my men were safe, unlike the Queen's Regiment, ten thousand yards away. Soldiers of C Company mistook their Chinese interpreter (each company in every battalion had one) for a guerrilla and, in the ensuing battle, killed six of their own men.

This was the last of that protracted food-denial operation. About fifty guerrillas had been eliminated, by kills, captures, surrenders or arrest of suspects. How many more would have been removed but for the brigade commander's insistence on our taking that corpse back to the rubber estate? The security forces had suffered one commanding officer dead, along with his escort, a major wounded, six British soldiers needlessly dead, a Gurkha with a broken skull and one jilted company commander. There may have been other casualties but I cannot remember them. What I will never forget is that, but for the grace of God and the Gurkhas' steadfastness and fire discipline, there could have been seventeen more.

Meanwhile, fifty miles away, efforts were being redoubled to prevent stores and supplies leaving the town of Seremban. That merited another code name (without which the planners feel naked) and 'Key' was chosen. Leaflets were to be dropped on the surrounding jungles to let the guerrillas know their desperate fate. Before the drop, however, the leaflets were all incorrectly printed with 'Quay', so the code name was changed to 'Pibroch', which made sense to nobody. Furthermore, the actual air-drop of leaflets coincided with the first-ever municipal elections. The voice aircraft tape to warn the guerrillas about their impending starvation, inviting surrender, was muddled up with the reminder to the inhabitants to cast their vote for town councillors! The good citizens of Seremban were indignant at the slur on their probity; I never did hear what the guerrillas thought but I expect their message gave them a giggle or two that raised their morale. This they needed as, despite such staff idiocies, government was, in fact, by then winning the war.

*   *   *

Large-scale operations never seemed to work well. One I particularly remember can only have been planned by a senior officer who must have taken part in the crossing of the Rhine during the war and so had no conception of time and space problems in the jungle. The operational area was the mountainous Cameron Highlands – rugged terrain much cooler than we had been accustomed to. There were reports that the Malayan Politburo had been building a new hiding place at the top of a 7000-foot peak called Gunong Plata. I was reminded of the First World War stories of seeing 'Russians with snow on their boots' when we were told, in all seriousness, that men, including Gurkhas, had been sighted carrying bags of cement into the jungle! Accordingly 1/7 GR was to surround the mountain and assault the Politburo on the peak, soon after aircraft had bombed it. A 7 o'clock in the morning the feature was bombed, but so difficult was the country that it took two and a half days' slog for the first assault company to reach the summit. The company found nothing at the top of the mountain, which was a cold, waterless outcrop of barren rocks. The cement, unlike the Russian snow, had melted away to leave no trace. The argument about the efficacy of air power in relation to ground power took on an added, and addled, dimension.

We were told to search the valleys and came across aborigines whose weapon was a slender bamboo cylinder, the blowpipe. Ammunition was a wooden dart, the tip of which had been dipped in black poison, made from the sap of the *ipoh* tree. We managed to capture one aborigine who approached our camp, presumably to shoot at us. He asked to leave and told us he would be back on the morrow. His reasons for not wanting to stay were, variously, to tell his father what had happened to him, to fetch some clothes, to get married and to fetch some food.

That night a fire was seen twinkling on the opposite side of the valley from us and I went to investigate. It was an incredibly difficult walk, and my brand-new pair of jungle boots wore out in eight hours. We found a guerrilla camp equipped with defensive positions and signs of a recently used firebrand. I could not determine whether the inmates had moved away at night or whether the firebrands had been used for aborigines to go fishing – not that it mattered by then!

That was our only 'sniff' of guerrillas: but at least we kept the blowpipe as a souvenir.

*   *   *

In another area, early one morning as we were casting around, I noticed some ash in a patch of undergrowth. I turned to the man behind me, Sergeant Tulbahadur Rai, one of the finest jungle men I ever had the privilege of commanding, and said that it must have been made by a Chinese.

Tulbahadur bent down, touched the ash with the back of his hand, muttered 'still warm', and dived into the bushes, almost in one swift movement. Before I had the chance to ask him what he was doing, he pulled out a guerrilla. I saw he had been wounded. The bullet had entered his flesh and I was horrified to see the squirming, glinting body of a maggot that was even then eating him.

I interrogated him in halting Cantonese. Other troops to the west had shot him two days before and he had wandered into our area. He was very hungry. I called up my sergeant major and ordered him to give the wretched man a tot of rum, first showing that it was not poison by drinking some himself. The guerrilla looked at me and enquired, in perfect English, 'Excuse me, sir, but is this whisky?'

It was the perfect squelch. He had been taught at the government English School in the provincial town of Bahau. Even though our Chinese conversation had been laboured, he was sufficiently impressed by a 'running dog's' efforts that he hid nothing during his long debriefing by the police. He had been a Bren gunner in an ambush against 1/7 GR in 1949, killing a number of our Gurkhas; punished for having a love affair, he had been demoted to carrying a rifle.

Capturing guerrillas was not just a simple task of physically apprehending them, with or without a struggle. They always had to be 'processed' so that, legally, the charge of carrying a weapon, which carried the death sentence, could be made to stick in court. If there was no proof of a soldier being detailed personally to carry the guerrilla's weapon, it could be argued in court that that weapon was not the one the guerrilla was alleged to have been carrying, so the charge was unproven.

I was in court once as a witness that, in fact, the weapon the captured guerrilla had been carrying was the one he was accused of possessing. At the end of the session the English judge put a black cap on his wig – an incongruity in that Malayan court room – and pronounced the sentence: 'You will be taken from here . . .' and paused, as did the interpreter. The guerrilla looked up, a happy expression on his face, presuming he was being allowed to go free. His hopes were dashed as the full import of the next part of the verdict was translated to him: '. . . to a place of lawful execution and there you will be hanged by the neck until you are dead. And may the Lord have mercy on your soul!'

Afterwards, in the privacy of his rooms, wig and black hat lying beside him on the table as he enjoyed a cup of tea, the judge remarked that he had a low opinion of army officers as they were not clever enough to be judges.

Like the guerrilla a little earlier, I had no answer.

*   *   *

One day we moved several thousand yards into deep jungle. Next day I took three men to look at an area near some higher ground. We travelled very light; weapons and ammunition only. We did not carry water bottles, as I believed they obstructed really quiet movement.

Two hours from our overnight camp, we heard the unmistakable sound of earth being dug by a *chankal*, a short-handled hoe. We crept forward and saw a cultivation, surrounded by a fence to stop pigs and deer depredating the crops. At the far side were two Chinese guerrillas, uniformed and even wearing their caps with the red star badge as they dug. I decided to tackle them and we moved slowly forward.

The area surrounding any cultivation is apt to be slow going. Felled trees and cut undergrowth make movement difficult and noisy. I therefore decided not to approach the two men from inside the jungle but to get into the cultivation and crawl up to a felled tree lying conveniently near, the easier to dispatch them. Gingerly we crossed a stile and – reminiscent of recruit training days – crawled forward between rows of raised and hoed soil. By the time we reached the tree we were all hot and sweating. We paused to get our breath.

The two men were thirty yards away, on a slope below us, heads bent so only their backs were visible. I quietly gave my orders: two of us would take the lower guerrilla, the other two the guerrilla above. 'Fire on my order!'

I steadied my body on the tree trunk, feeling very exposed, and brought my weapon, an American carbine, into the aiming position.

'Ready to fire?' I hissed at them.

They were.

I checked my safety catch, found it disengaged. 'Fire!'

As my target was only a man's back, I reckoned on three quick bullets through his ribs at thirty yards range would floor him. I fired. He put his hand up to his back and wheeled round, either to see what was happening or from the force of the bullet, an evil snarl on his face. I squeezed the trigger again and nothing happened. And suddenly I realised where I was: the dark woods around me, the clear open sky above and a weapon that did not fire. I pinched myself hard to ensure I was not dreaming, and squeezed the trigger again, of course to no effect. I tried to withdraw the working parts of the carbine but they were jammed. Instead of concentrating on killing the enemy, my soldiers turned their attention to me, so their aims were not true: human, understandable but very annoying.

As a result of the bullet case swelling so that it could not be removed except by force – so-called 'hard extraction' – my nightmare had come true.

*   *   *

By this time our combined efforts were meeting with considerable success. An entire guerrilla platoon was eliminated by kills, captures and surrenders. We tracked them for several days, at one time only a few hours behind them, and came across their camps. In one we found that they were so weak and short of food that their diet was leaves, and their stools were green. Even so, the terrifying capacity Chinese have to hold on to life was amply demonstrated. As we followed up, we heard the roar of a tiger. It was only Sergeant Tulbahadur Rai, an ace tracker, who could tell that what dimly looked like a tiger's pug mark was man-made. The end guerrilla had been turning round and 'making' pug marks but, unfortunately for him, he had made the 'tiger' walk backwards!

That evening we were so close to the enemy that we smelt the smoke of their fires. We deployed, using our noses to guide us. Once we actually saw the smoke come curling around a spur. At long last we were to have a resounding success. We had already killed a couple of guerrillas and now we slowly surrounded the area from where the smoke was coming, closing in as dusk fell. We were astonished to find absolutely nothing: no tracks, no camp, no signs of human activity, only the damp and insect-noisy jungle being swallowed up in the gathering darkness. As night fell, we sadly asked ourselves what had gone wrong.

Only next morning did we discover that we had been searching in the very opposite direction to the guerrillas' hideout, as some quirk of nature had blown the smoke in a semi-circle, clinging to the dampness of the undergrowth.

So we lost them. They crossed the main road twenty minutes before an ambush was placed to catch them. Search was hampered by three days and nights of solid rain. In the jungle, a couple of hours' rain in the evening meant that the trees dripped all night; seventy-two hours of rain makes conditions miserable.

We moved into a rubber estate and an A Company patrol captured a guerrilla just as a D Company patrol moved in. The man surrendered his weapon to my men but a crafty Gurkha from the other patrol called him over. The man obeyed and so was claimed by D Company. It was months before we were on speaking terms again! Even so the big prize eluded both companies as the guerrilla platoon commander was hiding in a stream all the while, watching what was happening with only his head above water, a mere two yards away from a couple of soldiers who filled their water-bottles. He escaped after dark but eventually surrendered. He showed us how he could walk through thick ferns without leaving a trace. It took half an hour for every yard and his deftness and sureness of touch as he moved was as nimble-fingered as any Chinese artist's.

We acknowledged him as an outstanding jungle warrior and a formidable adversary. The elimination of his platoon was a fitting end to 1954.

CHAPTER 2

In Gurkha Company
1955–6

By 1955 there was a definite change in the tempo of the Emergency. The guerrillas were moving in smaller parties in deeper jungle, contacts were becoming more scarce, helicopters more frequent. Gone were the early days of pitched battles and casualties. Now we were more dependent than ever on tracking, on reading signs, on a real knowledge of jungle lore. It was realised all too little that, in addition to luck, the fewer the numbers of the enemy the better the standard of soldiering required to deal with them. For the soldiers, however, there were few more disheartening occupations than endlessly flogging through the undergrowth that revealed no signs of any other human, fleeting or permanent.

The battalion left Seremban and moved south to Kluang, in Johore State: an unattractive town where tight-lipped men and unsmiling children reflected that the nearer to Singapore the tighter was communist control. Our first task was to search an area to the north-west of Segamat where a strong guerrilla presence was suspected. I doubted the ability of the helicopter pilots to put us down where I had requested, in such featureless terrain, using a small-scale map. Only on the fourth day did an Auster pilot discover we had been put down four thousand yards too far north. The newly appointed Brigadier Vickers had wanted to bomb that very area but was restrained from doing so by the CO, Chris Pulley. Initially I was blamed for poor navigation – but helicopter pilots started using the larger-scale map from then on!

As I had made no contact with the enemy nor seen any of their signs, I was ordered out by helicopter from another jungle clearing, 5000 yards to the south, within less than an hour's time. I had that postponed three hours and quickly moved on a compass bearing with the infuriatingly difficult angle of 127 degrees. Given a round number, the compass dial's thicker line would have been so much easier to read. Also, it needed less than a degree's mistake to miss a 50 square-yard hole in the jungle from 5000 yards away. I put my best sergeant, Tulbahadur Rai, in front and away we went, arriving exactly in the middle of the pick-up point with one minute to spare. The going had been anything but easy and we were all whacked.

We were quickly given more rations and moved into a fresh area. This time we had to walk in and, since it was from a known location, we did not get lost.

Our task was to investigate a guerrilla cultivation in deep jungle. On the way, I awoke one morning with a bad stomach. I was unwilling to make the usual early start so I told the men to cook and eat a meal, by when I hoped I would be in better fettle.

Almost immediately two guerrillas walked into view of a sentry who killed one outright. Cordite haze over a stream obscured the second man, who escaped, dropping his pack as he did. I fingerprinted and photographed the corpse, then ordered it to be buried. As the grave was being dug I examined the two packs and found ten letters, folded into small spills, and a mass of propaganda magazines printed in Chinese with English titles: *Freedom News* and *Truth* are two I remember. I felt that only the letters, not the propaganda material, would be worth keeping. I had taken back such a lot of similar stuff which had never been of any use so why burden ourselves with this lot? So, despite stringent orders to the contrary, I almost disposed of it – who would be any the wiser if I buried it with the dead man? In the end, however, I decided to take the bulky propaganda rubbish, as I had already reported it.

Our move to a landing site, to evacuate a sick man and fly out the documents, was as rough as any I had known. We took an air-drop and were ordered to walk out to the road where we would be picked up, twenty miles and eight days away. Four days later we were told that the documents had been sent to Special Branch in the Police Circle, in Segamat, where the exciting-looking spills turned out to be less than exciting – a bitter disappointment – and, as expected, the propaganda tracts valueless.

We continued patrolling to the jungle edge without incident and returned to our company base. There, surprisingly, I was thanked by Special Branch for bringing out those bulky tracts. It transpired that Special Branch, Johore, the next senior, had, at the last moment, asked for them. Their best man had cursorily glanced through them. At first he too had wondered why I had bothered to report their discovery, but then a worm of suspicion had entered his mind, so he had examined them with greater care and growing excitement.

Two days later he had discovered that the tracts contained an intricate code and had cracked it, finding that it revealed the latest Politburo directive for infiltrating schools, trade unions and local government. Every fourth word of the code was used to spell out the orders of the Politburo, the whole text being very cleverly managed to obfuscate the real message by making sense in its own right. Prompt action was taken to forestall these planned developments and much trouble was avoided in Malaya. It might otherwise have taken a year to have found out about it. Singapore, also a target, disregarded the evidence and suffered from student anarchy as a result.

I realised that neither I, nor anyone else, would ever have known about these plans had I thrown the tracts away; even so, I shuddered at the thought of what might have been the results of my initial impetuosity – and if I had not halted for gut ache!

*   *   *

Special Branch operations were seldom known to us; some of them were short-term, when informers were dealt with, others much longer. I give two examples of the latter. A very clever guerrilla, Tan Fook Leong – known to all as Ten Foot Long – was an ace operator. None in the security forces seemed able to match his ability. His elimination was the target of many operations for several years, all unsuccessful. Only when an agent told Special Branch where Ten Foot Long intended to send his portable radio for repair was a plan made finally to dispose of him. A 'bug' was installed in the guts of the radio which radiated a beam that aircraft could pick up when switched on. He was bombed to death. I felt that such a hero deserved a better fate.

In the second case a three-year infiltration of a brave Special Branch man into the guerrilla organisation came to fruition. This man, code-named 'Dover', had risen to be propaganda-cum-political adviser to a Regional Committee. He gradually shaped plans to lead the entire committee into an ambush. Communications with authority were tenuous and spasmodic in the extreme, involving a few trusted men working under great stress and danger. One Special Branch 'plant' was infiltrated to join Dover as his guide. It was hoped to eliminate thirty-two people when the guerrilla group came down from hilly jungle to an empty estate bungalow to collect supplies. All seemed foolproof, except for the safety of Dover and his guide. Both men were to join up with the Security Forces during the food lift. Dover was to be taken away, unhurt, being reported – for public consumption – as dead. The guide was to lead us back to the guerrilla camp.

The night was carefully chosen. Two hours before the guerrillas were due, one company of Gurkhas crawled into the killing ground around three tracks that met in front of the bungalow. The two Special Branch men were to be dressed in white shirts; the guerrillas would be wearing uniform. There would be plenty of time because the food dumped for the guerrillas had to be broken down into man-loads before being taken back into the hills. Suspense grew as the minutes passed.

Meanwhile three more companies had moved up to ambush positions on possible guerrilla escape routes. We in A Company, fresh from our exploits with propaganda messages, were to pursue any remnants and to attack the camp whence they had come, as another forty or so guerrillas were believed to be there, including seven wounded. Very much against my will, with us were two Chinese, a police inspector and a Malay Film Unit photographer, two aborigine trackers, a British soldier dog-handler and his dog. I was sorry for the photographer as, hapless man, he had just returned from his honeymoon and was in no fit state for any type of jungle operation. I was to pick up Dover's guide after the ambush and he would lead us back to the deep jungle camp.

On time we heard firing in the distance but not as heavy as expected. I made my way to the bungalow to learn that only one man had been killed and one wounded, then captured. All the rest had escaped. Apparently, at the last moment, the guerrilla military commander had balked at all his men being used for the food-lift, so that only half his force moved in. Somehow or other, too, white sacks had been provided for ferrying and, in the dark, a man carrying a large white sack on his back could not be distinguished from the two men dressed in white shirts. The guerrillas carried all the food away with impunity.

At 2 o'clock I was introduced to the guide who was having a meal and a glass of brandy. Reaction had started to set in and he seemed dazed. Yet, despite the obvious dangers, he said he was willing to return with two Special Branch men detailed as his escort.

I took them outside into the night, met my company and moved off into the rubber estate. Pitch-dark under the trees, movement became very, very laboured and the already tired soldiers were growing frustrated. Moreover, the slow progress of eight 'foreigners' was a burden to us all. I decided to wait an hour until dawn, have a quick brew of tea and then away.

Having a fair idea of where the guerrilla camp was, I moved quickly through difficult and tiring country to try to surround it and mount my assault. Then came the big disappointment: the guide had absolutely no idea where he was. I only realised later that the hierarchy of the movement relied entirely on their underlings for local knowledge and that this policy of minimal information was deliberately encouraged to prevent defections. That meant I could not pinpoint the camp, so delaying my assault. I had planned to be fighting a battle by 8 o'clock: it was cold comfort still to be searching for an empty camp an hour or so after noon. We tracked the enemy sedulously but, as I had feared, they soon split and we lost them, despite two more hours' patrolling.

It was evening by the time we cooked a meal and the soldiers were very tired. The photographer was nearly out on his feet, having to be pulled up the steeper inclines, his pack being carried for him; neither were the rest of the followers-on in any fit state for further movement. Even the dog had had enough. I sent them all back the next day. They were as thankful to go as we were to be free of them. We continued fruitless patrolling for another week before being recalled.

Dover was awarded a George Medal for his undoubted courage – it was not his fault that matters fizzled out so disappointingly.

*   *   *

One wounded and captured guerrilla had described a system of deep jungle courier 'letter boxes'; couriers never followed the same route between pick-up and delivery but they had to 'post' their correspondence in designated 'boxes'.

One such was known to be a good day's march into the jungle above the new village of Bekok and was loosely described as 'a large tree by a stream junction'. My company was detailed to find it!

The description could hardly be more vague but, by dint of elimination, I decided to concentrate on one area less unlikely than others. My reasoning was based on what lovers of military appreciations call 'time and space factors'. The area had to be far enough off the beaten track for safety, near enough the outside world for convenience and so situated that it could be of use in the main north–south guerrilla courier route or corridor.

The phrase 'needle in a haystack' must have gone through my mind as, at 2 o'clock one morning, I was awoken to a large mug of tea before moving off on as unlikely a mission as any I had ever undertaken. We were in the jungle by first light and trekked all day on a compass bearing that took us north-east.

By evening we had reached the suspected area and I sent out small patrols to make sure there were no guerrillas in the vicinity before we started to make camp. One patrol brought back news that it had sighted a large tree by a stream junction. Was Dame Fortune going to smile on us for once?

Next morning I went to see it: once it had been a very large tree, sprawling around a small rocky outcrop in the junction of two streams. Now only its large bole was left, entwined with creepers and encased in lichen. Even so, it would be too much of a coincidence to have found the correct place so fortuitously, so I sent patrols out at ten-degree intervals, like the rays of the sun, to cover all the territory in the area. In the forenoon eight patrols searched to the north and later on in the day six patrols went searching to the west. I guessed that there was little likelihood of there being any courier movement to the south or east. With no similar tree to raise the men's suspicions or hopes, I prepared ambush positions around the old bole. I based my plan on an outer ring some 200 yards from the tree and an inner ring actually watching it. By 8.30 on the third morning all were in position: two hours and ten minutes later we had a contact.

Two guerrillas were engaged by three soldiers. I ran to the scene of the firing and joined them. I had given firm orders that, if possible, a capture was to be made. Both guerrillas had by then been wounded and were running away. We chased them.

I glanced at one Gurkha, Parsuram Rai, as we surged forward and saw that his eyes were completely bloodshot. The lust to kill was in him and he had been, so he thought, deprived of his prey. We found the first man, lying in some undergrowth, unconscious, with a pierced lung and hit in other places. I quickly put an emergency dressing on his wounds.

Meanwhile I heard the second guerrilla open fire and shots being returned. It sounded as though Parsuram was engaged in a running battle so I went to help him. Apparently he had wounded the guerrilla in the leg so that he could not escape but, in approaching him, had been fired at from thirty yards' range. Parsuram had advanced another ten yards and been shot at again, so he had aimed at his enemy's right arm to prevent further firing. He had then captured him. The guerrilla was furious. He refused to talk, trying not to wince as we searched him, glowering fiercely, like an eagle. Aged about thirty, he was lean and strong. Parsuram's blood-red eyes were slowly returning to normal.

There was no point in staying put and it was imperative to get the two wounded guerrillas out as soon as possible for medical treatment and debriefing. Stretchers were made and we started off to the nearest place at which a helicopter could land. I asked our Chinese interpreter to talk to the guerrillas but neither would collaborate. Yet the expression in the eyes of the man I had patched up, Ah Chong, seemed trusting and, when I spoke to him, he answered. The other never spoke and seemingly willed himself to die, which he did that night. His corpse and the wounded prisoner were evacuated next day. I met Ah Chong when he was better. He seemed grateful for what I had done for him, saying that he would no longer be a communist, preferring to be a civilian instead.

*　　*　　*

On 9 September 1955 the newly elected Malayan Alliance government declared an amnesty but, by mid-October, realised it was not achieving the results it had so naively expected. Even so, we were suddenly ordered back to our old hunting grounds near Bahau. We had to search a large area of mountainous jungle, completely surrounded by roads, in the minutest detail. Unusually, the equivalent of four battalions were deployed in an area that had never previously occupied more than one company, a sixteen-fold increase. No reasons for such numbers was given.

For two weeks we plodded our way through forty-four map miles of jungle, painstakingly searching everywhere. We found considerable evidence of fresh and stale guerrilla movement but made no contacts. Our final destination was a mere quarter of a mile from a main road. We felt we were being 'flogged' for the sake of it. After another month of 'more of the same' we were given a better briefing, and finally understood the importance of our mission. A meeting of part of the Politburo itself, including the second-in-command, Yeong Kwoh, was scheduled to be held in the jungle not very far from Simpang Pertang, a notoriously pro-communist village. It was for this reason that almost 2000 men were being deployed.

Simpang Pertang itself was an unremarkable little place on a road junction. There were no able-bodied men there, only the old and the very young with their mothers. The menfolk were away, either felling timber or operating in guerrilla bands. Despite rigorous food checks and searches, food and messages were still leaving the village and reaching the guerrillas. Typically they were hidden under the false bottom of night-soil buckets, in the handlebars of a bicycle with the hand-grip replaced, and by women in unmentionable places.

Three weeks after full deployment it was decided to bomb suspected hide-outs. Intention of this was given on Radio Malaya, so quite naturally, the guerrillas moved. For three nights and two days the RAF employed 'maximum effort' to eradicate all the baddies: intensive searching revealed only the corpses of three monkeys and a pig. The rationale for broadcasting the information was, apparently, that the amnesty was still technically in force, so due warning had to be given. Well, yes.

The guerrillas split into two groups. Since they could only escape across the main road, perpetual ambushes with scout cars and searchlights (and bored British and Malay troops) were put on likely crossing places, the 'outer ring', while troops patrolled swathes of jungle considered likely to approach axes to the road, the 'inner ring'. Despite artillery and mortars being used in areas the troops could not cover, the guerrillas escaped harm by hiding near military bases.

One man was killed as he tried to cross the road but after that the guerrillas enjoyed, once more, the luck of the devil. A few nights later, both groups met up and reached the road. They saw the silhouette of a soldier standing in the cupola of his scout car. They watched him for some time and thought he might be asleep. So they sent a few men across to see what would happen. Nothing did. The soldier was indeed asleep: he had not been carrying a pack and flogging the jungle for the past month or so, he had not been patrolling or ambushing, nor had he been braced continually for a fleeting target, an emergency, a chance contact. All he was asked to do was to stay awake – which he failed to do. The guerrillas, including all Politburo members, crossed the road with impunity and escaped. I never heard what happened to the sentry, I was too sick at heart to find out; but I expect he returned to England none the wiser as to the results of his incredibly bad soldiering.

*   *   *

In the middle of March 1956 we were sent south into the Bekok hills, not all that far from the 'letter box'. Parts had yet to be surveyed and the expanse of white on one of our two map sheets was relieved only by a river in one corner. I had a hunch about the area, having thoroughly combed it over the months. On the first day I took a small patrol and discovered what I thought to be a footprint in a swampy area. Others thought it was a bear.

The next day I again took out a couple of men and moved north, once more finding a similar print. This was greeted with scepticism; most Gurkhas knew that British officers were bad at tracking. On the third day, having moved our camp farther north, I came across another print. As soon as we could we moved off, following the direction the three sightings had pointed to us. That night my sleep was troubled and I was afraid. By the time I set out on patrol I still had not shaken off the feeling.

We were searching in hilly country and I sent the patrols out at intervals of a hundred paces, parallel to one another, on both sides of a main watershed. Out one hour and back another, it was doubtful if any signs of activity would escape us. We were, by now, on the fringe of the white map sheet.

An hour later my patrol and the adjoining one converged on a steep ridge. It was time to return but the other commander said he wanted to go on farther. I said he could, for a quarter of an hour, as I wanted everyone to search another sector of the jungle that afternoon. I myself went back.

When the other man returned he was very excited. He had seen five pairs of black trousers hanging out to dry. He had gone as far forward as he dared, but as the whole jungle, unusually, was crackling-dry as a result of no rain, he had decided to return so that the enemy camp could be surrounded.

Now, by this stage of the Emergency, the RAF had developed a procedure for bombing. A marker balloon was flown near the area to be bombed, the troops were withdrawn, the bombers dropped their bombs and the guerrillas died: the procedure was known as 'Smash Hit'. Brigadier Vickers ordered that no troops should invest an enemy camp themselves but that, in every case, the bombers would be called in. He further added that he would court-martial any company commander who thought he knew better and tried a ground assault.

I was very conscious of the brigadier's edict. However, I was even more conscious of the fact that an Auster aircraft, completely off its own bat and unconnected with my operation, was even then circling the enemy camp. I knew that guerrilla procedure was to stand to if any aircraft flew overhead and to evacuate their camp if it flew around. I had to decide whether to call in the bombers, by which time there would more than likely be no guerrillas, or to try to surround the camp there and then and face official displeasure, possibly of a violent nature, if I made a nonsense of it all. I decided on the latter.

In the event we were unsuccessful. I was in an agony of suspense as the platoon detailed to assault from the right flank was too slow in making contact, and I felt I had to get a position where I could see them and signal an immediate move. The better to get an enfilade view, I crawled up the slope towards the guerrilla camp. A Bren gunner covered me and, as I lifted my head six yards from the top, he noticed that a sentry in the camp had heard me, and moved into a fire position. Having seen nothing, and none the wiser, I tried again, crawling up to within four yards of the alerted sentry, in my attempt to contact the missing platoon. I was deafened as the camp sentry opened fire on me, missing me by a hair's breadth. My own men then opened fire, aiming just above me, but only managed to wound one guerrilla. We followed bloodstains for some distance.

Battalion HQ were as unhappy as I was at my missed contact. They would have to bear the brunt of the brigadier's wrath until I got back, but that was their bad luck. I told them I thought I could re-contact the guerrillas and was going to continue my search. Their bleak 'Roger – Out' was a fitting end to a laboured conversation.

I chose another area to search and the CO gave me three days to atone. I worked my way back up the hills to an area to the north and well inside the white map, and reached it by the evening of the third day. Next morning I sent out patrols. I went with two men and soon found tracks for three guerrillas, with the middle man dragging his right leg. This made sense as we knew that there had been five men in the camp and at least two had remained. We inched our way forward and heard a noise, but was it men talking Chinese or the sound of sawing? No matter. Contact had been re-established.

I went to fetch a marker balloon and took three men back to between one and two hundred yards from the guerrilla position. I did not want to get any nearer and the inflation procedure was messy and smelly, needing water to activate the chemical that filled the balloon with gas.

As we were inflating the balloon, we heard men felling trees in several directions about us. The noise was the distinctive one made when cutting the delicious palm cabbage tree, and I presumed that this was a guerrilla forage party. The work was being done surreptitiously.

At last the balloon was inflated. I bound the neck with string, cut the neck below it and hurriedly got out of the way of the choking fumes still churning furiously in the canvas bucket. I poured the mess out onto the ground. The string was on a reel and the balloon was tugging upwards, so I played it out to the extent of the string, maybe 500 feet, secured the reel to the base of a tree and left, hoping our work would not be spotted, for we had left traces we could not disguise, and that 'Smash Hit' would be a success. We were ordered back 4000 yards.

That evening, shortly before 6 o'clock, an Auster flew over the target and dropped a smoke marker that the bombers – Lincolns and Venoms – could recognise from some distance away. On the hour they flew over and dropped their bombs; the earth shook and the hills echoed and re-echoed. They flew over again, strafing the area, and a number of empty cases dropped in among us. We were all very excited and none of us slept well that night.

After a pre-dawn approach march, we saw the jungle had been flattened but our intensive search found no firm traces of guerrillas. I was told, over the radio, that one of the aircraft had dropped its bombs unfused.

I could hardly believe my ears ... and then I remembered that the place where I had seen the guerrillas' entry into the bombed area was, itself, unbombed. That explained it. (Or did it? It later transpired that the Auster did not see my marker balloon and, despite there being no details on the white sheet, the grid reference I had sent was accurate enough for a fix. Had the wretched balloon been tied badly or had the guerrillas found it and cut the cord? I never knew.)

So the heart petered out of our search. The soldiers thought that, with all the air activity, the guerrillas would be miles away by then. Two days later I went out on a patrol and we managed to kill one guerrilla, who had nothing to do with the gang we had been after.

Back in our base camp in Labis, we washed the twigs out of our ears. The CO came down for a talk. He gave me a letter from home which I put to one side. He told me I had to go to Kuala Lumpur to discuss, with the RAF planners, how 'Smash Hit' worked when initiated by a company commander. I was to fly there and back with the brigadier. I read my letter while the CO talked to someone else.

A great friend of the family had seen me in a dream, about to die. She tried to warn me but my very dear elder brother, Timothy, who had been killed in the war twelve years before, and dressed in white, told her not to worry, that I would come to no harm. The dream was so vivid that this lady rang mother to tell her. I worked it out that the dream had occurred just before the guerrilla had opened fire on me, and started to sweat with fear, or delayed reaction, or something.

The CO eyed me narrowly and told me to watch my health. The moment was too private to tell him the real reason for my trembling.

*   *   *

My visit to Kuala Lumpur was not a success. I was received coldly by the top brass of the RAF who asked me why I had not previously used 'the bigger weapon', bombing? The senior man said that the ground forces' ratio between contacts and kills was so poor that bombing was the only answer. Brigadier Vickers said that he had had trouble in persuading his company commanders to use bombing but that now one of the most recalcitrant of them had been won over and agreed with him. 'Don't you, Cross?' 'No sir!'

The horrified hush that greeted that bleak rejoinder was only broken by the senior RAF man asking me why I did not agree with the policy. I pointed out that 'maximum effort' around Simpang Pertang had only produced three dead monkeys and one dead pig (a total I did not consider worth the tax payers' money), that the one success of 'Smash Hit' was a fluke and that, in my case, one bomb had been dropped unfused. The atmosphere became glacial. I was not worth talking to, they said, so out they trooped, all five of them.

Brigadier Vickers was so angry with me that he cancelled my return journey in his aeroplane and told me to make my own way back on the night train. There being no reservations, I slept on the floor until 3 o'clock when it was time to get out at Labis and had to wait until dawn, when the curfew was lifted and the gates were open, before I could reach my company base. (Vickers later wrote, in my Annual Confidential Report, that I was 'narrow-minded and dogmatic': he could easily recognise both symptoms!)

*   *   *

By now elimination by erosion resulted in our going for weeks at a time without a sight of the enemy, although we often found tell-tale traces. I spent much of my time in the jungle, more often than not patrolling, sometimes in ambush – which I hated, finding the immobility and the bites of creepy-crawlies a penance. On odd occasions our efforts culminated in surrounding enemy camps and attacking them. I had spent 432 days 'under the canopy', only spending S$0.29 during that time.

During these years I had come to rely on the men, to trust them, to believe in them, even for those last few yards, and have my care and affection reciprocated by them in a way that was exciting, satisfying and stimulating. I learned from them always – whether a point of jungle-craft or, in a camp of an evening, folklore. Apart from the soldiers saying that I only slept for two hours a night, with the rest of the time being spent in language study (completely untrue), I was seen as being more involved in jungle work than other British officers and, in many cases, than Gurkha officers. 'Why do you always go out yourself, and with so few men?' they would ask, not understanding that I was burning Jane out of my system once and for all.

If happiness is seen as ease, regular meals, a varied diet, dry clothes, no aching body and sleep in a dry, comfortable bed, then the conditions I normally found myself in were misery; but I was neither unhappy nor miserable in my task, except when thwarted by stupidity or untoward interference from senior officers. Once in the jungle, I found I could change mental gear. Consequently, I did not find being dirty, tired, sweaty, wet, smelly, in danger and far from base nearly as much a burden as might be thought. I never felt 'foreign' or in a minority among the men, but always part of the cohesive whole. I was doing a job, successfully I believed, and that gave me a sense of completion, as I could only see middle-aged, desk-tied soldiering from then on.

One evening in the jungle I received the highest accolade I can ever imagine from a Gurkha, who remarked that when I was with them they knew no fear. It certainly made up for having none of that which Napoleon felt was needed to 'conquer the world', bravery ribbons on the chest, which in my case, however often they were suggested to Higher Authority, never came my way.

So, in the end, from the ashes left by burning out the hurt of Jane with always just that little bit extra done and little bit more exertion made, a knowledge and experience of the jungle grew into a skill that had stood me in good stead – and would stand me in better, although at the time I would never have guessed it.

Part Two

MALAYA, 1961–3
Seven Veils

CHAPTER 3

Warp and Weft

31 August 1957. Malayan independence from Britain. Although in the ninth year of an Emergency, and 2000 guerrillas still in the jungle, independence, promised since 1952, was being celebrated. The threat was considered nugatory as the main plank from the communists' political platform, continued British rule, was no longer relevant.

The main festivities took place in the nation's capital, Kuala Lumpur. Dignitaries were plentiful and the British Crown was represented by the Queen's uncle, HRH the Duke of Gloucester. There was a march-past, led by troops of the newly independent country, epicene Malays, followed by once-colonial British soldiers, sweating through their jungle-green uniforms, stocky Gurkhas, police, scouts, guides and schoolchildren. Crowds of civilians – all decked out for the occasion in their smart, colourful clothes – flocked into the town to join in the fun. Despite the political ritual and cant, many of the easy-going Malays did not seem particularly interested in this change of their fortunes, or at least those of their new leaders, while the Chinese merchants and Indian labourers gloomily looked on the absence of the British at the top as likely to make them permanent second-class citizens. There was no Malay word for 'independence', so the Arabic word *Merdeka* was used instead, having first to be taught to the bewildered population.

Away on the east coast, a small convoy of British and Gurkha soldiers was on its way up to the town nearest the Thai border, Kota Bahru, and its ill-named Beach of Passionate Love. It had been feared that the guerrilla leader, Chin Peng, would try to disturb the celebrations by an armed incursion in that area, and seventeen Land Rovers and trailers stood by as transport for any military reinforcements flown in to take necessary action.

There had been a torrential downpour the previous night and, early on the morning of Independence Day itself, the soldiers dried out as best they could before driving northwards, through the town of Kuala Trengganu. They caused quite a stir. A large parade was being addressed prior to a march-past. The senior Malay was delivering the English version of his speech in a clipped, staccato voice: '. . . and now as we are looking after ourselves, having shaken the British off . . .', when the low rumble of approaching Land Rovers was heard. All heads craned as the convoy drove along the road abutting the parade ground. No other interest was shown until the seventeenth and last vehicle had been counted and was out of sight. Just having moved off, the spacing between the

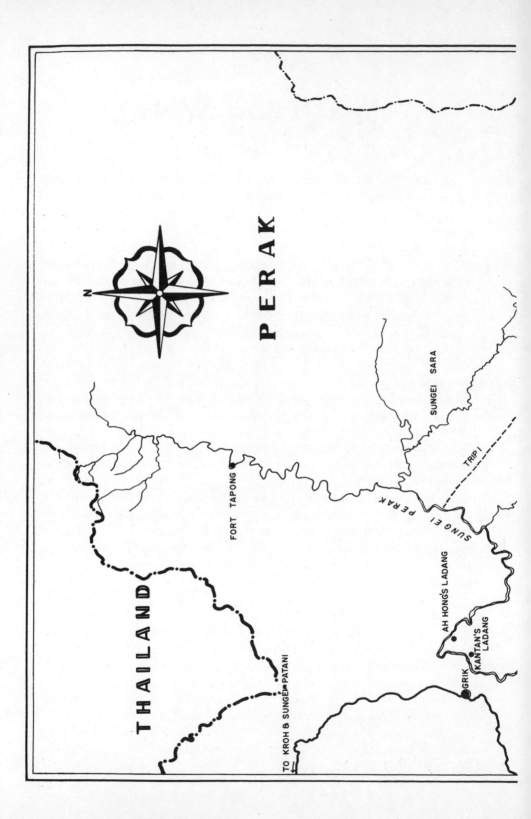

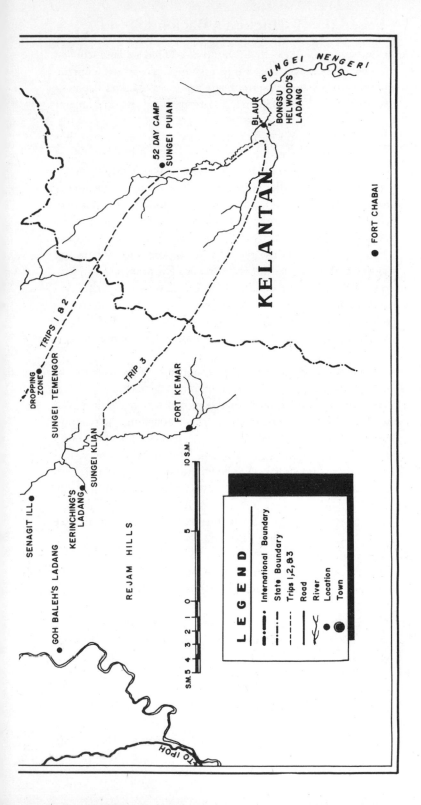

MAP 3: AREA OF OPERATION 'BAMBOO'. This shielded heartland
Malaya from any resurgent downward thrust from Thailand Communists.

vehicles was equidistant and very impressive. Damp and bored soldiers scowled as they drove past, giving an unwarranted impression of power and control. When quiet enough to be heard audibly, the reedy voice resumed its paeon of self-praise to the spectators and participants, '... from today we are on our own...'

Up in Kota Bahru the celebration parade had been, if anything, even less successful. A cage of pigeons was placed on a stand, in front and to one side of the main dais. Men in traditional warrior dress, carrying staves, were its escort. As the pigeons were liberated, an artillery piece was to boom out independence joy. The Chief Minister of Kelantan had, unfortunately, muddled the pages of his speech and reached the climax before expected. A gramophone record of the new national anthem, which had only arrived the day before, was started at the previously notified juncture, but alas the record was cracked and, not having been tested, no one knew about it. In the embarrassingly unrehearsed hiatus, before it had dawned on anyone to turn the thing off or to jolt it on a revolution, the minister realised that he had omitted some of his speech and turned the pages back, trying to find the missing passage. His fluttering hands were mistaken for the signal for the artillery piece to boom, which it did, several times.

There was no stopping it. Back was flung the lid of the pigeons' cage but so frightened were the birds by the noise that they remained where they were. The last boom died away and the shrill scratch of the record was becoming even more scratchy, when an old retainer, one of the warriors guarding the pigeons' cage, took the initiative. He raised his staff and repeatedly poked it up through the bars, trying to get the recalcitrant birds to fly. The birds, however, had different ideas. They bounced and shuffled to the far end of the cage, merely to be poked back again, ignominiously, by their staff-wielding tormentor. Only after considerable effort did he manage to get them airborne, but at least he had the crowd's sympathy as the ill-omened birds fluttered down almost at once and started waddling petulantly, looking for food.

Were these parodies of parades the only ill-omens at the birth of independent Malaya? As I took the convoy back – the whole business of moving north having been a false alarm – I asked myself if they could really manage by themselves.

Two years later the Emergency was declared over. The Malayan army, now known as the Federation Armed Forces, confidently took over chasing the rump of the guerrillas whose hard core still held out doggedly with the help of the aborigines. Their main base was in Yala province in south Thailand.

*   *   *

There were still thirty-five guerrillas on the police 'wanted list' when, in 1961, I came back on the scene with D Company, after a two-year stint in Hong Kong.

We were posted to the mining town of Ipoh, in the north of the country and, to our pleasure, unexpectedly warned soon afterwards for the deployment of two rifle companies in the Malay-Thai border region: so the rumours of the Malays not managing on their own were true after all!

The target of our activities was this thirty-five-man rump of Chinese guerrillas. An operation targeted against them, code-named 'Bamboo', had been in progress for three years. Military and civil intelligence was virtually nil. Despite much patrolling and ambushing, and Special Branch efforts to penetrate both the guerrilla organisation and the recalcitrant aboriginal population in jungle settlements, called 'ladangs', there was precious little to show for it.

As there seemed little likelihood of any orthodox military solution being successful, it was decided that a psychological approach was needed against the guerrilla support, namely the aborigines. The aims of 'Bamboo' were therefore twofold: clandestinely, to win over the aboriginal population and penetrate the guerrillas' organisation; militarily, to defeat the elusive armed Chinese remnants. Accordingly, the Department of Aborigines, through Special Branch, had been entrusted to wean the hearts and minds of the aborigines from the Chinese – whom they liked – and (not the same thing) to bring them over to the government, the Malays – whom they did not. This all required realistic, long-term planning, backed by steady, persuasive and sympathetic action to reverse the situation that had pertained for a score of years. Easier said than done, otherwise the Brigade of Gurkhas would not have been asked to help!

The area under scrutiny covered more than 10,000 square miles of rugged, jungle-covered, mountainous terrain between the Malay-Thai border in the north and the Cameron Highlands to the south, embracing the eastern part of Perak State to the west of the main spinal ridge, the 'divide', and the western part of Kelantan State to its east. This swathe of territory could be looked on as a communist bridgehead, one of influence rather than of physical occupation, from where the guerrillas could restart any nefarious activities, aided by friendly aborigines providing intelligence, porterage and some logistical backing. To achieve the military aim, groups of soldiers patrolled around the ladangs, hoping to persuade the locals to give information about the guerrillas so that counter-measures could be taken. Quite what Special Branch did remained a closed book.

For 'Bamboo', 1/7 GR was put under command of 2 Federal Brigade, the only non-Federation troops to be deployed, excluding occasional training parties of 22 SAS Regiment. As penetration of the aborigines was seen as the key to success, we were comprehensively briefed about these little-known people so that we could understand the difficulties and complexities involved in trying to work with them in any way, let alone weaning them from the guerrillas.

Malayan aborigines had been classified into as many as ten separate groups, all known as Sakai. This name became resented by the aborigines as it was pejorative, implying a person of inferior status, possibly even 'slave'.

The main group dominated by the Chinese guerrillas in north Malaya was the Temiar who, with the more southern Semai, form the Senoi. 'Senoi' is the Temiar for 'man'; they refer to themselves as 'serok', an 'inlander'. They, and also other tribes even less civilised, stretch north into Thailand. They live in communities varying from under a score to over a hundred. A headman ('penghulu') and a shaman have the most influence over a group, but many matters are decided by common assent.

Small, dark and lissom, they are very timorous by nature, and a show of anger by an outsider can undo months of work. Being animists, superstition prevails. We were told not to laugh in front of butterflies, not to flash mirrors in the open, not to touch anyone's head. Each person's god was in his or her head, and the larger varieties of butterfly were seen as souls in transit, while a mirror flashed in the sun was a magnet to lightning. Contact with the security forces had had some modernising effect on the Temiar, but traces of these beliefs were often to be found in the early 1960s.

The Temiar still lived in family groups and their dwellings were fashioned accordingly. The description of 'long house' gives a false comparison with the much longer houses in certain parts of Borneo. Houses were built on stilts and, except for the main uprights and the thatch, bamboo was used – indeed the Temiar were regarded as having a 'bamboo culture'. Rattan vines took the place of nails. The whole structure was rickety and, even though there were flimsy partitions between families, there could be no real privacy, even at night.

All were materially poor by any standards. Men wore a loincloth and sometimes a shirt. Women wore a shirt, rolled waist-high for comfort or with breasts covered, in front of most foreigners. They decorated themselves with rice straw in their hair and by daubing their faces with the red juice of one berry and the white juice of another, in a polka-dot pattern that I found most unattractive. All ages smoked and betel nut was very popular.

There was no beast of burden, no ploughing, no manure. For many the only wheel ever seen was that of a helicopter and for most their mother's was the only milk ever tasted. Food could be hard to come by. Apart from jungle produce, of which the Temiar had untold knowledge, their staple diet was tapioca and hill rice. To plant these crops, the jungle was felled. Starting from downhill, the upper trees were left only half cut through. When the clearing to be was adjudged big enough, the top trees were fully cut. The jungle collapsed with a horrific din.

The Temiar speak a primitive language thought to be an offshoot of the Mon–Khmer group, centred in Indo-China. Except for loan words, it is completely distinct from Malay. The archaic dual person is retained, Malay words are needed to count above three, while everything talked about has to be related to the stream – actual or notional – which lies in relation to the object, speaker and listener. Time and distance mean nothing. Any period more than two days in the past is undesignated; similarly, any future happening more than four days ahead is too remote to need specification. Distances, depths and heights are all expressed by the same word. Even the concept of an animal is too much to understand, so individual animals have their own names, as do trees: I later found myself struggling to remember fifteen species of bamboo and not knowing which one I was trying to refer to! Yet despite their vagueness as to time, the Temiar have words that span six generations back, indicating that in some ways they possess long memories.

During the Emergency efforts had been made to win over the recalcitrant Temiar from the Chinese guerrillas, whose commander, Ah Soo Chye, was reputed to have eleven wives scattered around various ladangs. Contact between security forces and the Chinese was very rare, and thus Chinese influence remained strong.

The Temiar have a creed that could be summed up as 'anything for a quiet life'. Coolness – because they wanted to be left alone – inherent fear and latent antipathy all extended to a certain degree towards the security forces, as these were government men. Thanks to the efforts of a few dedicated Europeans, this reserve had been broken down by the time we got into the act. The only real military problem was the actual deployment against the guerrillas. For the troops, periods spent in the jungle had a certain value for training purposes, but palled heavily after a time. Monotony, discomfort and squalor, often seemingly to no purpose, were hard to combat. And up to the end of 1961 there had still been no positive results for over five years. It was a stalemate.

We were razor-keen to show that the battalion could succeed where all others had failed; Malays, Australians, New Zealanders, British and even surrendered guerrillas, known as Surrendered Enemy Personnel, SEP, who went back in as cops, not robbers. If, at the beginning of it all, I had known what it would entail, I would never have become as involved as I did, not would I have guessed that I had enough mental or physical stamina to endure the strain. Then, and two years later in Borneo, I was steadily sucked into the vortex of events created by my own impetus, but so gradually and so tantalisingly, with something concrete only just out of sight, that I kept on to two bitter ends.

In this first fifteen-month saga it was as though a veil, almost in reach, hid my target and once that had been lifted, I could see what it was I had to do. Without the Gurkhas to sustain me, I could never have achieved it. Had I enjoyed the backing of all my superiors, I could have done much more.

I never guessed that there would be seven veils, nor what I would find after the seventh had been lifted . . .

CHAPTER 4

The First Veil

The continued implementation of 'Bamboo' was to break this stalemate and achieve positive results. Its functional headquarters were in Ipoh, where police, military and civil authorities met periodically to discuss the situation and try to maintain momentum. Here also was the very efficient, Chinese-run Special Branch, which kept tabs, as far as possible, all over the 'Bamboo' area. The Department of Aborigines was based in Kuala Lumpur.

Although Ipoh was the mainspring of 'Bamboo', day-to-day running was done in the small riverine town of Grik, a hundred miles to the north.

In late October 1961, A and C Companies went up to establish contact with the police and to deploy around the ladangs. We in B and D Companies wondered if it would all be over by the time our turn came.

We need not have worried. Only gradually did we realise just how little impression soldiers could make on the aborigines. The Chinese guerrillas had been in continuous contact with the Temiar ever since 1942, since when there had never been a period of more than three months without some guerrilla representation either in the area as a whole or on a specific ladang. Over the years, the propaganda and mode of conduct of these Chinese had impressed the Temiar. The guerrillas had detailed written instructions on how to behave towards the aborigines. The Chinese also helped them where and when they could, they understood them, they spoke their languages (which the Malays who came into contact with them did not) and, above all else, they had been there for a long time and were an accepted part of the order of things. In China, Mao Tse-tung had spent thirty years in the wilderness before achieving victory. His representative in the Kra Isthmus, Chin Peng, had only spent twenty. Was there a parallel and, if so, was it only the Chinese who remembered it? Temiar and Chinese mixed well together, Temiar and Malay did not. Why make an effort to change the devil you knew and liked, and did not regard as a devil, for one who proclaimed he was not a devil yet behaved suspiciously like one? Information about the guerrillas was simply not forthcoming.

Once only during the past five years had a guerrilla been killed, as the result of a feud that had its roots in some personal quarrel. Ah Soo Chye, Chin Peng's deputy in Malaya, had not been seen by security forces since 1956, and any reports about him that did trickle back were invariably so old as to be of no military value.

When the guerrillas entered areas they suspected might harbour security forces, they moved in with a frontal screen of aborigines who, in turn, had their dogs roaming ahead. Apart from conventional security forces who had tried, and failed, to penetrate this combination, there was an extraordinary outfit called the Senoi Praaq. This was a collection of aborigines who had been 'taken off the trees', given a uniform and a rifle and assigned to quasi-military duties on the main ladangs in Perak and Kelantan. Their name was the Temiar for 'Fighting Men', but a more unwarlike bunch of fellows would have been hard to find anywhere. Their inception was a bold idea, but that was the only bold thing about them. In spite of everybody's efforts, all reports were depressingly and repetitively monotonous – NTR; Nothing to Report.

So we who were left behind in Ipoh need not have worried. As the truth dawned on us, frustration bred. Operations were stereotyped, with liaison between ourselves and the police becoming strained. Unless there were a breakthrough, with something constructive happening, the Chinese were assured of a continued presence in north Malaya. Chin Peng's advance party would be poised for a second push south – something the Malayan government did not want and would not tolerate.

*   *   *

In late November 1961, B and D Companies went to Grik to relieve the troops who had been there for a month. The camp was outside the town on a small hillock overlooking a short runway. Very hot by day but pleasantly cool by night, it consisted of wooden huts. The town itself was small and lay three miles away from the Sungei {river} Perak, across which were the aborigines and, possibly, the guerrillas.

I found relations cool between the young, inexperienced, outgoing company commander and the local Special Branch officer, and the troops' morale low. Special Branch tended to ignore the military, whom they regarded as too impatient for quick results, whereas its own painstakingly slow projects often took months or even years to materialise, let alone pay dividends. In this case, unfortunately, the outgoing company commander had tried to work on his own behind Special Branch's back and this stupid gaffe had soured relations.

Working strictly to orders, we deployed across the Sungei Perak and based our troops on several ladangs. The river is one of the largest in the country and contains many nasty rapids which were only negotiated by the skill of the boatmen. Even so far inland it was often over a hundred yards wide.

Temiar headmen in the area were Ah Hong, Kantan and Goh Baleh. I went with a platoon of my Gurkhas and made camp near Kantan's ladang. The day after our arrival we went to visit him. The little collection of shacks was squalid and the people timid, insignificant and very dirty. My heart dropped when I saw what material we had to work on. No wonder, I thought, nothing had happened for so long. And the Temiar language was so different. Maybe our

Malay was too fractured for them to understand, despite their living so close to the Malay-speaking community in Grik.

Kantan came into my camp to meet us that evening and, realising that first impressions can be significant and even useful, I made a note in my diary soon after he left. Giving the Temiar greeting in Malay, he sat down and made himself very much at home; there was no need for us to try to make him talk. What impressed me was the apparent ring of truth in all he said. He claimed that he had not set eyes on or heard of communist terrorists for seven years. He talked at length, sometimes direct to me in Malay and sometimes with the Junior Civil Liaison Officer (each sub-unit had a Chinese JCLO attached to it to interpret) also in Malay. He was very prone to mood, scowling at the idea of our thinking he knew more than he would tell, and our hint that the terrorists used him to buy things in Grik, as the police suspected. He laughed happily at my attempts at Temiar and at my whistling like a bird. I noted down that his eyes gave him away when he was lying, that he had the mind of a child but the shallowness and guile of a monkey.

After he left, I realised that a month of such meetings would drive us all so demented as to impair our judgement. However, these were early days yet and we had to be patient.

I ordered a boat and moved upstream to visit Ah Hong. I went with a Chinese SEP, Ah Fut, who knew the area, and two soldiers, a radio operator and my batman, Tanké Limbu.

This ladang was bigger than Kantan's and we were lucky to find Ah Hong at home. As soon as he discovered I had no Malays in my party, he made his wife roast some tapioca for us and we all sat down near the river's edge to eat the stuff. The only news Ah Hong could give us was of five guerrillas, who had supposedly visited a Malay village on one of the larger tributaries of the Perak, namely the Temenggor, to the north. However, when pressed for more details, he said that the guerrillas were in Thailand, which was of no help. I was later told that Ah Hong was regarded with mild suspicion as he was always on the move. My comments on our meeting were that we had established friendly relations, but nothing more. We had been given a sop and now he would hope to be left alone.

I spent the night there and next morning moved back south, past Kantan's pathetic little plot, downstream to Goh Baleh's ladang. Here B Company had a camp and the aboriginal settlement was a much bigger concern, boasting just over a hundred souls. Goh Baleh himself was a shrewd man with personality, who neither cheapened himself like Kantan, nor gave facile answers as did Ah Hong. B Company was well organised, with a small medical post, and unlike the other two settlements I had visited, some of the aborigine women had come into the camp, bringing their children with them for treatment. As Goh Baleh was never alone, I did not have a chance of talking to him about the guerrillas.

It was essential that no public pressure be put on the leaders. Suspicion would immediately be generated, motives for our visit would also be suspect, and the headman would never dare commit himself publicly. So I contrived, the next morning, to talk privately with him. He answered that he thought there might be guerrillas in the deep south near a place called Rejam, but he could not tell for sure. He hesitated to put himself in a position to be blamed for inaccuracy, but even that snippet – it could not be called information – could not easily be acted upon because there were two areas, widely separated, both known as Rejam.

I returned to my base near Kantan's ladang. The northern man had said north, the middle man had said nothing, the southern man had said south. My message to Ipoh was 'nothing to report'.

Ipoh, on the other hand, had a message for me. Lieutenant Colonel Richard Kenney, the CO, wanted to visit a ladang and the very next day I was to meet him at the boat point opposite Kantan's place. We would then go downriver to Goh Baleh's ladang. Privately I felt it a waste of time, but one does not argue with any commanding officer, even as nice and understanding a man as Richard. We had first met when we all came from our Indian Army units to the British Army in 1948. Now, thirteen years later, our friendship had ripened. So we went to visit Goh Baleh, happy to be together again. At B Company's camp we behaved like normal visitors: pleasantries, a brew of tea, a wander around the perimeter, a talk with the Queen's Gurkha Officer platoon commander and the soldiers. Having been briefed on the complete lack of information, Richard Kenney sent for Goh Baleh and when he arrived we had more pleasantries. Then Richard, on the spur of the moment and for no apparent reason, observed: 'I hear some people have come from the north.'

This remark drew a most interesting reaction. Goh Baleh became quite worked up. He said that his son-in-law, a man named Soraya, had indeed arrived from the north only a day ago and had gone to his own ladang farther downstream. He had not bothered to inform Goh Baleh, either as headman or as his wife's father, and this was wrong. We had obviously touched on a raw spot and it needed canny exploitation; but Goh Baleh then dried up and merely asked us over to his ladang that evening for a dance.

The JCLO informed us that Soraya was a known guerrilla helper and his presence could well mean that he was spying out the latest military influx with a view to preventing the guerrillas from coming too near. It further transpired that the Rejam referred to by Goh Baleh was already being investigated by a platoon of B Company. The implication was that the guerrillas would now probably bypass the riverine posts and lie up in the other Rejam, where caves were. This was so nebulous that it hardly warranted being acted upon, but if the guerrillas were not going to be interested in the ladangs once they knew Gurkhas were in the vicinity, it might be a good opportunity for us of D Company to go north up to the Thai border to see what we could find.

Richard gently reminded me that, apart from having to get Brigade's permission to leave the ladangs, the area between Grik and the Thai border was
vast and possible routes through the area defied counting. My rejoinder was
that anything was better than squatting near a rural slum and with that we
both ate our evening meal, then went over to the ladang. We got there after
dark and the whole atmosphere was very friendly. We sat outside and a fire was
kept burning to see by. Maidens sat on one side and sang. Their voices were not
inharmonious and the pieces of bamboo they used as an orchestra produced an
enjoyable, simple clunking cadence in time with their song and the dancers'
footsteps.

As was inevitable, I was called out to dance and felt a complete fool as I was
put in line between two women and made to follow suit. Left, left, right, right,
round and round, it was not difficult, and the dim, flickering light hid my face.
The music did not drown the sound of the soldiers' applause and I managed to
get my own back by hauling some of them in to join me.

Next morning we went back to Grik to attend a meeting of the staff from
Brigade and Special Branch. It was for this meeting that Richard had come, and
his visit to the ladang now allowed him to put 'Bamboo' into some kind of
perspective.

He presented a plan that involved part of B Company moving south from
Goh Baleh's place to lodge with Soraya, and to ambush the area between there
and the Rejam hills where the caves were situated, while D Company moved
north, aiming for the Thai border. During discussion about this move I was
warned that no enemy courier routes – implying a line of country rather than
any particular track – had been identified for the past five or more years. To me
that showed a lack of a proper security force patrolling programme rather than
an absence of guerrillas.

The meeting took place on 6 December and on the 9th I received orders to
move north by river, some fifty miles, and then to patrol up to the Thai border,
paying particular attention to the area immediately east and west of the upper
reaches of the Sungei Perak. A fleet of boats with outboard engines would leave
the main boat point at 7 o'clock the next morning; all we had to do was to get
ready and be there on time.

A combination of Richard's tact and my own record from Emergency days
had been enough to put us on the offensive. The veil of operational torpidity
had been lifted.

CHAPTER 5

The Second Veil

At 5 o'clock on the morning of 10 December 1961 we were up, drinking our tea, prior to our move. By dawn we were at the boat point, the men told off into boatloads, life jackets ready and weapons tested. Eight boats were needed and, by 8 o'clock, an hour after we were due to have been on our way, none had arrived.

I managed to contact the Malay captain who was the Brigade Liaison Officer and spoke to him in English, more as a protocol gesture than otherwise. He drove off in search of the contractor whose duty it was to supply the boats. By then a few Malay boatmen had turned up and, in an effort to get matters organised with a bit of speed, I chivvied them along, this time speaking in Malay. At the same time a group of Senoi Praaq passed by and, showing off more than anything else, I tried to find out their destination, using simple Temiar. In Nepali I told the men that I foresaw a change in our proposed timetable and, before I had finished, the boat contractor, an ample-bellied Indian, arrived in his car. Trying to instil some urgency into the proceedings, I spoke to him in Hindi. His driver was Chinese, so I vented my feelings on the hapless man in Cantonese. It only then struck me that I had used six languages within the space of half an hour. But it was not only being able to get things moving by using those languages; I noticed a look of deep respect in the eyes of those whose knowledge did not extend to the tongues I was using. Unconsciously, the germ of an idea was generated in my mind on that morning and, although I did not realise it, I had already taken a fundamentally vital step forward in the right direction on the 'hearts and minds' front.

By 8.20 two boats were ready to move, so I told my Gurkha Captain that I would go ahead there and then, while he was to organise the rest of the company in tactical groups and send them upriver as and when boats became ready, and we would meet at the place previously decided upon, possibly that night and certainly on the morrow.

At first, in the cool of the morning, it was fun to be on the river. At least we were doing something positive and unusual. The countryside on either side was cultivated by small holdings of rubber and tapioca where not covered by tall, rank grass, called 'lallang'. The jungle had been cut back. Small villages and isolated homesteads dotted the scenery and we came across fishermen as well as folk bathing.

Within two hours the boat accompanying mine had completely broken down, so I radioed Grik and left it where it was. There was no hardship as it was self-contained with arms, ammunition and rations. We pressed on alone. It was all airy-fairily unmilitary and typically Malay: we stopped at two houses near the river's edge, once for the boatman to have a meal and once for his coxswain to get some victuals. This allowed us to stretch our legs. Our progress was further slowed by several breakdowns. As the hours passed we grew uncomfortably hot, for there was no awning, and very cramped. The river wound around the contours, with a strong current in the main channel. Occasionally we came across rapids that needed considerable skill to navigate.

By evening, instead of being well north with my company, I was barely halfway. Another boat joined me at dusk: two boats and eighteen men! It was no use being annoyed, there was nothing that could be done, at that stage, to hurry things up.

Next morning we reached a police fort, some forty miles north of Grik, at a place called Tapong. The Malay 'kampongs' on the river's edge had petered out long before, and there should have been nobody north of the fort, as the limit of aboriginal cultivations was also well to its south. Jungle pressed down on both banks. I called in and met the commander, a Malay inspector who, with a Sikh, gave me a cup of coffee and an invitation to spend Christmas with them. They told me the limit of their patrolling north from the fort – well below my destination.

We continued upstream, the river now considerably narrower but more turbulent. We had one very shaky moment when it fell more than two feet between large rocks. We had to climb over this fault and I doubted whether it was safe even to try. I would have preferred to get out and walk around the hazard; apart from stretching our legs, it would ensure no drowned weapons. The boatman, in a fit of misplaced confidence, dissuaded me from doing so and was half-way up the incline with a powerful head of water against us when the engine failed. The boat was immediately slewed sideways and caught the whole force of the current. Water poured in. Luckily we did not capsize but were swept back down into the comparative calm. There was near panic in the boat until the soldiers saw a large fish swimming around in the water at our feet and their foraging instincts prevailed. I was not going to risk another attempt, so we got out and walked. My unspoken comment on the whole journey up till then was 'haphazard with more hazard than hap'.

We reached the boat limit before dusk on the second day and could do little until everybody else had arrived. However, we could, and did, search around and almost immediately found very obvious traces of camping. We reckoned that two or three guerrillas had been there quite recently, basing our judgment on the state of some dried blood from an animal carcase that we came across. We also found a number of tins that had been untidily thrown away not more than two months previously. The police had said that they had not visited this area for a long time, yet here was evidence of movement that no self-respecting guerrilla would leave. I opened my radio with Grik, asked for records of security force movements to be checked, and waited, with growing impatience, for the rest of my men to arrive.

At 7 o'clock the next morning I was sitting by the side of the river, which was only about fifty yards across and swept round in a wide curve. I suddenly heard a noise that sounded like the mewing of gulls from the far bank. A long snake was being swept obliquely across the river. It had bumps equidistantly spaced its entire length. Only when it reached the near bank did the bumps separate and become monkeys. As the river was too wide to cross by jumping from tree to tree, each had held onto the tail of the animal in front as the current carried them over.

The last boatload of men arrived at midday on the third day, in some rain, and they were very glad to get out of the boats. I gave the last boatman a sample of the tins and a note to take back to the police.

We had a quick brew, sorted ourselves out and moved north. We soon came across definite evidence of guerrilla movement: a camp eighteen months old, on the site of an old security force camp. And at 4.40 that evening, we encountered footprints of two men, one wearing hockey boots, the other barefooted, who had moved north that very morning.

We immediately started ferreting around and informed headquarters, who also became very excited. Tantalisingly, we found no more footprints. A platoon from another company was flown in farther north next day, on the odd chance that I could direct them to intercept the two men, whom I suspected were a Chinese guerrilla courier with an aborigine guide.

We only carried five days' supplies so, before we could continue as far north as the Thai border, we needed resupplying: food, radio batteries, jungle boots, many of which did not last more than ten days, and clothing. We reached a hole in the jungle where we took our resupply, putting out ambushes until after the drop.

I had a radio message that a thorough check of troop movements revealed neither a police nor military presence in the area, but that there was a considerable black market in Thailand based on time-expired rations issued to the security forces. It all pointed north and led me to believe that the guerrillas were deliberately disguising their camps to resemble those of undisciplined soldiers: it was as good a deception as many others and from then on we took nothing for granted.

After our airdrop I asked for a map sheet of southern Thailand to be dropped. An Auster flew up from Ipoh, by now 150 miles away, and the pilot felt that a round trip of 300 miles for a piece of paper depicting a confined area we were not allowed to enter was asking a bit much. However, I was delighted as I found, when I joined it to my Malayan map, that a village and some cultivations were shown ten miles over the border, on the axis of our advance. No other such details were shown elsewhere, so I decided to move forward on a line between my present location and the one cultivated area in Thailand shown on the map.

We moved off and, a couple of days later, reached the border. There, 200 yards short of it, I was amazed to see three limes lying on the ground. However hard we searched the locality, we could find neither lime trees nor footprints. The limes were in a straight row, placed, not fallen, and were fresh. Later on we found another three, similarly set on a track, but many months older and nowhere near any other lime tree. Who had placed them and why? There were no such trees anywhere we searched. I sent a radio message to the Intelligence Officer to find out where lime trees grew, wild or cultivated. He queried my message, seeing no point in such esoteric knowledge that seemed to have no bearing on what I was doing. Richard Kenney came on the 'blower' to ask if my query had any relevance. Although there was a lot of interference which made voice contact difficult, I prevailed and Special Branch were asked for their opinion.

I had to take another resupply and this time two parachutes fell into the river, one containing the signal batteries. The long-suffering Auster flew in yet again to bring us some more. We then moved up to the border. On the way we again heard high-pitched animal noises and this time we had the rewarding sight of three otters fishing in a stream. Game abounded in the area: we recognised the spoor of bear, elephant, rhinoceros, tiger, deer, pig and snakes. One patrol found a large patch of trampled and bloody undergrowth, and a pig and a python that had fought to the death.

Near the border we again found evidence of guerrilla movement. We deduced that there had been two groups, one of three or four men who had come over from Thailand, and patrolled as far as we had reached before returning. We reckoned that their footprints were three or four days old. The other group could well have been those whose footprints we had come across on 12 December, as there were two men, one in hockey boots and one barefooted. We found their prints on one side of a large boulder and I sent for the corporal who had led the patrol up to that point only the previous day. The footprints were fresh and the painful implication was that these two men had spotted the soldiers as they moved upstream and had hidden behind the boulder as the patrol passed by. Recrimination was useless and unfair, nor did I allow myself the luxury of it. Even so, I felt very sad at missing such a chance. It was intriguing to think that those two men had placed the limes as a code to those who had come over from Thailand, maybe as a message in case physical contact was impossible. Time and space considerations, however, could mean that the two men from the south had gone into Thailand and the group from the north had merely been patrolling. But, then, surely those limes were no coincidence.

We were warned to fly out by helicopter on 30 December. As we prepared the landing site we found plentiful evidence in the surrounding creeks of a Police Field Force group. There were many tins that had been dumped after airdrops. I spent some time foraging and found another large dump containing unopened tins of food; other tins had been opened with a knife, the scavengers obviously having no tin openers. It had all been well picked over by guerrillas from over the border. The dump stretched for 400 yards each side of a stream. I also found a pair of boots of a pattern that only Police Field Force units wore. All the dump lacked was a photograph of Lord Baden-Powell in shirtsleeve order and, of course, any guerrillas.

The soldiers' reaction was understandably critical. Why did we flog out guts out, insisting on an uncomfortably high standard of everything, when others were so ill-disciplined as to make such a frightful mess, besides giving away so much to the enemy? But at least it was obvious why there had been no positive results for so very long.

Later there were recriminations among the police hierarchy, alleging that I had made it all up and was being beastly to them; yet they could not deny the evidence of the boots.

The answer to the limes riddle was there were no trees in Perak, but some in Kelantan, near a large ladang belonging to a headman called Bongsu Helwood. News was also passed of aborigine movement from Kelantan in connection with a suspected guerrilla meeting, location unknown.

We had found the guerrilla courier route, from Thailand to Perak and Kelantan.

Having lifted one veil and gone on the offensive, we had uncovered another, one of ignorance, so we now knew where to focus our attention with definite knowledge – the first for five years. But although my company had lifted the second veil, there was nothing to suggest that I was to become personally involved.

CHAPTER 6

The Third Veil

During January 1962, A and C Companies ambushed and patrolled up in the north, near the Thai border, as well as south in the area of the ladangs, but with never a sniff or sign of anything faintly hostile. By February it was once more the turn of B and D Companies, so back I went to Grik. This time a squadron of 22 SAS was in the area, nominally in a training role, but very deployable for all that.

Until this juncture the movements of the security forces had been controlled, to a large extent, by Special Branch. One area that had been 'frozen' belonged to a certain Kerinching who had, at one time, carried a shotgun in the guerrilla organisation and had been on very friendly terms with Ah Soo Chye, the 'senior' Chinese guerrilla in the whole of 'Bamboo'. It had been hoped that, by not having to worry about troops in the vicinity, he could have freedom of action if the guerrillas wanted to contact him again. He had surrendered his shotgun to a remarkable Chinese, one Goh Ah Hok, who was the JCLO with B Company and who had twice been awarded the British Empire Medal for gallantry. Now that there was fresh evidence of hostile movement, Special Branch felt that Kerinching could furnish some more details. With Goh Ah Hok present, Kerinching would suffer troops on his ladang, and a platoon of B Company was sent there – a five-hour boat journey, followed by an hour's walk.

For the first few days, Goh Ah Hok jollied Kerinching along and confined the conversation to pleasantries and reminiscences. On 7 February, Kerinching volunteered that the guerrillas had gone to Thailand and would contact him on their return. The information was passed to me in Grik, and to Richard Kenney in Ipoh, that same day.

Events were considered to be taking a favourable turn by Special Branch who said that Kerinching, even by confessing as little as he had to Goh Ah Hok, would never pass on rumour. The desire for positive results and for a follow-up to my December findings prompted Richard Kenney to send me to Kerinching's ladang the very next day to see what I could glean.

A boat was arranged for me and Tanké Limbu on 8 February. The first part of the journey up the Sungei Perak was familiar, but the ride up a much narrower tributary, the Sungei Temenggor, was new. The jungle closed in on either side and we could have been ambushed from almost anywhere along both banks. The boat grounded several times and the boatman had to get out and push. At last we reached a place where the map marked a 'halting bungalow' where we

Above and below: Compass and map in the jungle are as necessary for controlled tactical movement as are white stick and guide dog to a blind man.

Above: Had these Vietnamese soldiers under training in the Jungle Warfare School been on operations their lives might well have depended on sticking some vegetation into their hats to break up the outline.

Below: The Commandant listens to his Vietnamese students at the end of a day's jungle exercise.

Opposite page: Cooking techniques may differ but a 'hot brew' is universal.

Opposite page, top: The Commandant pins Jungle Warfare School Graduation Brooches on successful Thai students at the end of their course. A member of the Gurkha Independent Parachute Company carries the brooches on a cushion.

Opposite page, bottom: Gurkhas were normally very patient when acting as 'exercise enemy' against those who, in the heat of the moment, sometimes forgot they were not operating 'for real'.

Below: Jungle fighting is the nearest thing to night fighting by day. So close is the range of vision that ears have to take over from eyes much of the time.

The helicopter, more than any other vehicle, changed the face of jungle fighting by covering miles in minutes when such distances would otherwise have taken days. They were also battle winning in their ability to fly in reserves quickly when needed.

Above: All-round observation and the passing back of orders in silence is possible when the leading scout uses hand signals. Here 'halt' is being signalled and will be passed back in similar fashion.

Below: Dry paddy; slash-and-burn cultivation is common in Sarawak. As a waste of valuable timber it is unexcelled.

Opposite page: Gurkha Demonstration Troops acted as 'baddies' and 'goodies'. When this demonstration of captured and wounded guerrillas was shown to certain journalists, the Commandant was even accused of 'teaching torture'!

From above the jungle looked like a sea of cabbages. The skill of the pilots in flying their aircraft, looking for suspicious signs below or giving troops a 'fix' as to their positions, was fully appreciated by all who operated on the jungle floor.

The officer in charge of all the Rangers in the ARVN (the South Vietnamese army) visited his men on jungle training. Here a point is being explained by one of the British instructors.

The same officer is seen here talking to the officer in charge of the Jungle Wing, Major 'Oscar' Whitamore.

Opposite page, top: During his time as Commandant, the author received an average of eight visitors every five working days during his three-year tenure. Here a VIP from General Headquarters is being shown the type of well that Viet Cong guerrillas would hide in during the Vietnam War.

Opposite page, bottom: The Gurkhas of the Gurkha Independent Parachute Company were so proud and thrilled to get their 'red berets' when linked with the Parachute Regiment that one or two of them slept in their new hats on the first night.

Below: The author is bid farewell by his senior staff on leaving the Gurkha Paras.

Men of the Gurkha Para Company jump in simultaneous 20s from an RAF Argosy at 900 feet. One minute behind is a second Argosy with forty more men, flying at 800 feet. Never before had there been a British jump involving simultaneous 20s in Asia. Uniquely, not one man of the total eighty needed checking in pre-flight or in-flight. It was this demonstration of efficiency in the air, and later on the ground, that earned the unit permanent Order of Battle status. (Robin Adshead) stopped and I thankfully stepped ashore. Met by a guide, we set off into the jungle, down a well-worn path. Twenty minutes later the jungle fell back and a valley devoid of any trees opened up. Pre-war the area had been open-cast tin mining, but all had fallen into disuse, with only the concrete base and one low wall remaining to show that a bungalow had stood by the river's edge.

The jungle closed in again. We reached the platoon base, and as I walked into the camp I got a warm welcome from the Gurkhas: I noticed Goh Ah Hok sitting on one side with a Temiar who seemed, from his stately bearing, to be a man of some importance. I dumped my pack and went over to Goh, using my Cantonese to good effect, remembering how easily even a few sentences of a language not understood by a listener can sound impressive. I was quite aware that Goh did not speak Cantonese, but he knew what I was trying to achieve. The Temiar listened impassively and was then introduced as Kerinching.

Later on, after a meal, Goh, Kerinching and I sat down for a talk. As I had yet to come to grips with Temiar for detailed conversations, we spoke in easy Malay. I had been warned by Goh to listen, not to ask Kerinching to repeat himself, not to press him and not to show exasperation. I had little hope of getting anything useful by myself, so let Goh guide the conversation.

By the end of an hour my head was in a whirl. I had been told many things and even though there was no means of knowing whether Kerinching was telling the truth, at least he had started to talk. Maybe my initial burst of acting was paying dividends.

I learned of three places where the guerrillas crossed the Sungei Perak, who of the 'big three' – Ah Soo Chye, Lo See and Tek Miu – wore khaki and who wore green, how their aborigine screen moved, how warning of danger was passed, and even how they preferred sleeping. Kerinching then closed up and refused to divulge any more, as though he had said enough for one time and now it was up to us.

I had made out to Kerinching that I had come to help him, so he would be suspicious if I left too soon. I sent back the information I had gleaned and spent the next four days in and around the ladang, trying to become friends with the people. On my second day, Kerinching asked us to burn down his main house, owing to sickness. So we set it ablaze and heard the fleas jumping, click, click, as they jumped away from the fire twenty yards off. The aborigines moved to some temporary, and very squalid, shelters. I changed the platoon's ambush and patrolling programme as the men were being overtaxed. All the while I tried to think how I could improve on what had been done so far. And on 11 February I heard about Senagit.

Senagit was a relative of Kerinching and they had shared the shotgun before Kerinching's surrender. He had married a girl from Kelantan, from the ladang of Kerinching's counterpart over the main divide, Bongsu Helwood, whom the communist guerrillas had made headman even before the Malayan government had. If there was one man as powerful as, or even more powerful than, Kerinching, it was this Bongsu Helwood. Senagit was therefore a link between the two communities and, an added attraction, had been Ah Soo Chye's friend, guide and cook for the past nine years. He had been wounded by a security force patrol and he remained faithful to Ah Soo Chye. Special Branch learned that Senagit was somewhere in the area, probably on a mission for Ah Soo Chye; and on my making inquiries, I discovered that he had fallen ill and was even then downstream from us.

That evening I asked Kerinching about Senagit. It was here that I came up against a barrier. Kerinching was unwilling to discuss him with me. His eyes became shifty and his talk evasive. I knew that forced methods would not work, so I made arrangements to leave for Grik the next day. I also knew that Kerinching was due to pay one of his infrequent visits there the day after, to meet one Ismail of Special Branch, and I wanted to prepare my ground.

Back in Grik I found that a young doctor, Captain David Hopkins, had arrived with the SAS. I arranged with him and Ismail for the two of us to return with Kerinching to see the stricken Senagit, provided Ismail could get Kerinching to agree. This he managed to do. So, on 14 February, we went back upstream, in two boats, one for David to get back to Grik and the other for the rest of us to go as far as the Sungei Klian, near the site of the 'halting bungalow'.

We reached a spot on the Sungei Temenggor where Kerinching bade us halt. He clambered up the bank, followed by David and myself. He again told us to wait and searched around for the sick man. Having found him, he returned to bring us forward.

The man was a pitiful sight. Any grandiose ideas I had entertained of Senagit were dispelled as I looked at a pathetic little runt, scantily clad, lying on a small platform of split bamboos under the cover of some leaves. His eyes were large and bright with fever. His hand trembled and he was plainly both ill and frightened. His skin was unhealthily dry and flaking. A woman, his wife from Kelantan, lay near by, also sick. Kerinching muttered something to them.

David Hopkins took out a few instruments from his haversack and Senagit was so terrified he would have run away had he had the strength. I tried to ask questions but Senagit only understood Temiar and Kerinching would not cooperate. Eventually a diagnosis was made, malaria or typhus, so a crash course of pills which would help both and hinder neither was decided upon. The pills were placed within easy reach of Senagit and his wife, and I looked up my phrase book and gave the instructions: *Nai ish nai ish neq kalai neq keldel*, which was the nearest I could get to 'three pills three times a day'. *Nab ong*, I added, when David asked if I had specified with water.

Before we left, I tried to make Senagit understand that I would visit him again soon. We reached base at dusk. The Gurkhas were very interested in what we had done, but indicated that they held out no hope for a successful outcome as far as the guerrilla situation was concerned. I was more optimistic, but was worried at Kerinching's obvious dislike of Senagit's meeting outsiders. I felt that if only I could get Senagit to Grik without Kerinching being there, I might have a chance to find out something positive.

Next evening Kerinching walked over from his new temporary shack to cadge cigarettes and talk to Goh. I acknowledged his arrival, but pretended to carry on reading. They started talking and I heard Kerinching say, very softly, that he did not think any good would come of treatment without the needle. 'Why,' he asked, 'was the doctor brought all the way from Grik without a needle?'

Goh made some soothing remark, but Kerinching was not mollified. I then put my book down and went to join some soldiers who were not in earshot. A germ of an idea had formed; I needed my conversation with the Gurkhas to be seen and remembered, just as I wanted Kerinching to associate my having been with them and not with him and Goh.

Two days later Kerinching and Goh were sitting talking. I went over to them, and, ever polite, they let me join in.

'Heh, Old Man,' I addressed Kerinching respectfully. 'In two days' time I am going downstream to see Senagit.' I had waited until then because I knew that even he had no real idea of any time of more than four days ahead, and I needed four days for my plan.

'I hope he is better,' replied Kerinching, smiling weakly.

'If he is still ill I propose to take him to Grik for treatment.'

'He will not go to Grik,' came the flat refusal. 'If he is still ill the doctor must come upstream again.'

'Do you want Senagit to have the needle?' I asked.

'Who said he wanted a needle?'

'You yourself did.'

'When?'

'Two days ago with this Chinese here.'

He was beaten and he knew it. He did not want to go to Grik again and I told him that the needle could not come upstream. So Senagit had to go downstream. But there were conditions and I had to promise to conform. Senagit would go, but I would have to go with him and stay with him. He would only be there for two days and no one else would talk to him. I would have to bring him back myself. I agreed, and the thought struck me that Senagit would probably refuse to accompany me.

'Never mind,' said Kerinching. 'I will send my grown-up son, Sutel, with you to Senagit. What he says, Senagit will do. Senagit will go.'

So, on 20 February, I went downstream to Senagit, taking Tanké and Sutel as authority, with myself as an expectant surety. We nearly failed to reach him owing to boat trouble and when we did he was so scared at the thought of going that his hand-rolled leaf cigarette missed his mouth altogether. I felt that I was in for a struggle but, obligingly, another man walked out of the trees and made his way towards us. He radiated confidence. His name was Rijed. He was Kerinching's brother and he said he would go down to Grik with us. So we were six; two boatmen, Senagit, Rijed, Tanké and myself. Sutel stayed with Senagit's wife.

We reached Grik just before dusk and there was insufficient time to examine Senagit. Instead, we fixed him a bed by himself in a hut, gave him a 'needle' and a sleeping tablet. The needle merely injected purified water, but honour was satisfied – we had 'gone through the motions'.

Next morning there was a proper medical examination and a very bad dose of malaria was diagnosed. Penicillin was injected and a course of vitamin tablets recommended. We then turned to the serious business of trying to make Senagit talk.

In my wilder moments I had envisaged my interviewing him using pentathol, the so-called truth drug, but when I put forward such an idea, there was so fierce a reaction against it that I felt rather a cad for suggesting it in the first place. Instead, two SEPs were produced, neither of them recently surrendered. I had already met one of them, Ah Fut, but not the other, Ah Kong. If Senagit knew either of them, he kept it to himself. I tried all ways: talking in different tongues, hinting, cajoling, anything but showing impatience. Nothing would budge Senagit and I reluctantly called it all off because I could not afford to turn him sour.

I took him back to his little hut, had him treated and then contacted the CO on the radio. I was bitterly disappointed and wanted to wash my hands of the whole matter. Richard Kenney wisely cautioned me against breaking my word, telling me to take the man back upstream. He added sagely, 'Only good can come of it.'

Luckily for me I could in no way foresee the outcome of Richard's words.

Another million units of penicillin and a sleeping pill that evening, with the promise of going home on the morrow, made Senagit look happier than he had all day. Next morning we went down to the boat point and, once again, set off upstream.

I was sitting up in front, next to Senagit and, for the first quarter of an hour, said nothing. On an impulse I put my arm round his skinny shoulders and said, in Temiar, 'Senagit, you are a good man.'

'You have a good heart, but you make your mouth look like a chicken's backside,' was the surprising rejoinder.

'What to do?' I countered neutrally.

'When I am ill again, I will send for you and the doctor will make me well.'

'Yes,' I said, thinking of the effort needed to do only that which we had done. I hesitated to commit myself, so I changed the subject.

'Senagit!'

'Yes.'

'Will you go fishing with me?'

'Yes.'

'Will you go fishing with me for fish with two legs?'

'Yes, when I am strong, if the Old Man lets me.'

'Senagit, I go with you, for you are a good man.'

'Old Man, I go with you for you are a good man. But the other Old Man will let me go or not?'

The third veil had been lifted. The fourth would prove much harder.

CHAPTER 7

The Fourth Veil

So there was my problem. I had, so it seemed, made an ally of the one man who had recent connections with Ah Soo Chye and also a link to Bongsu Helwood, the man made 'penghulu' by the guerrillas before the government so appointed him and whose name was mentioned in connection with those limes. First, could I persuade Kerinching to help me? Second, despite his having addressed me by the honorific word Tata – literally but baldly translated as 'Old Man', a most unusual honour – could I trust Senagit? And third, if I did prosper, could I persuade officialdom, with all its prickliness, to let me plan, then act, on whatever resulted from Kerinching, allowing Senagit to go with me? We were due for a change over a week away. I doubted if my relief could easily take my place. Somewhere a price would have to be paid. Could I discover Kerinching's price and who would pay it?

I pondered as we journeyed upstream and scarcely noticed the rapids as we nosed our way into the water cascading over the faults in the rocks. It was cooler when we reached the Temenggor and I was glad to stretch my legs when we arrived at Senagit and Rijed's temporary shelter, while the two Temiar went ashore to collect their womenfolk. They approached their lean-to shelters, but nobody was there. I felt out of my depth and was assailed by a sense of helplessness that I was to know so well later when I was being swept along by events. Yet neither man seemed upset by the absence of their women. It left our boat that bit lighter and we made good time to the Sungei Klian.

At the camp Kerinching was waiting for us, like some primeval clocker-in. I felt he would not be best pleased by the disappearance of the two wives, but he evinced no outward manifestation of any feelings. The soldiers were interested and waited patiently until I was ready to tell them. But there was nothing really to be told, just a silly conversation about fish with two legs and some basic doctoring that also involved purified water and sleeping pills. That evening, not for the first time, gloom reasserted itself.

For the next day and a half I hardly moved. A wooden bed-frame had been made for me and I had a paperback novel to read. I held it in front of me so that people would not think I was idle and sleeping, but I scarcely saw the text, much less read it. Thoughts crowded one another as I picked them: Thailand fifty miles north ... the main divide to the east with no pass below 4500 feet high ... and so far ... would radio work? ... how many ladangs and how many head men, 'penghulus', were there? . . . who trusted whom? . . . what was whose price? . . . what was Kerinching's price? . . . who would go? . . . and if they went, who with? . . . and where? . . . and when? . . . and resupply? . . . and sickness? . . . and maps? . . . and boundaries? . . . and . . . and . . . It was endless and any tentative solution to one set of problems merely raised doubts about others. The only answer was to sleep on it all and hope that some solution would be obvious the next morning.

Alas, all that happened was that I slept badly and my mind was as far from any solution as it ever had been. A mug of tea, a walk down the hill to the stream to shave, the morning radio schedule, 'November Tango Romeo – nothing to report'. Back onto the wooden platform, eyes closed, mind in neutral . . . and suddenly I had a flash of inspiration, a moment of truth. I sent for Goh and told him to contact Kerinching. I turned my new idea over in my mind as I waited for his arrival.

Kerinching came with Goh. I told them to be seated and I then started: 'Heh, Tata. I think and hope deeply you help me. For your help this I promise. If we have success I will pay you one thousand "ringgits".' One 'ringgit', or Straits dollar, was worth roughly one-eighth of a pound sterling: a thousand to him was about a million to anyone else. As the Temiar could only count up to three it was an impossible amount to visualise, but it had to be worth having. 'If we do not have success, if we have bad luck, I will say nothing, I will not be angry. Will you help me?'

I waited, on tenterhooks, and finally he said, 'Tata. Yes, I will help you. Why did nobody ask me like that before? I will give you three men who will be yours. You will take them where you will, they will be trusted men.' He had three conditions: 'Only you will go. If another, I will not send my men. I do not know, I do not trust, I do not like. Only you.'

He paused and I waited for a second condition. I was surprised when he said, 'You will not wear jungle boots. You will not have andrup' – a corruption of the word 'airdrop'.

Again he paused for so long I feared he had changed his mind. But he continued, 'Only take a few men with you and no one else must know.'

'Who will you give to go with me?' I dared not presume, nor hint. Kerinching smiled as he turned to me and said, 'Senagit will go with you because he knows where the "bad men" might go and he recognises their signs. Sutcl and Rijed will go as well, to let you see I mean true for other headmen and yourself. So you will all go and fish for fish with two legs. If you have good luck, you have good luck. If not, so, what am I to do?'

I thanked him sincerely and explained why one man had to know, namely Ismail of Special Branch. 'Otherwise who will give the reward if I am far away?'

'Yes, bring him here. I will talk with him and you.'

I looked at my watch – 11 o'clock on Saturday, 24 February. I called over to the Radio Operator, 'Heh, Sig-nel. "Fetch Sunray."'

Richard Kenney came on the set a few minutes later and, warning him to expect a long message, told him all I knew and all that Kerinching had stipulated.

*   *   *

Two days later, Kerinching, his wife, two Gurkhas and I walked down to meet Ismail on the Sungei Temenggor. It was nearly dark by the time the boat arrived from Grik and, as it was the month of fasting, none in the police boat had eaten all day, so food first, then talk. I told the Gurkhas to cook our meal, as we had arrived only a few minutes before Ismail. Kerinching's wife had already started to prepare their evening meal of tapioca. It was a simple exercise in economy of effort, I thought, as I looked on.

She had brought with her a rattan back basket, containing bamboo cylinders for water, and tapioca. Earlier on she had carried the bamboos into the water and, legs apart and skirt above her knees, washed them out as she stood, then filled them. Later she built a small fire to bake the tapioca. Having peeled the tubers, she had to clean them. Squatting down, holding a bamboo container between her knees lest the water spill, she put them within easy reach. Tilting the container up to her mouth, she took a swig of water, replaced the bamboo between her knees and picked up the pieces of tapioca one by one, holding them a little away from her. Squirting the water out, jet-like, onto each piece, she deftly cleaned it before her supply ran dry. Finally it was put into the ashes to roast, with a slight dowsing of the flame until it dried off.

After our meal we settled down for the conference. Ismail asked me to listen and he drew out of Kerinching his ideas for success. It was a fascinating study of tact and leadership and, in the end, a simple plan was produced. If Ah Soo Chye was in Perak, a 'penghulu' called Sagor would know. If he was not in Perak, he would have to go to Kelantan where Bongsu Helwood would know. In either case my three men would spy out the land while we lay up. They would arrive in ladangs as though they had no connection with anyone else. It was for that reason that my group had to be small and had to remain hidden, hence no airdrops. By wearing hockey boots instead of jungle boots, any aborigine finding our tracks would put us down to guerrillas and not security forces. It all made sense. Kerinching also said he would let any troops remaining on his ladang know if Ah Soo Chye came while I was away.

Finally it all came to an end. Ismail, sitting next to me, excitedly nudged me. 'We're through!' he said. 'Now, at long last we have the key, or rather,' he corrected himself, 'you have the key which opens all doors. Maybe you don't realise that this has never happened before – never.'

He went on to embrace Kerinching and, after a few pleasantries, the meeting broke up.

We went to settle down for the night. I moved over to where my two Gurkhas sat, weapons over their knees. I sat down with them.

'*Hunchha, hola.* All may go well,' I said. 'We talked much and the "bare one" is satisfied. Maybe all this time with mangy dogs and jumping fleas has not been wasted. Now I am tired.'

The Gurkhas looked at me in the flickering firelight and one said, 'We, too, hope for success. Now let us sleep.'

*　　*　　*

Back in Ipoh I had three weeks to plan everything. I was lucky it was so long because it gave Senagit enough time to recover his strength, apart from sorting out my own problems. Richard Kenney accepted my absence for two months and higher formation had no objection, nor had Special Branch. However, I did have difficulty with the Department of Aborigines, who were possessive, if not jealous, of their mandate and resented what they saw as my intruding into their affairs. In fact, an Englishman named Norman Herbolt made a special journey from Kuala Lumpur to Ipoh and tried to dissuade me from taking up Kerinching's offer. His parting words, spoken with animosity, deliberation and sincerity, were, 'I hope you fail'. This man was to prove a disruptive influence, especially after Richard Kenney had left, with the new man not knowing the background and, it seemed to me, veering much more towards Herbolt than to me, his own company commander. Luckily for my peace of mind, I did not know then how much discrimination I would encounter.

My problems gradually became sorted out and fell into six main categories. Once I had appreciated all the limitations, I had some hard decisions to make.

The terrain worried me. The area I had initially been given was 1200 square miles, neatly divided into two by the main range of Malaya. The lowest pass was 4500 feet above sea level and I had to face considerable differences in temperature, as I started out at only 500 feet. There were many fast, deep and unfordable rivers where rafts were needed for crossing.

Rations were the biggest problem. I knew we could not carry enough by ourselves. I doubted out ability to forage much and I reckoned that hunting would betray our presence – the one thing I could not allow to happen. I aimed to buy some produce from ladangs, my three Temiar making the transactions, and carried S$100 in one-dollar bills and S$50 in small change. It was quite a weight. I had received a list from Special Branch of where tapioca patches were to be found as this seemed to be the only food that we could use for bulk. I had made enquiries about tapioca and regarded it as a last resort. Its disadvantage was that, to get sufficient calories and vitamins, forty pounds of the stuff were required each day and that, I was told, was more than a cow's daily intake of grass. Vitamin pills were obviously important and some hard tack, chocolate and biscuits, both supplied in the rations, would also be very useful.

The cumulative effect of a poor diet was worrying me, so I asked the Medical Officer how little food we might need each day and still keep functioning. He said five ounces a day would keep a person alive, so I planned a daily diet of five ounces of rice, with half an ounce of tinned meat or fish from the rations we carried, and anything extra to be bought or foraged. I knew we could have vegetables from the ladangs, as the aborigines grew calladium, sweet potatoes, taro, gourds, bananas, sugar cane, eggplant and, surprisingly, spinach.

In addition I had to make arrangements for my three aborigines as they could not be expected to be self-supporting when working so intimately with us. In the end I planned on making twelve days' rations – and then by no means all the items in the ration scale – last for forty-eight. So much for permission to be away for two months!

Carrying all we needed in the way of weapons, ammunition, rations, clothing and medical requirements posed a weight problem. We could not get any lightweight rations so our food, though good, was bulky and heavy. Some of us carried Bergen rucksacks and others, like myself, carried two packs strapped together on a light alloy frame, a 'manpack carrier'. Both methods utilised a head-band that helped distribute the weight. We also wore our equipment. It was cumbersome and heavy, but effective. We weighed ourselves before setting out and found we were carrying between 103 and 108 pounds.

We had no special radio equipment and the communication problem was what to do if our set became unserviceable or the divide masked us. I requested a search aircraft if we were silent for three days and suggested certain smoke and panel signs.

The last two problems were interwoven: my men and sickness. I based my tactics, hence the size of my team, on three groups of three, with myself available to go with any group I considered necessary. The principles on which I based everything were fourfold: secrecy, security, surprise and simplicity. All that we did would have to be simple enough for our screen of three aborigines to react properly in the event of a chance encounter. I was not so concerned about their behaviour when they were away from us, only how they would operate as part of a team.

Although I had a paper strength of well over a hundred men in D Company, my choice of soldiers to take with me was restricted to fifteen men only. I could not touch one of my platoons as the soldiers had recently been trained as parachutists with a theatre role, nor men due for home leave in Nepal, nor men due to go on courses or posting. Nor did I want my most recently joined soldiers.

Most Gurkhas, and all who are properly led, are tractable and tenacious. I consider them better than other troops. Having stayed on ladangs, there had been enough time for the chemistry of relations with the Temiar to mature. Even so, human stamina would most likely be called on in great measure: there was no place for frailties. It would be a case of mind over matter; men rising to the challenge. I had to have men who were fit and strong, tight-corner men, men who would sleep rough, be ready to tighten their belts and be prepared, if sick, to be left behind alone. My men had not only to get on with one another, but also with me. Our close proximity and the unnatural strains resulting from such a mission would mar it if we could not live together.

I selected nine men and called them to me. I gave them a thorough briefing and told them that, were we successful, the consequence could be that a Gurkha battalion's presence near the border became a permanent requirement and that was very important as even in those days there were rumours of cuts in the Brigade of Gurkhas. I also told them that there was no compulsion for them to go on this operation; I would in no way think less of a man if he opted out. I parodied Winston Churchill by saying that all I could offer them were toil, sweat, hunger, boredom, dirt and probable failure. I turned to the senior man, Sergeant Hastabahadur Rai, and said, 'Hasté, I'll give you a few minutes to make up your minds and give me your decisions.'

They must have talked it over before, because the answer was immediate and unequivocal. 'We all go.'

So, apart from ensuring my company was ready to be without me for a maximum of two months, we were nearly ready. We practised certain contact drills, based on what Kerinching had told me and zeroed our weapons. We packed up ready to go and on Saturday 17 March, we left Ipoh for Grik, yet once again, Richard Kenney wishing us well.

*   *   *

I met up with Ismail and, on Sunday, we all boated upstream. I left my men to make camp in a deserted stretch that was to be our point of entry where the aborigines normally did not venture. Ismail and I went on up to Kerinching's ladang to fetch our three Temiar, as arranged previously. Ismail wanted some last-minute talk with them to ensure they all had as clear an idea as possible of what was happening. The whole plan nearly foundered because Rijed wanted to go hunting instead of coming with me, but after some frustrating moments when all seemed about to go awry, Ismail managed to get matters under control.

We almost struck another snag with Senagit's wife. When I had taken him away downstream, she feared that he would never come back to her again and, so convinced was she that he was dead, had gone to get solace from Kerinching. She had been overjoyed at her husband's return and subsequent recovery – she herself had not been nearly as ill as had he – and here was I, back once more to take him away from her. We dissuaded her from going with us and told

Kerinching to keep her with him. The very last thing we wanted was for her to go across the divide into Kelantan, getting there within ten days, and telling everybody all about what Senagit was doing and with whom, thereby spoiling our every effort to maintain secrecy.

Late that evening we five met up with the Gurkhas and Ah Fut. The Temiar were surprised to see him and I told them he was to go with us for only part of the way to help us learn our new tactics and practise them. We gave the three Temiar their rations and something to carry them in. I told them that once they were finished, there would be no more except what they could pick up from the ladangs we came across. 'You have been warned!' We then settled down to get some sleep.

CHAPTER 8

The Fifth Veil

On 19 March we began our long journey. We had no idea how things would turn out and were glad to have a few days in what should have been a tranquil area so that we could 'shake down' and practise our immediate action drills — what to do in the event of a head-on collision with the guerrillas or other aborigines, and how to avoid leaving tracks that could be recognised as those of a heavily laden military party. To counter the danger of a chance contact, we made the three Temiar walk between thirty and fifty yards ahead of the first soldier. In front was Senagit, who knew the country in the greatest detail, followed by Rijed and Sutel. Senagit and Sutel were normally out of sight of each other. In the event of a contact, Senagit and Rijed would engage the person in conversation while Sutel came back to warn us. We would then sidestep as quickly as possible, take off our loads and await Senagit and Rijed's return with the strangers. This manoeuvre was important because, until we had exact details worked out, the aborigines were naturally scared that we would hit them if fire was opened at the men they had brought back with them. In smoothing out this difficulty, Ah Fut was invaluable. To counter the danger of leaving traces, we resorted to such dodges as walking in streams or walking backwards, where possible, over soft ground.

Once we were within 5000 yards of any headman we wished to contact, we were going to lie up, send the Temiar forward and, if they could enrol his help, he and I would have a meeting. Having negotiated his price, the headman would organise a detailed search for guerrillas with his men and, finally, we would take necessary military action.

If the enemy could be dealt with in isolation, then we could, and would, resort to firearms. If they could only be contacted on a ladang among the women and children, we would have to surround them at night, using cudgels and close-quarter tactics. Realising that there were so many possibilities made me unwilling to confuse everybody by trying to plan for all contingencies. Instead, I laid down broad principles, hoping to have enough time to make a workable plan if the occasion arose. Seldom can a military mission have been more vague or tenuous.

* * *

By the end of the first day we had covered just over a mile on the map and were exhausted. Around 500 feet above sea level it can get very hot and, moving

93

along a compass bearing until we got into country that Senagit knew, we found ourselves traversing large tracts of secondary jungle. Trees were low and, in places, there was only tall grass. Heat mounted up and we plodded our way through. We made camp that night on the edge of a tapioca patch. We had tried to disguise our last few yards by walking backwards but, with over a hundred pounds weight on our backs, the results were pathetically obvious. Having had a meal of rice that morning before the boats left us for Grik, we ate an unappetising wad of baked tapioca for our evening meal. It was tasteless and none of us felt any the less hungry for having eaten it, albeit our bellies were full. It did not bode well for the future.

Early next morning I sent Senagit and Rijed to try to make contact with the nearest headman, called Betong. It was bliss not to be moving so soon after the previous day's exertions. I was still confident that the area of our search would be confined to west of the divide, so there was no hurry. We nibbled at tapioca for our morning meal and had a taste of milkless tea at midday.

The two Temiar came back in the afternoon. They reported that they had met a senior headman, called Bunga, who asked them about tracks. They had retorted that they did not know of any security force movement and they were only going to meet friends. Both were plainly unhappy about the situation and all our fears were confirmed that evening when eight local aborigines arrived, armed with spears and blowpipes. We looked the picture of guilt and the investigating Temiar stood over us as we sat there, wondering how to deal with this unexpected turn of events. So I told them a story about a patrol of soldiers being lost – after all, the SAS were somewhere to my north – with their radio unserviceable and, as helicopters were coming to take them out on the morrow, we were trying to track them with three of Kerinching's men.

The eight Temiar, among whom were both Bunga and Betong, were unconvinced. They pointed to our feet and almost angrily asked why we were not wearing jungle boots. It seemed that they had come across our hockey boot tracks and immediately suspected guerrillas, hence their investigation. I told them that, had we worn jungle boots, our tracks could have become muddled up with those of the lost ones. This they accepted and assured us that there were no lost soldiers anywhere near. So, in my turn, I assured them we would now be returning to the big river the next day, as our mission was obviously fruitless.

At that they became very friendly. They were wonderful specimens; big, strong, healthy, with clean teeth and no blemish on their skins. After they had left us, we had a talk. My three aborigines reckoned gloomily that Sagor was bound to be informed of us by the morrow at the latest, so our presence would be known and our security prejudiced. My answer was there would be heli-copters on the next day overflying us on a north–south axis and that we would leave as though returning to the Sungei Perak. After some time we would jink back again and continue on our original line. By this subterfuge I hoped that we could still contact Sagor without rousing his suspicions. We had been discovered six miles to the south-west of Sagor's ladang: we would probe forward from six miles to the south-east. Getting there was a problem because, although we did not expect to meet anyone on the way, we were moving against the grain of the country. Had I known the consequences, I doubt I would have made that decision. However, I had a map with the reputed tapioca patches marked on it, one being only two or three days' walk away, so we rerouted our advance in order to reach it.

The doctor had said we could exist on a diet of five ounces a day, so I decided to stick to that amount from what we carried until we came across some tapioca. After all, we had enough biscuits for two ounces each day for a week and a similar amount of chocolate for twenty-three days. With the rest of our food, we should be able to last out these next few days, even though the daily amounts were, in ounces, rice 5, ghee 0.2, fish or meat 0.6, sugar 0.1 and salt 0.5.

I could not know that we would be a month before being able either to increase our daily ration or to find tapioca again: twenty-eight days and fifty miles.

So we left early the next morning, moving to the west until we came to a stream running laterally. We trudged down it for a while, going south, before stepping out onto the near bank and moving east again. We walked slowly and, mid-morning, I stopped for a rest and to open the radio. I was just congratulating myself on having jinked successfully when four of the previous evening's group walked into us. We were flabbergasted. They did not stay long and after they had gone we all succumbed to acute gloom. Ah Fut, who was more lightly burdened than the rest of us but not as fit, was for returning. I pointed out that only we ourselves knew of our intentions, so we would carry on.

The next four days were misery. We took much longer than I had reckoned. Our hockey boots slipped on the slopes of the hills and offered no support walking in the boulder-strewn streams. Our ankles were an ideal target for leeches: every hour when we stopped we took about ten of the beastly things off each ankle. On the move our loads were so awkward that keeping upright was a constant challenge. The highest pass we crossed was just under 2000 feet, but the going was slow beyond belief. Every evening we drooled over our meagre rations, and our loads, so teasingly containing our food, in no way seemed to lighten. I would send out a couple of my Temiar screen to patrol the area forward and, if they picked up no traces of man-made movement, I was satisfied we would be safe for the night. I detailed no sentries; we were all so tired we were asleep before darkness fell.

By 24 March we were forced to presume that the tapioca patch we were looking for was overgrown and had reverted to jungle. It was a blow because our stomachs were still not used to eating so little. I made a more comfortable camp and, the next day, sent off two groups: Senagit and Rijed to the north-west to contact Sagor, and Ah Fut, with three Gurkhas as escort, to a point on a tributary of the Sungei Perak nearest our location. I had also arranged for some more rations to be delivered in the boat that took Ah Fut to Grik, not that we could happily increase our present weights, but purely to top up what we had consumed to date. As for the two aborigines, I expected them to spend three nights in Sagor's ladang. This was based on the normal speed of Temiar custom: first night, social pleasantries; second night, probing; third night, details.

Ah Fut was very pleased to be leaving us. He had patently hated every minute of the journey, but his presence had been of great value. Down on the river they met the boat with no difficulty and my friend, Alastair Rose, whose company was then in Grik, had also sent some supplies: rice, biscuits, plaster, gauze as well as fresh vegetables and a couple of live chickens. The three soldiers were tired after their journey and we welcomed our enforced inactivity so that they could rest before moving off again.

While we were waiting for Senagit and Rijed to return, we continued to search for the tapioca patch and any other edible produce. We went fishing, but the streams only had tiddlers in them which, even so, were a welcome addition in the evenings. Sutel found a small tortoise which, to our disgust, he rolled up in leaves and roasted alive; he ate everything but the dirt and the shell. A little later one of my soldiers, Kubirjang Limbu, found a large centipede and handed it to Sutel to eat. It was his method of expressing disgust, but the gesture was lost on Sutel.

Meanwhile I took the opportunity to learn Temiar properly. I had a book that gave a vocabulary and examples of Temiar speech and found to my amazement that I absorbed it all with no difficulty. It may be that hunger, by reducing the need for blood in the belly, somehow had a beneficial reaction on the brain. Whatever the reason, when the two men eventually returned after an absence of six days, on 30 March, they were surprised at my fluency.

I had told them to return in three days if there was nothing to be gleaned, but to stay longer if plans were to be made. By the evening of the fifth day we were happily speculating what information the two men had found. We greeted them warmly when they came back, carrying some tapioca and a fish, and waited for them to tell us the news. But there was none and I learned, the hard way, that the Temiar never count the day of departure or arrival. Three days meant, to them, three full days at the ladang. To us this worked out at five days. When I asked them about the sixth day they saw no sense in the question, which I did not labour, remembering that their language only specifies one, two and three — not even four, although, for example, there are that number of fingers on each hand!

What they did have to say, however, was that Ah Soo Chye was not in Perak.

Taking this at face value, there was only one place to go – Bongsu Helwood's ladang in Kelantan, on the Sungei Puian. I searched for it on the map and showed it to the soldiers. There was a stifled gasp of disbelief, if not horror, at the distance; a mountain range and forty-five map miles away. To us it seemed as remote as the moon.

It was 30 March and, except for the few bonus items of food we had received and gratefully eaten, we had been on quarter rations for ten days. We had not been pressed for time till then, merely being very tired and hungry. From now on it would be much harder. I had presumed that Senagit would lead us by an easier route, to the south, but he said he only knew the northern one, which seemed, from the map, to cross the more difficult terrain. As there would be no tapioca in mountainous country, there was no hope of a full belly except by eating into our rations – the one course I dared not adopt as we were going to operate more tenuously than ever. I decided I could 'top up' the rations by airdrop, just before crossing the divide, provided it was by Auster and nothing larger and noisier. We could have at least one good meal before we started climbing, and it would give us a chance to get some fresh clothing.

I had a long discussion with Senagit about the next stage of our journey, slipping in a question about Sagor's reaction to our being found by the aborigines. He said that Sagor had not heard of our meeting. So much for taking counsel of our fears! Sagor was also reputed not to have seen Ah Soo Chye for two years, but by then I was beginning to suspect the Temiar phrase for anything further back than two days – *nai ish hatop* – could mean any time from three days to ten years. It also appeared that Ah Soo Chye used the northern route and had a couple of secret ladangs in the mountains.

Three days later we reached open ground by a river, suitable for a dropping zone. I felt that the risk was justifiable if the news of no guerrillas was true. I told the soldiers to ask for what they wanted and each one requested a bottle of rum. I told them that that would take up valuable space and weight, but they were adamant, so I included nine bottles of rum in my airdrop demand.

On our way to the dropping zone we searched for where I had been told of an old enemy camp but we were unable to find any traces so we discredited the report. However, we did find one of our tapioca patches: it had recently been harvested, with aboriginal movement to the west three days previously.

Our resupply drop was nearly a complete failure. The Auster was sent to the wrong area by the young British officer who had gone to Grik to take my place, and had to search a large area looking for us, thereby prejudicing security. I had requested a considerable amount of hard tack, namely biscuits and chocolate. For some inexplicable reason somebody had decided to 'freedrop' most of our requirements. Thus all our food, and unbelievably the rum, was dropped without a parachute; and the one commodity that was parachuted – rice – fell into the river and became soaked, so could not be properly cooked. The rest –

ghee, containers, radio batteries and rum bottles – lay smashed with their contents useless, and the hard tack a mound of mixed-up mush. We rallied and salvaged as much as we could: four and a half potatoes each, three-fifths of the rice (two men being nearly swept away during the frantic effort of quick recovery) and one-third hard tack which we collected, picked out the bits of wrapping, added boiling water and consumed as a travesty of hot soup. At least it was nourishing, which was all that mattered. The Gurkhas rallied heart-warmingly. Sergeant Hastabahadur said, so that all could hear: 'We can't recall the pherry pherry,' so called because of the idling note of the engine, 'so let's get on with what we have. After all, it's a bonus.'

We moved off east towards the high hills of the divide between Perak and Kelantan on 4 April, along a good track. This soon started crossing and recrossing the river instead of going alongside it, which was very tiring as our heavy loads unbalanced us by making our centre of gravity higher than usual. The water tugged at our legs and balance became so difficult that it was only by clinging onto one another that we managed to cross the river at all. I counted twenty crossings in the first thousand yards, after which the level of the water dropped, so fording the river was less of a problem.

I was glad when Senagit guided us up a hill, but the steep gradient had us all gasping as, not only were our loads very heavy, but we were weak through lack of food. At the top of this first climb we sank to the ground, blown, with sweat pouring off us, even, it seemed, from the inside of my eyeballs. And we had another thirty miles of this type of terrain in front of us.

Later that day we found guerrilla footprints, which the Temiar tracked until they were lost in a bamboo grove. We were surprised when, on being shown them by Senagit, he seemed to follow them in the reverse direction, but his sharp eyes had understood that, in the softer ground, the guerrillas had walked backwards. The verdict was that they were not Ah Soo Chye's gang but Tek Miu's. They had gone from north to south three days before. I wondered if there was any tie-up between these and the aborigines' tracks we had met near the last tapioca patch. I reported the whole story on the radio but communications were atrocious and I despaired. If they were bad while we were still on the west of the divide, it boded ill for later work. I decided I could not spare more than one day searching and following up the tracks since whoever had made them would probably be well away by then. I eventually got the message through and other troops were sent to where the guerrillas were thought, by our aborigines, to have gone.

The next three days were even harder. We climbed steadily. The weather closed in and we were in mist and rain for most of the time, making our loads heavier still and the ground more slippery, to say nothing of making the leeches even more voracious. Our route took us along slippery streams and thick jungle, clambering over the many fallen trees and jutting rocks. The nights were perishingly cold, and the one we spent near the pass at 4500 feet sheer misery as, to cut down weight, we each carried only half of one lightweight blanket.

My target was about four miles short of Bongsu Helwood's ladang. By now our journey was very exacting: time and space meant nothing, every footstep was a challenge. We had to walk carefully, remembering security, weapons at the ready, keeping a good look-out as, apart from anything else, we had the problem of physically propelling our weakening bodies without mishap. If a man fell, he lay on his back unable to move, like a sheep, until kind hands helped him wriggle out of his burden, turn over, arrange his load, and pull him to his feet. A twisted ankle up in those mountains would have been devastating. We looked forward to our hourly halt with almost sensual pleasure. Every other emotion, even hunger, was ignored while we were on the move, the terrain so difficult and our burdens so heavy and cumbersome that everything else was blotted out. The fierce joy of removing our loads every hour was only blunted by the pangs of hunger that then assailed us.

Senagit, as guide, was wonderful. We could not have made the journey without him. I had developed a great regard for him and we were well on the way to becoming firm friends. His knowledge of the country was invaluable as the map was inaccurate and had patches of white, marked 'cloud', over our itinerary. I learned that I was the second European he had ever seen and the first to whom he had ever spoken. The other two Temiar were slower to respond to me. As for the soldiers, I can sincerely say that during the whole operation my regard for, and esteem of, Gurkhas never stood higher. A challenge was there and they rose magnificently to it.

Up on the divide, radio communications were good and I received a long message to the effect that Ah Soo Chye was in Kelantan and had visited ladangs to the south of Helwood's territory, giving pep talks and trying to arrange a meeting of all 'penghulus', but security force pressure was preventing it. This was very encouraging but none of us dared voice any optimism. We all felt so dwarfed by the vastness of the jungle, our task, the odds against us, as well as the gnawing hunger, that we were content to take each day, hour and minute as they came.

On our journey down the eastern side of the divide we heard the roar of the Sungei Puian, the river we were destined to follow, over an hour before we reached it. I was appalled when I saw what we had to cross. The river was about twenty yards wide, very fast-flowing, and full of large slippery black rocks. The only bridge was a fallen tree that lay across it. On the near bank the wide bole gave firm support. It narrowed and jinked in the middle, with a branch reaching across to the far bank. The water surged a few feet below and, handicapped as we were with our unwieldly heavy loads, one slip could well have been fatal. Looking at it, I doubted by physical ability to cross over. For the first time on that journey I felt afraid.

The three aborigines walked over unconcernedly. Barefooted, they were in no danger in slipping on the damp surface. I watched, fascinated, and saw, when they reached the jink, that the whole tree wobbled. Kubirjang and Hastabahadur, both physical training instructors, went over next. I found myself halfway along the queue. I must have looked as scared as I felt, because Kubirjang recrossed, having deposited his load safely on the far bank, and said he had come to fetch my kit.

Was it sheer bravado that made me say I would carry over my own kit and start forward? I inched across, fighting against being mesmerised by the rushing, surging, pulsating water, roaring over large, black and shiny rocks, ice-smooth by aeons of punishment. At the jink I faltered and glanced up. There, on the far bank, stood Hastabahadur, waiting for me, arms outstretched. I shuffled forward, sweating with fear, hating it all, myself, the operation, the hunger, the danger, the lot. I suddenly found I was forcing a whistle, a tune, from my lips and was amazed to hear that I, the seldom church-going, was whistling 'There is a green hill far away'. I reached Hasté and fell into his arms. He felt my convulsive trembling. 'Sit down and rest,' he said, 'I'll look after the others.'

I was across. It took several minutes to stop trembling and I rejoined my men. Senagit smiled at me and said, *Laös ong, jeruq*, and I agreed that the water was wicked and deep.

We made camp not far away, all moving unnaturally slowly. Later that day I told Senagit, Sutel and Rijed how I envisaged they should make contact with Helwood. I believed our presence was still a secret and that caution and cunning were needed. I expected no contact with any Senoi Praaq as I had been assured a free hand and given clearance. I understood there were six extra men who lived on the ladang who were to do with a medical post that the Department of Aborigines had established there.

My three men left early the next morning, 8 April. The three days they were away lasted five and during that time we rested. We had been on short commons for twenty days and our stomachs had shrunk. There was nothing to do all day. We brewed our gill of tea early morning and midday, more to give us something to do than anything else. By then we knew that water distends the belly and gives an illusion of fulfilment, but, with hardly any tea leaves left, we had to make do with cold water.

Every evening at 4 o'clock we had what was by then a ritual: we cooked. We hung around the cooking pot like hungry dogs until the saliva in our mouths made us turn away. Not a drop of anything was wasted, not even a grain of rice. Misers with their gold could not have been more careful than we were with our evening meal. Once it was cooked, I tried out different ways of eating it. If one ate normally there was never enough, so I decided to eat it grain by grain but gave up, as I lacked the self-control. I then tried to eat it so quickly that it would give me indigestion and I would not want to eat, but there was no joy that way either. And when it was gone we knew that we would have no more for another day. We could not hunt as our tracks would give us away. Fish were very scarce, but one day we did catch some small frogs and there were enough for two and a half each. I found them bitter.

Come sundown there was nothing to do but sleep and try to forget it, for sleep, although being a poor substitute for hunger, does pass the time. By now, physically we were nearly beaten. Each night dreams plagued me. In one guise or another, food and drink would be offered and accepted. Manners would be forgotten as I would grab what was being given, but always it would vanish by the time I had brought it to my mouth. I would then wake in vexation and my tummy would be going round and round, spittle drooling from my mouth and tears oozing from closed lids. Inevitably I would look at my watch and it would seldom be later than 9 o'clock. Sleep would come once more with equally vivid dreams and I would wake up again maybe two hours later ... and two hours after that and ... I decided it were better not to have my watch on my wrist, in an attempt to ignore time. I have not worn one since: I keep it in my pocket. Every night I dreamed of my elder brother, Timothy, who only ever came to me under the greatest of stresses. He gave me comfort, telling me to stick it out, that I had it in me not to give up, that the men were relying on me. We also talked as though we were boys together once more.

Yet even during waking hours I found myself thinking way back into the past, reconstructing events I had lost for thirty years: my first day of kindergarten; my first lesson on money with cardboard coins, which I wanted to spend and cried when I found I could not; my first visit to the lavatory and the deplorable shame of being unable to do up my braces at the back, not daring to tell the teacher. Jokes shared with mother, sitting on her knees, poetry, pieces of schooling like paradigms of Greek irregular verbs and Latin gender rhymes ran through my head as though escaping a beating depended on it. I asked Tanké one day what he was thinking about. 'I'm back in childhood,' was his answer.

Lack of nourishment was making itself felt in other ways. Men became giddy and blacked out; we all defecated minutely, if at all; and none of us could concentrate on anything for any length of time.

Two days after my three Temiar had left, we received a bombshell. Radio communications with Ipoh and Grik, surprisingly, were no problem and we were informed that it was known by all in Helwood's ladang that we were 6000 to 7000 yards north, because my men had been interviewed by a Senoi Praaq officer and had told him all. I was dumbfounded, not understanding how this situation had come about. I had been promised that nothing of this nature would occur: was all our labour in trying to operate secretly and use guerrilla tactics to have been in vain? Waiting for my men to return was now even harder, especially as another message had arrived saying that it was suspected that a large meeting was soon to take place in an old ladang near Helwood's, with the guerrillas and many 'penghulus' taking part.

The three aborigines rejoined us late in the evening of 12 April. Their news was mixed. On the one hand it seemed that Helwood would cooperate, but was not allowed off his ladang. On the other hand, there were twenty of the Senoi Praaq there, whose commander's message to me was that if he saw us come to the ladang he would shoot us. This was the first time I remembered the words of Norman Herbolt when he came to see me in Ipoh and remarked: 'I hope you fail.' Had he engineered all this to spite my efforts?

There was nothing, at that stage, but to continue as though all was well. So we moved downstream next day and bought some tapioca, the first time we had passed a patch for a month. We made camp half a mile or so from Helwood's ladang and I opened my radio. I complained bitterly about the Senoi Praaq detachment and got an answer on that same day that they had been confined to their camp and told not to shoot us.

I received another message saying that Helwood had left for Fort Kemar, in Perak, with thirty-two people, including some women. So I was very surprised when he and half a dozen others walked into my camp the very next day. One was so much older than the rest that for some time I presumed he was Bongsu Helwood. In fact he was a man called Kalusa, a great friend of the guerrilla Lo See. He had had considerable influence when younger, but was now well past his prime and, so I learned later, went slightly mad every full moon. Helwood himself was a much younger-looking man than I had supposed. We spoke for two hours and he had a very business-like approach to my request for help. He said he would send men to search for Ah Soo Chye. They would report back after two weeks. We haggled over the price and he would not allow his men to go for less than three 'ringgits' a day. I had to ask Ipoh if our sources of money could stand the sum involved: thirty men for fourteen days at S$3.00 a day costing S$1260. The sum was agreed.

It was at this juncture that Richard Kenney handed over command of 1/7 Gurkha Rifles to a man called John Heelis. John and I had known each other since 1947. Regrettably, we had never properly hit it off together, try hard though both of us did. I knew he was a more difficult man to work for than Richard, to whom I bade farewell over the radio, with heavy heart, wishing him good luck and thanking him for all he had done for me. When Heelis spoke to me we exchanged pleasantries and I said that I needed luck to complete my mission. Yes, he answered, he would need luck in his new post – not the answer I was expecting – but I realised that he could have little, if any, idea of what my group had been through. Nor, fortunately for me, did I know what mischief Herbolt would cause when he and Heelis got together.

My original time limit was withdrawn and as the need to starve was no longer valid, I requested an airdrop. This was easy as the Senoi Praaq garrison was regularly supplied by air and an extra parachute for us would make no difference to the aircraft's load. However, even when it did come, much of what I had requested was not dropped. When I queried this I was told that they did not think I meant what I had said! Before the drop came I had increased the rice ration by buying from Helwood. It was being milled, so he told me, and I could not have it for a couple of days. It was delicious when we got it. On 17 April I increased the ration to 7 ounces daily and, with our stomachs getting used to food again, to 10 ounces two days later. We also bought vegetables. The men visibly brightened and I instituted a daily programme of physical training, school and certain aspects of jungle warfare. We only had one big meal a day as we still found two large meals most painful, so we nibbled tapioca in the mornings.

*   *   *

After Helwood and his men had left us I briefed the men. Sergeant Hastaba-hadur was the only one to make any comment. 'I don't trust that one. He will deceive us. My blood has gone cold.'

Next day when Helwood came to see us, the men were training in the undergrowth. He looked scared and asked me to keep them near camp, because his search party would be afraid. I received a message saying that Special Branch had reason to believe that Helwood was not to be trusted as he was really working for the guerrillas at my expense. Helwood, not realising my suspicions, starting asking for S\$4.00 a day for his men and told me he had sent out forty and had briefed another twenty to go. I informed Ipoh of his action and was told I was bound by the original agreement. I was also informed that I had only a fortnight before I had to return. This I passed on to Helwood, who seemed genuinely dismayed. He said that security force pressure made Ah Soo Chye move around and if he knew exactly where the Chinese was, he could call him in for an ambush.

We moved camp farther downstream. This made it easier to collect the airdrop and to visit the ladang. In order to show the folk there that I was not afraid I walked the 200 yards from our new camp to the ladang unarmed. The ladang itself, on the junction of the Sungei Puian and the Sungei Blaur, was large and had many houses. There were three buildings for the Department of Aborigines, used for medical work. It was here that a grand X-ray programme was being organised for all Temiar for miles around. It gave me a good chance to meet and talk to all the headmen: it was also very useful to Ah Soo Chye for the same purpose!

We received our airdrop on 24 April. That day I had another long talk with Helwood. It was frustrating to a degree and, although we spoke at length about searches and areas, I now firmly believed he was stalling. I tried to get proof from Senagit who, along with the other two, was living on the ladang. I was on the point of asking him, when we were disturbed by a crowd of aborigines. They would not take the hint that I wanted to be alone with Senagit, nor could I afford to get angry. So I started singing 'Suzanna's a funny old man' with appropriate noises. This convulsed them and when the laughter was over they went away. I began to talk with Senagit once more, only to be interrupted for a repeat performance. After the third rendering I did manage to ask Senagit, who said he would let me know. Scarcely had we finished speaking when all the aborigines came back for yet another encore. Nothing loth, I obliged.

On 25 April, the next day, Rijed brought two scraggy chickens to our camp for us to buy and with a message from Senagit. He nervously took me into a nearby thicket and told me that tracks for five guerrillas had been found on the other side of the river, leading from the ladang. Helwood had ordered his men not to tell us. I was further informed that Helwood had told the Senoi Praaq detachment commander, an elderly Malay called Ismail, who had been in the Malayan Navy. There was obviously an amount of intrigue going on, but I could not get to grips with it. I felt weary of the whole business. It seemed a waste of effort for everything to have turned out so scrappily after so much endeavour. So I went down to the ladang to talk with Helwood. I did not meet him as he was organising the X-ray programme, which seemed an unexpectedly good cover plan to meet and resupply Ah Soo Chye and his gang. I had to admire Helwood's gall. Ismail suggested that I give Helwood one more chance. This went against the grain of all my military instincts. He told me that the evidence of guerrillas had been passed to him five days previously by Alang, Helwood's brother, and not the previous day as I had been told – if indeed both reports concerned one set of tracks. Ismail further advised me to concentrate on yet another 'penghulu', named Setia, to which I agreed but without much enthusiasm. I decided to play it my own way.

Next morning, helicopters made half a dozen trips into the ladang with the X-ray equipment. I went over to Helwood and told him that I had had a dream the night before; I then relayed back to him the information that his brother, Alang, had passed on to Ismail. I requested his men to be sent in the direction of the tracks. He looked thoughtfully at me but was non-committal.

Our airdrop came in that day and gave us something positive to do. Towards evening Helwood paid me a visit to tell me that his men had found the tracks I had dreamed about but had forgotten to inform him. He was sure I would be very angry. I looked at him without speaking for a long moment, then said, very coldly, that I regarded my dreams not coming true as seriously as breaking a taboo and left it at that. The soldiers were so sick at Helwood that Kubirjang put a curse on him and volunteered to go and seize him and dispose of him by drowning. Reluctantly I forbade it.

I received a visit from another aborigine whom I had not yet met: an elderly man called Mudak. This man had a grudge to settle with Helwood as the area on which the ladang was situated did not belong to Helwood, but was part of Mudak's hereditary area, or 'saka'. He had been dispossessed when the Department of Aborigines amalgamated several ladangs at Blaur.

Mudak came with Rijed the next evening into our camp and sat down next to me. He said he would tell me the truth, but that if Helwood found out, he, Mudak, would be poisoned. I obtained a lot of information, which Rijed confirmed, that Ah Soo Chye had visited Helwood twice recently, each time taking 60 pounds of rice. This explained the delay in our buying it and Helwood's request to us not to stray far from our camp. Other commodities given to the guerrillas included salt, tobacco, chicken and a dog. Ah Soo Chye, who carried a pistol and a sub-machine gun, wore dirty khaki drill uniform with four red stars in his cap. He and his gang had gone north. The names of the other three were given, as well as their weapons and their proposed itinerary. I pulled out my map and, spreading it on my knees, studied it intently. I asked Mudak when all this took place and I was told that it was a night when a dance had been held. I thought back and remembered the day I had walked to the ladang unarmed. That evening there had been lots of noise, singing and plonking of hollow bamboos. I also remembered being told it was a warm-up party to be given for us: and all the time Ah Soo Chye was 200 yards away. We had been completely hoodwinked: Hastabahadur had been right. As the enormity of it all slowly sank into my brain, Mudak's eyes dilated and a look of horror came over his face. I glanced up and there were Helwood and Alang standing over us, and the map still spread out. My one thought was to save Mudak.

'This man came here with a headache and I was so interested in the country to the south I started asking him questions,' I lied glibly. It was fortuitous I had my medicine box by my side. I pulled out two pills and some water, telling Mudak to take them. He rallied gratefully, but inaccurately, by rubbing his stomach and not his head, saying how much it all hurt. I intervened quickly and, in his haste to do justice to this providential escape, he choked on the pills and had a paroxysm of coughing. He left in a hurry, but the other two remained for half an hour. We ignored them.

Next morning, after talking it over with Ismail, I sent a message to Heelis, telling him all, that I refused to pay Helwood and had devised a scheme of publicly discrediting him in front of his people. Ismail had promised to act as witness when I addressed the ladang, on the pretext of paying them, but in fact speaking about dreams and breaking of taboos, a plan I knew I could make work.

I was not prepared for the answer: not only had Herbolt forbidden Ismail to talk to me but he had convinced Special Branch that I must not even speak to Helwood. I was instructed to pay his men, even though the situation had developed so unexpectedly. I could hardly believe my ears and sent back a sharp question, asking which side Herbolt was on.

Next day Helwood was ill. We were all sure that Kubirjang's curse had worked. I was sent for and he told me he had news that Ah Soo Chye was in Perak as his camp had been found a long way upstream by the search parties.

It was time to pay out and leave. I asked for money to be sent in by helicopter. Again something went wrong and it came in ten cent pieces, weighing nigh on a hundred pounds. The pilot could not even lift the sack containing it out of his machine. Later I was blamed by Heelis for insisting that the aborigines' wages were to be sent in this form – it had been a hard job to get so much small coin – and I was too sick at heart to argue. I disbursed it: the equivalent in sterling would be £156 in sixpences. Alang had lined up to receive his money but, as he had done no patrolling, I refused to pay him.

On 8 May we packed up and moved down to the helicopter pad. Waiting for the helicopter to arrive, yet another aborigine sidled up to me. I recognised him as Mudak's lieutenant, Duwin. Speaking in a perfectly natural voice, he said that all Mudak's men were angry that I had been deceived and that if Ah Soo Chye came back he personally would undertake to walk over the divide to Grik and let me know. When anyone came into earshot he kept his voice at the same level, pitch and tone and spoke about the crops.

So we flew back. It was like being on a magic carpet, so unreal was the sensation. We were all worn out and bitterly disappointed at the final outcome. But I was extraordinarily proud of my men: no grumbling, not a day's sickness and no giving up. I put this down to a great sense of purpose, combined with rigid health discipline. We had been away for fifty-two days and I was a stone lighter than when I had started. My last entry in my log read: 'Returned to base. Nothing to report.' I thought my efforts were all over and done with, but events were to prove just how wrong I was.

CHAPTER 9

The Sixth Veil

Back in Ipoh, the doctor examined us in detail. Our haemoglobin blood count was down to the level expected in a woman who had aborted, so we were given an iron tonic. The soldiers took some leave and I settled down to work on the backlog of company work, writing a report for Special Branch and reading my mail. Once more the welter of peace-time priorities sought to overwhelm us and an internal security exercise made us traipse down to Singapore for four days. The General Officer Commanding the Federation Army, Lieutenant General Dato Sir Rodney Moore, and the General Officer Commanding 17 Gurkha Division, Major General W.C. Walker, came to speak to me there. They requested me to return to the Puian-Blaur area and I agreed. Apparently Head of Special Branch had asked for me, even before I had left the Blaur ladang, but Heelis had opposed it. After the Singapore meeting, Head of Special Branch wrote to the Commissioner of the Royal Malayan Police, Claude Fenner, asking for me again. This was passed on and became official, as far as my release from other duties was concerned, in late June. I also learned that, as a result of the report I wrote when I first came out of the jungle, plans were being made to reorganise the Senoi Praaq completely, converting them into an intelligence-gathering force rather than a fighting formation.

Two months after I emerged from the jungle I had put on weight but could only manage one meal a day. I grew stronger and won the battalion quarter-mile in fifty-six seconds. Life was returning to normal.

*　　*　　*

Although Special Branch wanted me to go back immediately, I told them I needed time for preparation. My reports of Ah Soo Chye's movements had been confirmed from other sources; Rijed and Sutel had returned to the Sungei Klian area with Kerinching, and Senagit had stayed on at Blaur. That gave me the genesis of my new plan: Senagit to control all search movement, in conjunction with Mudak and Duwin, in the Blaur area, while my small groups would hide up not far away and take what military action was needed. Working out Ah Soo Chye's likely movements, I reckoned that he would be back once within a three-month period and so I would have to be self-sufficient for ten weeks. My two Klian men would take me over the main range again and leave me to negotiate with Mudak, somewhere in the high hills, on the Kelantan side. I went to Grik, talked with Special Branch, and moved to Kerinching's ladang where I explained my plans. That done, I returned to Ipoh and announced I would set off once again on 15 July.

I picked another team, retaining only one man of the first group. I was determined to be better fed this time, so planned on eating 10 ounces of food daily, not much of an increase but significant in weight when calculated for the time I planned to be deployed – ten weeks. It meant that I had to use a carrying party. Even so, my own group would still be saddled with kit bags strapped to the carrier frame, with packs above and small dixies for communal cooking atop the pack. This made our loads very unwieldy but, as I envisaged a shorter approach march than before, followed by a period of lying-up, I thought we could just about cope. In fact none of us were laden lighter than 120 pounds and some men carried 130 pounds, which was, in most cases, more than the man himself weighed.

Entry was to be by helicopter from Grik to as near the western slopes of the divide as possible, and I asked to be put down in the same place as had been used for the abortive Auster drop in what now seemed a previous existence.

Heelis said he was not happy at my going as he felt the lack of a British officer in D Company; but he believed that, apart from a lucky chance contact, a further long and patient wait by me presented the best possible chance of success. An added fillip was that the whole battalion was to be committed on 'Bamboo' towards the end of the year.

I had a very long talk with my new CO, asking him why restrictions had been placed on my conversations with Bongsu Helwood and with Ismail. Herbolt was indeed behind it, motivated as far as I could gather by jealousy. After that, I went to see Special Branch again to put the record straight. I tried not to be bitter about the way Herbolt was carrying on, but it had rankled so much at the time – it did still – that I had wanted to give all the Temiar a warning to stay uncivilised; once civilised, you had to fight your friends before you could fight your enemies. I gather Herbolt was 'spoken to'; like so many people who would never have been given such a position of trust had he remained in his own country, he had an inflated sense of his own importance. He left me alone for a while, but was again to prove a thorn in my flesh later on.

Heelis did not come to say farewell to us on our departure as Richard Kenney had done, but the Gurkha Major did. I remember his dismay at seeing we were so heavily laden: no resupply for seventy days is some challenge. But apart from staving off hunger, there was another powerful incentive for withstanding hardship. Rumours were flying about that Gurkha battalions were to be axed. Were we successful on our mission there seemed a good chance of saving at least one battalion, and indeed the Prime Minister of Malaya would later tell his counterpart in Britain that Gurkhas were essential for long-term border stability.

*   *   *

On 18 July 1962 I went back to Grik with my nine men and the carrying party. There I met Kerinching, Rijed and Sutel, who had been forewarned. Kerinching was most upset at not having been paid for my previous escapade, failing to understand that I could only pay for 'porters' who had worked for me and had to be classified in order to receive their wages. I told Ismail of Special Branch, who restored Kerinching's good humour from another fund. The other two were happy, having previously been enrolled as 'porters' and been paid. They were again kitted out and given rations. The helicopters were confirmed.

Two Sycamore helicopters flew over from Butterworth next morning. The pilots had a last-minute briefing from me but baulked at the weight of our kit. No one had thought to tell them how much they had to fly in, and their payload was small. I patiently told them we could not leave anything behind and apologised for the breakdown in communications. This they accepted with good grace.

Eventually we took off at 10.30 that morning with the first three loads being roped in, and were successfully ferried in by 3.45 in the afternoon. The ground needed clearing of undergrowth before the helicopters could land, as their tail blades had a very low clearance. No one felt any extra confidence by finding a crashed Sycamore lying on its side when we had cleared a landing approach.

I had known that another long walk, this time of twenty miles, would be hard, but I had not fully appreciated how much difference the additional fourteen or so pounds would make. We ate from the carrying party's rations and, since we had been spared a tedious approach march, it only took us three days to cross the divide. The journey was marred by heavy and incessant rain which made our burdens even heavier, so we were glad of the chance of a rest and to dry ourselves out. We camped two days' walk from Helwood's ladang. I sent my carrying party back, having had to switch one man from each group, and my two Temiar forward. The extra few ounces of food daily made a great difference, as did living up in the hills, well above 3000 feet, where the air and the stream water were fresh.

We stayed where we were for the next eight days, during which time we lived off the rations brought by the carrying party. We had some physical training and periods of schooling each morning, and practised the type of manoeuvre that might be used for surrounding a small group of armed men, by night or by day, in a house, the ladang or the jungle.

Our first visitors were Senagit and Sutel. Senagit was delighted to see us and made a very good impression on all my men. He had told Helwood he was going fishing. Helwood and Alang had been very angry with my three Temiar for helping me and with me for not paying out certain of their men. Apparently everybody in the ladang felt that they were entitled to payment; indeed, I remembered one man, a cripple, scarcely able to walk, who had lined up on my pay parade.

The Senoi Praaq detachment had been withdrawn and Helwood, who previously had needed permission to leave his ladang and, if this was granted, to explain his itinerary, was now free to go without let or hindrance and was, at that moment, upstream collecting rattan and vines.

Senagit was hopeful of a successful outcome to our efforts. Whatever his comings and goings, Ah Soo Chye was bound to attend the feast that was held to celebrate Iwoh, the rice harvest. Until then his movements were a matter of conjecture, in that he might bypass Blaur, meeting Helwood in the jungle. I learned that Iwoh was still some time off, so it was more than likely that there would be a meeting or two beforehand, though there was no guarantee that the next one would be held 'at home'.

Senagit told me that Duwin was the person who could best select a site for hiding and that it would be up to three of them, Senagit, Duwin and Mudak, to coordinate efforts in the search for guerrilla movement and for keeping us informed.

Senagit and Sutel spent two nights with us and left early on 26 July. The next evening Rijed, Duwin and Duwin's brother, Pedik, arrived. They said that they had heard of some guerrilla movement away to the south-east about a month previously but sensed it was not Ah Soo Chye's group. They told me they envisaged us working, not by attacking guerrillas around any ladang area but operating in the jungle, which I was relieved to hear. The area around a ladang is difficult for silent movement as there are always fallen trees and thick secondary growth to negotiate. We were going to move to an area much closer to Blaur, but not as close to the spot where we had originally made contact with Helwood. However, we had to wait until Mudak arrived as we would be hiding within his 'saka'. Once ensconced by Mudak, we would be safely off the axis of movement up and down the Sungei Puian and only his men would know our whereabouts. It was then that I learned that Duwin was Mudak's son. From a security angle I was unhappy that a quarter of the population at Blaur should know about us, but there was nothing I could do about it, apart from stressing the need for secrecy. As the Temiar vocabulary does not run to the word 'secret', this also presented difficulties.

The second group only stayed one night. It was useless growing impatient at their apparently dilatory endeavours; this was the pace we had to work to or work not at all. Next evening four Temiar arrived, Mudak, Pedik, Senagit and Rijed. They brought us chillies, tapioca and bananas. We discussed plans and the chances of enemy movement during the next two months. It seemed that there was absolutely no way of telling if Ah Soo Chye wold come; but the longer he was away, the greater was the likelihood of his return. I gathered that eight of Mudak's men were to be used to search probable areas for enemy movement. We would discuss details later. One difficulty to be over-come was to know where the men were going, as the map gave Malay names and the searchers only used Temiar names. It was all so tenuous that, more than once, I realised how easy it would be for Mudak to jolly us along, being paid money on the pretext of patrolling, giving me false reports and all the while doing nothing. I tried not to dwell on this because if I believed this, it would sap my trust, and that would show in my face, speech and actions. I could not bear to think that what we had done to date might be wasted by unwarranted suspicions, yet the thought was there, at the back of my mind and, so I gathered later, in the minds of those not so intimately concerned with it all, back in Ipoh.

On 30 July, early, we added to our already heavy burdens the remains of the ration dump that even the four Temiar who were to guide us could not carry. Nothing was to be wasted. The journey that day still carries recollections that haunt: 126 pounds, nine hours for maybe only four miles. In the middle was the crossing of the Puian that had been such an effort the previous time. The whole day was one walking nightmare, the horizon limited to one step at a time. My body reacted sluggishly to the cruel weight it carried and muscles screamed with agony on some of the steeper slopes. We were led down and across streams, with small groups of us hanging drunkenly together as the current tugged at our legs and the slippery, stony surfaces mocked our attempts to find purchase. And it was all done on an empty stomach – wrongly in retrospect – but I wanted the rations to be consumed, if possible, according to my original timetable. The last few hundred yards were up a stream. Until then Mudak had followed behind us and, where he could, disguised the marks left by our feet. He and his party now dumped the rations they were carrying and moved straight back to Blaur, promising to be back in two days' time, in the morning. We moved off the main river, up a small tributary and I chose a campsite for the night in the junction of the two waterways. My idea was to make any follow-up by unfriendly people as difficult as I could. The sheer sensual ecstasy experienced when we took off our heavy loads was only equalled by a meal and a sleep. We were sore from being squashed all day and stretching out supine was unexpectedly painful.

Next morning we were still tired and stiff, but had to get organised in our proper long-term hideout before we could afford the luxury of resting. We hid the rations the Temiar had carried and disguised our occupation of the camp, partly by mudding over the scars of the saplings we had cut at ground level. We walked upstream in the water for half an hour and I chose a new campsite. Nowhere was as flat as I would have liked but this had the requirements of a good hideout: tucked away inconspicuously, with water and good escape routes. We each made two trips ferrying our rations to and fro. On our final journey I made it my job to erase any footprints that remained and, once we were concealed, I sent men back to the stream to place large stones so that a watering party could work without disturbing the ground around.

Our final task was to move up the line by which we had originally entered the area and, walking backwards, to plant living camouflage as we went. The path we used for water and washing was along a dry stream-bed we had only later discovered. I felt we had taken all the precautions we sensibly could and now it was just a question of waiting. I had established communications with Ipoh and could hear them plainly, but since I used Morse, conversations were limited and one-sided. I heard from the CO that the battalion was to be deployed from mid-September and plans were being made to keep troops off Helwood's ladang. I felt that it would be a good idea to have somebody there who was of the battalion, as it made life so much easier for me. I told Heelis my thoughts.

On 1 August, the day after we established ourselves in our hideout, I sent two men down to bring up our friends, but they never came. The following morning I went down and did a stint. They eventually arrived at 3 o'clock. There were nine of them, including Mudak, who said he would visit me again after three days. They brought some tapioca and bananas, the latter great, long, black fruits, a cubit in length and a meal in themselves. We had by then checked our rations and discovered we were two packets of tea short. I feared a hunting party might find them, but Mudak was unperturbed. As he had been bringing up the rear, I dismissed it from my mind. We discussed a number of points, such as collecting their pay later in Grik and not having it flown in, the possibility of Ah Soo Chye coming in August, and if not August then September, or October, or November . . . and how often they would patrol and whereabouts. They were in good spirits and before they left I gave Rijed four penicillin tablets and a bottle of Chinese cure-all pills for his sick wife. These items were from a small stock of presents we had brought with us to keep the aborigines 'sweet'. From a security angle, I queried the food supply and was relieved to be told that produce was always to be brought from an individual garden some distance from the main ladang and not from the main ladang itself.

Our camp was the size of a tennis court and we were asked by the aborigines not to stray outside. One reason was to prevent our leaving footprints and the other that if we were to be used, it could be in a hurry, so it were better we remained concentrated.

Despite being on quarter rations we had just enough food each day to keep the pangs of hunger away and provide us with a full enough belly. If we ate less in the evening, we could make gruel in the morning, but after we had tried it once, we gave up the idea. Besides which, the aborigines brought additional provisions which we ate in the morning. We also carried the invalid food called Complan which gave us strength. We kept it for use after the first fortnight and one man, Panchamani Tamang, a cheery fellow, was immediately sick.

We rested for the first three days and morale was high. On the third day we heard considerable helicopter activity over Blaur which caused me some concern, as did a very inquisitive Valetta aircraft which flew around us. I learned that some Federation Army Engineers had been flown in with materials to enlarge the helicopter pads and landing sites.

We soon settled down to a routine. This was important as boredom was bound to be our chief enemy. I carried a notebook and three language books: Chinese, Malay and Temiar. I knew that I would have time and enough to spare, and one way to occupy my mind was to make up English sentences containing key words and then translate them into those three languages, plus Hindi and Nepali. Our daily programme was a small brew of tea just after first light, physical training – we built a beam to hang from – followed by a snack of fruit or tapioca. During the morning I would take school, which consisted in the main of English, Malay, Temiar, Cantonese, mathematics and general knowledge. Each man had his own notebook. One form of English was playing 'I spy'. We each took a turn and Panchamani kept us all baffled with his 'I ishpy with my eye' (I could never get any of them to use the word 'little') 'something beginning with G'. None of us could guess and after some five minutes we were told 'green' was the answer! We had another brew at midday and some afternoons we played quoits with a rattan ring or practised making pig traps. Occasionally we would go and wash in the stream below the camp. The main feature of the day was our evening meal. After that we would take turns to tell stories or riddles until it was dark. The nights were very, very long.

Senagit advised us to set an ambush not far from the camp overlooking the stream above the water point as Ah Soo Chye was reputed to have come that way in the past.

We stood to one evening early on when we heard suspicious noises. It sounded like someone pushing his way through the undergrowth. We searched cautiously, weapons at the ready, until darkness forced us back and we all spent a night wondering which way tracks would lead us and how many men there were. Investigations by daylight revealed pig, which was very disappointing.

I ruminated, during that morning, that we were pigless and without anything to show for our operations against the enemy. These gloomy thoughts continued to nag me dully. Just before noon, when the ambush was due to change, we were all startled out of our skins by the reverberation of a rifle shot. We stood to, expectantly, only to find it was our youngest soldier, Rifleman Purnahang Limbu, letting off a round by accident. He was ditheringly contrite, the rest of the soldiers scathingly angry and I emotionally drained, not just because of the rifle being uselessly fired, but also by the potential harm arising from the breach of security. Recriminations were useless and the damage could not be undone. Not only that, but I expected Senagit to visit me that day and he never materialised. Angry or frightened, was my guess. I felt great relief the next day when he reported that he had heard nothing and that the reason he had not come was merely that he was out foraging. But there were no more accidental discharges!

We continued to receive visits from some of our nine helpers who, besides bringing news of areas they had checked for guerrilla movement, almost always brought us something to eat – fruit and tapioca being more usual than fish, and even, on two occasions, live chickens. The security angle concerned me but the men were so happy to have fresh meat and a change of diet that it somehow compensated for the risk. I paid for all the produce with the money put aside for this very purpose. I liked to think that the Temiar would not have brought anything that entailed danger.

We had no rain for the first nine days. This, at that altitude and so near the divide, was unusual, but thereafter it rained daily and most nights, from 6 August to 2 September; not all the time, but heavily once every twenty-four hours, with a persistent drizzle, which made drying out a problem. Life became uncomfortable as well as dull. What little activity we could indulge in was severely hampered. As the rains continued, the aborigines came less and less, partly because all movement across the Sungei Puian was dangerous and partly because even they disliked getting wet to that extent. As the days passed, slowly – oh how slowly – with the nights even more protracted, a new danger appeared. None of the forest had time to dry out and large branches or even whole trees would become waterlogged and no longer able to maintain their own weight. We listened, every nerve tingling, to the creaking that heralded such a fall, each of us hoping that there would be time to run away to safety. Hearts in mouths, we awaited the rending, tearing sound ensued by a sickening thud, then stunned silence following a particularly near miss. It was far worse at night: after the tree had fallen, we would call to one another, 'Are you all right? Is anyone hurt?' Relief would flood in with a 'We're all right, it fell just outside the camp.'

Some of the waterlogged branches were unable to take the weight of the monkeys that normally scampered about them. We would hear crashing, a chattering scream, a horrendous thump, then silence. On average, we heard a tree crash down once every twenty-four hours.

By then even falling twigs were a menace to our shelters. The issue water-proof sheet, or poncho, was comparatively heavy to carry and was too narrow effectively to keep out rain. I had brought oilcloth, cut wide enough for a dry sleep, but it was delicate and could not stand up to small missiles being dropped on it. During daylight, sticking plaster could be applied to keep what little bedding there was dry, but at night there was nothing to be done but get, and stay, wet.

Occasionally I received news of the outside world: who was going to com-mand which battalion; Russian probes to the moon; and some political grouping to be called Malaysia. Not knowing how long my batteries would last, I would not allow the radio to be used for anything but daily contact, normally no more than a minute or two.

One day during the early part of the rains, we went down to the stream to fetch our water later than usual. The water was muddy and unfit for drinking or cooking. As we had some tapioca, we ate that for our evening meal. Thinking to give the men a treat, I ordered that we eat the next morning what we had missed the evening before. It was unusual to prepare for a meal so early but it made a change. I could not foresee the result of the unaccustomed food; within half an hour seven of us were asleep and the other three comatose.

On 17 August we finished our dump and starting taking rations from our kit bags. By then I had managed to save a few ounces each day to make a reserve, should we need it. This was not a very popular move, even though the extra fruit and vegetables we got from the aborigines was a compensation.

We had a visit from Senagit, Rijed and two others on 24 August. They brought spinach, maize, sweet potatoes, taro and bananas. They said Helwood had gone upstream to the high hills on a hunting expedition. He had taken some women in his group. They seemed to think that it was very probable that he had had a meeting with Ah Soo Chye. Although there were ten people in his party and rations had to be taken, the amount of food they had carried was suspicious. One or two of the women were believed to be Ah Soo Chye's wives. I then learned that when Ah Soo Chye had visited Blaur on 24 or 25 April he had slept with Temiar women, but his men had not been allowed to. Once again I wondered whether we had been outwitted. I told Senagit to find out, either by directly asking the womenfolk or by Mudak using his son, whether a meeting had taken place. If it seemed possible that Ah Soo Chye had been contacted and was even then heading up to the Thai border through Perak, I would also bug out. I told him to come back within three days with the answer. If he had found out positively that a meeting had been held he was not to bring anything for us to eat. If no meeting had taken place, we would buy whatever he brought.

By then we had been thirty days in the jungle and seventeen in our 'tennis court'. Most of us felt dizzy when we stood up suddenly and all of us soon became very short of breath. Morning exercise was, by now, confined to a few bends and stretches. The ground was slippery as a result of the incessant rain and we were too weak to do much else. We only failed to take a few minutes' exercise during an actual downpour. When we walked the few yards to the river for a wash, it was an unpleasant labour. I was also plagued by a leech bite on the ankle that became infected. I finished what little ointment we had brought with us, so I told Senagit to get some from the medical post at Blaur. He said that the dresser insisted on seeing the infected part; I told him to say it was for his wife's crotch. So he brought me the stuff, having done what I said, reporting that it was the same excuse Ah Soo Chye made when he sent aborigines to get medicines from security force medical packs. The stuff, a green ointment, failed to do the trick, so during periods of sunlight I exposed my ankle, hoping that would help cure it. When it did not, I burned it out with a blazing ember. All I achieved was a different sort of infection which took three years properly to heal.

By then the rain had eroded our latrine and the faeces were washed down the normally dry gully that led to the drinking water. The camp was in danger from falling timber. I felt we ought to move, but to cross the Puian under prevailing conditions would have been more dangerous still. There was no point in leaving if we were going to return to Perak soon.

Mudak came the next day, carrying eggplant and tapioca. We had a long talk. Helwood had returned and Mudak agreed it was quite likely that Helwood had met Ah Soo Chye, although he had assured Mudak that no meeting had taken place. Mudak, in turn, feared Helwood was deceiving him. I was no further forrader!

I decided to stay where we were on the off-chance of Ah Soo Chye coming our way, but thought it wise to send Rijed and Sutel back to Perak, where Kerinching might have some firm news. In that case, they were to go to Grik and inform Ismail, who would let me and the battalion know.

So I told Mudak that I would like to see Rijed and Sutel, and how dangerous our camp was getting; to spend the rest of the time in it – I had rations for another twenty-nine days – was not a happy prospect. Mudak volunteered to cut down any dangerous-looking trees, but I feared it would draw attention to us. I decided to search for another campsite myself.

Next day I took some men out with me, but found nowhere that seemed to have advantages over our present site. Fallen trees were everywhere, in fact the farther afield we went, the worse it seemed. I decided to stay put: lethargy and weakness affected my decision to some degree. We picked some bamboo shoots and had a pleasant evening meal. I calculated on remaining where we were until 21 September, but if Ah Soo Chye were to arrive as we left, I had a reserve of food until the end of the month. If nothing else, I was learning patience.

Thus August 1962 passed. Rijed and Sutel left for Perak. Our days monotonously ticked by – ambush parties out and back, rain, rain and more rain. An hour or two of sun and an attempt would be made to dry out clothes, radio set and weapons. As the sun only filtered through in small patches, we had the choice of moving everything to keep pace with it or leaving the stuff where it was and waiting for the shadows to move off. There was no sickness, but we had grown wan and long-haired. Stories came less easily and conversation was more trivial. There was no quarrelling and gradually our mental horizons shrunk to our physical one: a frond had grown longer, the ants' nest was less busy, the frog was croaking at a different time.

September began as wet as August ended. Senagit came with some vegetables and said Kerinching wanted him back in Perak. I asked him to let me check on the radio, because I badly needed him to lead us back over the divide. We would be severely hampered without such an expert guide, even to the extent of running out of rations before we found the helicopter site.

Senagit showed us how to cook some nuts that were falling in profusion near by. We roasted them and ate them whole, then tried mashing them with the wild chillies Senagit had brought. This was a new 'chutney', so beloved by the Gurkhas. The nuts had a curious taste which was not unpleasant and, once we knew they were not poisonous, I let the men wander up to about 200 yards away, searching for them. It gave them something to do as well as supplementing their daily diet.

It was interesting to watch the soldiers: for the most part they accepted the hardships quietly and with fortitude. However, there was one man, Rifleman Prembahadur Rai, who had not been among my original choices. He had been one of the carrying party and I had exchanged him for one of my 'first eleven', who admitted, as we made our approach march over the divide, that he was not up to the task – and who had been transferred to the Gurkha Military Police by the time I got back. Prembahadur was a strong man and a potential NCO. He had not received my initial briefings, nor had he prepared himself mentally for extended hardships generally and hunger in particular. Compared with the others, he was greedy, and when first getting accustomed to hunger soon after the departure of the carrying party, made himself ill by overeating some wild chillies we found. Now this same man spent his whole time collecting and cooking nuts, gorging himself to the point of again making himself ill. I showed no sympathy at all.

I had not seen Mudak for some time and asked where he was. I was told he was sowing his rice and I realised that this was the crop that everybody referred to when they asserted Ah Soo Chye would come and celebrate its harvest at Iwoh. The complete lack of any understanding of time and their inability to express any but the simplest matters in their language made the Temiar despairingly difficult to deal with. The rice crop of the previous year was being harvested when I first went into Kelantan in March, and the way all the Temiar spoke about the next crop being sooner than later had misled me into believing there were two crops a year. This was not the case, so it was not now, September, that Iwoh would be held, but six months later, in March 1963!

By 11 September I finally decided to leave the area on the 21st, and requested a helicopter to lift us out from where we had been lifted in, on the 25th. Two of my soldiers were due home leave and our battalion's annual Dashera festival was scheduled for early October. After the effort all the men had put in, I did not want them to miss it. Some troops had also been assigned elsewhere in the 'Bamboo' area and I had submitted a plan for part of my own D Company to live with Helwood and shadow him wherever he went. As the battalion as a whole was already committed, I regarded my exit from the jungle as a temporary measure and would arrange a meeting with Mudak and Duwin on my return, news being given to them by an aborigine whom I would bring with me from Perak.

Ensuring Senagit came on the appointed day was a problem. As soon as I started to explain and count days absent, he became confused. So I took a piece of string, made ten knots in it and taught him to undo one knot every morning and come the day there were no knots left. He was thrilled with this brilliant idea, but doubted his ability to remember even that. I jollied him along and he departed in high humour after practising it and getting it correct.

The remaining days creaked slowly by. It appeared that Helwood had moved south to arrange a timber contract. I envied his freedom of movement. There was now less rain, but we were all weak and I was worried lest the return journey over the divide should be too much for us. I had to walk back, because I still believed my security was intact and that my method of conducting operations was still the best, nay the only method to use against Ah Soo Chye. We were faced with a twenty-mile footslog, and had to be ready after that to return to the Blaur area once more on foot.

On 20 September, one day before it was necessary, Senagit and a friend of his, Anjang, returned to our camp. We had received that very morning a radio message to say that Ah Soo Chye had been seen on the Sungei Sara in Perak – north of the Sungei Temenggor – about one month before. Senagit was most interested, as to him it indicated that there had been no jungle meeting between the guerrilla leader and Helwood. We would have to move back as though we expected a contact, for Ah Soo Chye could well be on his way over to Kelantan even as we were returning. There was no point in staying in camp any longer, so we packed up. It was a curious sensation, after living there for fifty-three days and fifty-two nights, to be taking our shelters to bits, throwing away the plaited leaves we had woven, dismantling the stone fireplace. I was conscious of a feeling of relief, simply glad we were all fit enough to start the journey back. A reaction might yet set in, but we still had to be ready for that chance encounter. No relaxation was possible.

Red hot skewers pierced my knees as we moved off, practically in slow motion. It was 1 o'clock and an afternoon stroll was as good a way as any of getting accustomed to walking. Our loads were light and, once we had the use of our legs again, the journey back was comparatively simple. The only really difficult place was the tree crossing that had previously caused so much distress, but we managed to ford the river without mishap.

The next two days were much easier. We averaged 2000 yards each hour and reached the helicopter site in fourteen hours of walking. This included crossing the final stretch of river, now much swollen, twenty-one times, starting off ankle deep and finishing wet up to our navels. We met with no evidence of guerrilla movement.

At 11 o'clock on 25 September, ten weeks after we had been flown in, we were flown out. The one helicopter that came for us was piloted by Flight Lieutenant Peter Davis, who had been with me in 1/1 GR. He had won the Military Cross on the North-West Frontier of India for his action on Sunday, 15 June 1947 – this was one of the very few, if not the only, bravery award ever given without a supporting campaign medal. It was wonderful to see him again and I knew if anyone could get us out safely, it was Peter.

Once out, everything seemed, on the surface, to be normal. We were greeted rather as curios; our faces were fish-belly white, except where the sun had caught us as we awaited the helicopter. My soldiers resembled Japanese and my eyes had a hunted look in them. Our hair had not been cut since we left Ipoh. The normal noises of everyday life frightened us and, having spoken in nothing but soft tones for so long, we soon strained our voices.

We went by truck to Ipoh the next day. I had seen some new postage stamps when in Grik and decided to buy some at a post office on the way down. I was taken by surprise at the shocked look on people's faces, as well as being told that those particular stamps were no longer an issue. That made me realise that life had passed me by, as indeed did many later conversations. People could not understand my not giving what they believed to be a simple answer to a simple question. My reticence was taken as a slight but, when pressed, all I could mumble was that I had been out of circulation for some time.

D Company was firing on the range when I arrived at Ipoh. I sought them out. 'Saheb, what have they done to you?' some of the Gurkhas asked. 'Saheb, why are they trying to kill you?' others queried. Sympathetic clucking ensued and, having met up with them again, I went to collect my mail, all ten weeks of it, and walked slowly to my room in the mess.

The next few days were a burden as I painfully adjusted myself. Heelis kindly offered me leave 'in the bright lights', as he put it. This I did not want, as I felt that, once I had reverted to a certain standard of normality, which I still equated with softness, I would be in no condition to return once more to Blaur. Far better, I felt, to resist temptation in the knowledge that I could continue the task that it seemed only I was fated to do, than to risk wasting the fifty-two plus seventy days of hardship, let alone the extraordinarily protracted and tenuously fragile relationship so patiently built up between myself and the Temiar. Heelis wrote me a stern note, telling me I was boring all and sundry by talking about it. The letter, doubtless sent with the best of intentions, may have been prompted by his wife who, kindly according to her own standards, had invited me over to their house for a Sunday curry lunch party. I must have reacted ungraciously, although I thought I had camouflaged my true feelings, when she said something unthinkingly about giving me a rice dish, after I had endured a rice diet for so long.

It was still all very difficult.

*   *   *

Within a week of my return I was at a Dashera party. It was the evening of the main battalion nautch and I was comfortably settled in an easy chair awaiting the curtain to rise and the show to begin. An army officer connected with Intelligence had also been invited and his was the only empty chair. He arrived late and eventually came over to tell me he had just heard that Ah Soo Chye had visited Helwood's ladang three or four days, maybe a week, ago, possibly even as I was flying out. Although I had half expected such an occurrence, I now felt at a complete loss and sucked dry of any strength. I put it as far to the back of my mind as I could, but the whole vexed question continued nibbling at me. During an interval some unkind remarks were made by a couple of my brother officers – who had 'known' all along I had been hoodwinked – and I relapsed into moody contemplation.

As soon as I could, I paid a visit to Special Branch in Ipoh and had a talk with a senior and sage Chinese. His information was that the guerrillas had allegedly congratulated Helwood on keeping troops away and to the south. I had hidden more than 5000 yards to the north and the guerrillas were reported to have approached Blaur from the south-west. To me this was indicative that guerrilla movement was coincidental with, and not occasioned by, my departure. The guerrillas were also seen to be carrying American-type weapons, believed to have been captured in Vietnam, and wearing khaki-coloured uniforms. There was also something fishy about the report as to which Temiar Ah Soo Chye had met, but I could not place it. That was only fathomed much later when I queried why Kalusa, the moon-mad friend of Lo See, was reported to be working for me. It transpired that Herbolt had not distinguished between Kalusa and Mudak, and was spreading rumours about me that simply were not true. This he admitted much later on: unfortunate remarks made by Heelis – some when I was in the jungle – showed that Herbolt's influence was stronger than my reputation when it came to assessing the true situation.

At the time, however, I accepted what was said at face value, partly because there was no alternative and partly because I felt that the protest would be taken as a pointer that I had no real faith in Mudak and his men. Although I had almost had enough of it all, my inability to obtain concrete results spurred me on to continue my quest for the elusive Ah Soo Chye. I had originally gone to Special Branch expecting a polite thanks, and maybe scarcely veiled scorn at my blundering attempts. I was not prepared to be told that they thought I still had an 80 per cent chance of success, whereas no one else was thought to have any chance at all. Despite being gratified to hear that, it seemed that I was destined for another hard slog.

CHAPTER 10

The Seventh Veil

There remained the question of when I should return to my jungle hideout in Kelantan. The monthly guerrilla movement pattern would have allowed me to stay a little longer in Ipoh, regaining my strength completely, but Special Branch evidently had some ploy designed to lure Ah Soo Chye into the Blaur area well before the three months were up. Already one week had elapsed since my return. Would I please be back in the jungle in three weeks' time?

This meant I had to move sooner than any of us had envisaged. I made a quick journey up to Klian and contacted two of Kerinching's men, Rijed and a new man called Abush. I told them to go over the divide as soon as possible, contact Mudak and get him to start another pattern of movement. If Helwood had any suspicions that security forces were in the area he might have Mudak's men shadowed and, on finding nobody in hiding, would, I hoped, make subsequent operations much freer.

*   *   *

Two weeks later, on 26 October, I arrived in Grik for the third, and surely the last, time of asking. Planning had been much easier. The whole battalion was deployed on various ladangs and an airdrop to them could include rations for me. A little careful planning might result in my being topped up at intervals. I feared that my old route would, by then, be prejudiced, so I decided on a different one, the more southerly of the two, which looked easier from the map. This was ten miles longer, involving a thirty-mile approach march, as well as having to cross the divide a thousand feet higher, at 5500 feet. Our loads were lighter but still weighed over 100 pounds. I took eight men, including one from the first group, Tanké, and one from the second.

After one night in Grik, we moved by boat to Klian. I had done what I wanted, namely to liaise with Ismail and buy gifts, such as fish hooks and twine, for the aborigines. At Klian I met up with Senagit, Sutel and another man, Anggah, who said he was happy to go with me.

Despite strictest orders to the contrary, the Malay boatmen did not stop where I had told them and took us on to a small settlement farther upstream. This angered me because we ran into a party of aborigines there who were making their way to Fort Kemar, to the south, and our 'long-range' loads excited their suspicions. I told them I was going due north, this side of the divide, up to the Sungei Sara, but I was not believed as they duly reported to the authorities at Fort Kemar that I was bound for Kelantan.

The actual crossing took five days. It was uneventful, but the going was unbelievably difficult as it rained the whole time, we had to negotiate many landslides and we were going against the grain of the country. More than ever was I filled with admiration for the Gurkhas. Every step was a burdensome effort yet they were ever patient. I had increased the ration compared with the time before by including packet soups, but the heavy rain, and the fact that some of the rivers we crossed came up to our chests, meant that forty packets of soup, nine lots of rice and six of sugar, were ruined. My aborigine escort took us to a place they recommended we made camp. They then left us in order to contact Mudak.

The area was vile. Originally I had been told to prepare for a three-month sojourn, so I had bought many packets of vegetable seeds. The planting of these and the need to be nearer the main ladang complex had brought us into a belt of country that had, at one stage, been cultivated. Now it was full of sandflies and mosquitoes. Moreover, it sloped and walking was difficult. I realised it would drive us mad to live there for any length of time, so I resolved to get the aborigines to reconnoitre another site as soon as they reappeared. We were all miserable. I was told, over the radio, that I might be withdrawn after three weeks. Had that been the case I would have had to ask for a helicopter, as I could not face a walk back over the divide.

Not knowing how long we would be in that dreadful place before the guides returned, I decided to obliterate the marks of our entry into the immediate area from the stream we had walked up, by once again planting living camouflage along the axis of our movement. Control of smoke was a problem: it was the one way we could keep the plague of insects at bay, but we dared not use it by day. We daubed ourselves liberally with anti-mosquito oil throughout the day in an effort to keep calm, but at night the sandflies flew through the mesh of our mosquito-nets and made sleep very difficult. The second night we lit small bonfires under our bivouacs, for we were sleeping in hammocks, and managed to keep them off us.

Six Temiar, including Mudak, arrived at midday on 5 November, our third day. They disapproved of our campsite and one of them went looking for a more suitable area. Meanwhile I asked Mudak some questions the CO had told me to put to him. I did not then know that Mudak, having been mistaken for Kalusa, was under suspicion, hence the reason for such questions, even though I had been so fully debriefed in Ipoh. Mudak sensed something was wrong during his long-range interrogation and was grieved.

Part of my message back to battalion HQ read: '. . . Mudak not heard of communist terrorist visit of 25 to 30 September and all his men surprised when I told them . . . Helwood does not know of [my] previous stay . . . I am willing to remain whole time but cannot make another long approach march. If three weeks time limit really necessary suggest either another party takes over or call the whole thing off . . .'

While this message was simmering in Ipoh, I was visited by some aborigines who brought fern tops, beans and tapioca. I planned that they come and make our own little plot where we could sow our seeds and get some sunshine. I also instructed them how to go to the nearest military unit for the resupply and establish that they were our men — for the other Gurkhas did not know them — by introducing themselves with a handshake, left hand to left hand. We practised, amid great mirth, but when they reached the camp where our rations should have been waiting, there was nothing for us. The Intelligence Officer had forgotten to include us in the ration indent! The aborigines were told to wait until an emergency drop was arranged.

For the next four days I brooded on the possibility of my being withdrawn. Now I was safely ensconced it seemed a pity to change the situation if there were no overriding reasons. Accordingly I sent another message to Ipoh which read: 'Obvious clash of opinion of value of my mission, suggest following before final decision taken: A. Following persons to be consulted by you', and here I listed several Special Branch officials, including the sage Chinese in Ipoh. I continued: 'B. Suggest you plus Special Branch representatives visit Helwood's ladang to assess situation . . . C. Facts are: 1. Best chance of kill still through Mudak. 2. Mudak still only aborigine of authority willing to work for government with system now in operation. 3. By my living with Helwood, Mudak's continued cooperation doubtful. 4. No information Ah Soo Chye in area when self and Mudak present since promise of help. 5. What other project helps the Brigade of Gurkhas? D. 1. Paddy sown by 14 September, half ripe by 31 October. Harvest should be from 17 December. Plus six weeks wait gives 28 January as deadline. Pity waste all efforts on whim of another. 2. If no joy suggest officer plot situation eased by my going on home leave as soon as possible.' This last thought was put in as my name was down to be a Recruit Company Commander in 1963.

It was a long message and had to be sent by Morse so it took several hours to pass. I had no worries about batteries as we had a resupply line. To pass the time we planted some of our vegetable seeds where an area had been cleared. I had had a shopping spree. There were packets of broad beans, long beans, mustard, spring and Spanish onions, six kinds of tomato, black and white squash, parsnip, marrow and eggplant. That left lettuce, carrot, leek, okra, silver beet and pumpkin to be planted another day.

Senagit popped in to see us and said he personally doubted the report of guerrillas visiting the Blaur area. I had, by now, much faith in his opinions, but had to choose my moment to talk with him only when others were not present. The general view was that Ah Soo Chye would return for Iwok in two months' time.

Parts of my long message were queried by Heelis: why could or would Mudak not tell when Ah Soo Chye would return to the area and why had he no information concerning the guerrilla meeting?

These questions made me realise that my CO was thinking along different lines from mine. I sent an answer. I said that all nine of Mudak's men were in Perak when the meeting took place. Aborigine security was on a need-to-know basis while events were still hot. Mudak thought that many aborigines' reports of guerrilla movement were made only to earn Special Branch reward money. Therefore, as there was no positive indication of a meeting, there was an initial reaction of ignorance. Now there were fifteen men working continuously covering the area. I had stressed to Mudak this was his last chance of so much security force effort and he understood the urgency. 'At present I am not worried,' I ended up. 'If least bit dubious efficacy of Mudak, I will inform you.'

Next day, 14 November, part of our airdropped rations were brought over, with the remainder promised ten days later. I had food until 19 December. We sowed the rest of our seeds. All seemed set fair next day, when permission was received for me to stay until the harvest and, if I considered it necessary, even later.

It was then I had a message from Goh Ah Hok, the JCLO, who had been in Helwood's ladang with part of my D Company for some time. He called me to the set and said that Alang, Helwood's brother and the man more in with Ah Soo Chye than Helwood himself, wanted to work for me. Goh added that it was common knowledge in the ladang that I was in the area. I was very disturbed. Goh ended up by saying that a tall aborigine had recently visited the ladang and that he was a 'spy'. I later learned that he meant he was sent by the Department of Aborigines, in other words, by Herbolt, and had leaked the news of my hidden presence. I savagely presumed this was all part of Herbolt's 'hope you fail' campaign. I never did comprehend how such a man was allowed to flourish unchecked by his superiors.

I also learned how my second sojourn had eventually been twigged: I had paid all my men, who had gone to Grik and bought a watch each! None knew how to tell the time but a watch was a status symbol, all the more conspicuous when only a loincloth was worn. It was obvious, too, that those aborigines who were still pro-Ah Soo Chye had no watch, no status symbol, no prestige. Those whom I had subverted possessed all three.

I later fetched Goh Ah Hok back to the set and asked him if Helwood knew that brother Alang had defected? Answer: no. I asked more questions: did Alang suspect Mudak and Duwin? Who were the bad security risks? Who was the 'spy'? How long had Alang known about me? Was all lost?

Goh Ah Hok could not answer my queries straight away but would contact me later. I wondered how to deal with the situation. Maybe I could get Alang out of the ladang and employed elsewhere by Special Branch. I could pretend I was moving myself. I could send back all my Perak aborigines. I could show myself in another area. I could arrange for dummy airdrops elsewhere. I could pretend to take Alang into my confidence. I had to discuss the whole situation with Mudak urgently.

I slept on this and awoke with a tentative plan: I would split my force, leaving five men at the camp in ambush and move with the other four far south to a place called Gemala. I would first go to Blaur, and meet my own company officers there, as well as the new reinforcements from the Training Depot, who were due to fly in shortly. I would persuade Alang to go with me to Gemala, dump him there with Special Branch, continue south and then wheel round, having dyed my face black so as not to be recognised as a European from a distance, and walk back, a total of sixty miles.

I sent the gist of my plan to battalion HQ and had it approved next day. I arranged to meet Heelis in Gemala; would I give him a firm date and place? I was also to meet two special branch inspectors in Blaur on my way through.

I fixed details of splitting the party and eventually started off on 21 November. I had arranged to take the radio operator and one other man with me the whole way, plus two more men as far as Blaur to bring back rations for the stay-behind group and also to act as guides later on. It was the twenty-sixth day of that phase of the operation and the 148th of the series. The bad diet, the long journeys, the heavy weights had all taken a greater toll of my strength than I had realised. We only had just over a mile to go. We started off at 11 o'clock and I expected to be with the rest of my soldiers at Blaur by noon. All the previous evening I had heard helicopters shuttling in with reinforcements, landing and taking off only a short distance away.

I was carrying about 50 pounds. We were due to pick up rations at Blaur, so we left what we had with the stay-behind group, whose task was to ambush the small stream near our camp, along which guerrillas had been known to walk. I would rejoin them, I thought, in two or three weeks' time. They knew where to go in an emergency – 2000 yards away. I was not worried when I left them.

After about twenty minutes I realised that I was at the end of my tether. The ground had sloped gently downhill, but now it levelled out and even rose slightly. As I walked along I suddenly found I could not manoeuvre my right leg in front of my left leg. I stood, legs separated, looking down at them, wondering how I could get them to move. My men waited patiently. Seconds ticked by. One said, 'Come on Saheb, let's get going,' but nothing happened. I mumbled something about trying and with a supreme effort brought my right leg forward. I looked up at the men, confident that I was all set to move. But I was wrong. I was still stuck. I had forgotten the simple truth that, when the right leg is in front, the left leg must be behind. I did not know what to do, nor did I greatly care. I sat down in a crumpled heap and waited half an hour for some strength to drip into my body. We were only a few hundred yards from our objective.

Later I was pulled to my feet and I stumbled on. I was defeated, completely and utterly. I was empty of any feelings, except the realisation that I was beaten, physically, mentally and operationally. All my efforts, all my high hopes, all my stubbornness, all the military stupidities I had had to fight against – all to no avail. I had lost. I staggered on. We followed the line of the Sungei Blaur, the river that met the Puian, not so very far away. The ladang where my company HQ had established itself was at the junction of these two rivers. The Blaur was smaller than the Puian, but fast-flowing and full, at that point, of black rocks. Its banks were high and steep. I lost my balance and slipped. I hung to a sapling that somehow held my weight and looked down longingly at the rushing water and wicked black rocks thirty feet below. If, then, I could have guaranteed going head first and knowing no more about it, I would have let go. But all that might have happened was a broken limb or two and a leaderless group of Gurkhas. I hauled myself up with a strength I did not know I had and blundered on.

Five hours after we started I thought I saw a man washing at a ford in the river. As I looked at him he became blurred and began revolving. Then he was not there, yet I could still see him. It was all very strange because he had gone when I looked again. I peered around and saw where he had gone. He had climbed some crude steps up the far bank. We had arrived. We linked arms and lurched across the water, splashing each other as we faltered. Then we were on the other side. My men said they were going up the steps, and invited me to go with them. I found I was sitting down and had shut my eyes. I was quite happy, thank you. They could climb where they liked. I would sit down. Why go any farther? I could, surely, will myself to fly up the bank. Anyway, it was worth trying ... but it did not work and with a deep sigh, I stood up and hoisted myself up those steps. Hands, knees, feet, they all had their uses when you knew how. Slowly, so slowly, I went up. There were not more than a score, but they were too many to count.

I got to the top and there were my men whom I had last seen in Ipoh. I heard an intake of breath as they saw me. I looked at them and, for a brief moment, none moved. I swayed forward and the soldiers quickly closed in to help me to a rough seat. One I had known for ten years was in tears as he looked at me and two others walked away so as not to see me.

I could not stand, nor sit, nor lie. I crouched forward, put my head in my hands and sobbed. Dirgaman Rai, my Gurkha Captain, soothed me and ordered a man to brew some tea. Kind hands removed my pack. I wiped my eyes and sat, motionless and unsure what to do. I was only conscious of not having to move. I drank three mugs of tea, but I could not eat. I was led to a wooden platform and more kind hands helped to undress me. Night must have fallen because it was dark. Sleep must have come some time during the night, but angry red swirls of aches seemed ever present. I was myself again next morning: very sad, very stiff, very weak, with my walk to Gemala an utter impossibility.

I spoke at length to Goh Ah Hok. I had been told by Senagit that Alang was afraid I would take vengeance on him for having tricked me the previous May. Goh, on the other hand, reckoned that Alang and Kalusa were more likely to produce positive results than Mudak or Helwood. I had almost lost all faith in my part of the operation. If I had, at that eleventh hour, so patently failed, how could I hope to salvage anything?

I sent a message to Heelis, saying that I would no longer meet him in Gemala, that I needed a few days to reappraise the situation and would he come to Blaur to meet me?

Later that day, Goh Ah Hok, myself and my two Gurkhas – the other two had picked up their rations and gone back to the ambush – toured the ladang area. I had decided to show my face as I could no longer keep my presence secret. Our visit was cursory. The ladang was a quarter of a mile from the campsite and an easy path led there. I met three 'penghulus', Helwood, Alang and Kalusa, and merely greeted them. I appeared neither angry nor happy, just neutral. I had no idea what effect I would have on anyone, but I wanted them all to see me.

I got back to my camp, worn out. I lay on the wooden platform in a secluded area thinking and wondering where I had gone wrong, unable to bring myself to believe that all was finally lost. As I lay there, musing, Goh Ah Hok came across and called me. The senior aborigines wanted to talk, there and then. Goh's plan was to have a meeting, I not speaking in Temiar, trying to catch any remark they made to one another. I agreed. The meeting was brief: the sum of it all was the aborigines saying that, although they were friendly with Ah Soo Chye and Lo See, they could arrange to bring them to an area to have them killed by others. It all sounded hopeful, but I was not convinced. I arranged for another meeting the following day, when I would talk to them – let them dance to my tune. Meanwhile I had to settle my account with Mudak and his men for the patrolling work they claimed they had done. It came to a little under £100 and I asked battalion headquarters to send the cash with the CO and the Intelligence Officer, when they came to see me in six days' time.

Next day I held a grand meeting of all the four 'penghulus' in the ladang: Helwood, Alang, Kalusa, Mudak and my own friend Senagit. Goh ah Hok was also present. It took a long time and I had to show continuous tact and understanding. But I obtained what I wanted, which was for them all, individually and in the presence of the others, publicly to promise to help me initially, and later the government, to eliminate the communist guerrillas. I invited their ideas and I made them all speak. Again I promised a reward for success and a recommendation that, when loyalty had been shown, an aborigine could once more carry a shotgun, a privilege I knew they wanted, but which had been disallowed by government. I further stressed that, as Helwood had been a friend of Ah Soo Chye, I did not expect him to take an active part in any elimination plans. He seemed most relieved at my pronouncement. Mudak, I felt, was a spent force: somehow I had offended him by not paying him certain moneys to which he thought himself entitled. He had brought me thus far and I was most grateful to him on that count, but he had shown himself greedy. By bringing the planning onto an 'all ladang' basis, I guessed he would fade out.

I gave them a meal and I expected them to return. However, they stayed and discussed the plans earlier put forward. This was a very hopeful sign, as normally a meal signified the end of any proceedings. They wanted me to hide again, disguising myself. There was no point in my deciding to do anything until my meeting with Heelis; but meanwhile a number of aborigines, including Alang, came to see me and apologised for deceiving me earlier in the year. They were afraid, then, as they did not know me; now all was different. They knew, liked and trusted me and would not hoodwink me again.

Five days later Heelis flew in by helicopter. He objected to our campsite and was shocked by my general appearance. I was not happy about the campsite either, but it had been chosen before I got there and it was on one of the few flat pieces of ground near the ladang and clean drinking water. It had been an aboriginal graveyard and whether it was because we were in such weakened condition or because of our remoteness, we all experienced emotions ranging from unease to alarm at one time or another in what appeared to be ghostly circumstances. It was agreed that I should stay another three weeks, while Goh Ah Hok went on leave and came back as the continuity man. Meantime, I was to lift the ambush I had left behind. None of the seeds, incidentally, ever sprouted! I would then be relieved by C Company. During the remainder of my time I was to consolidate the enthusiasm shown by all and sundry, also getting them used to the idea of my leaving them.

By now all the Temiar knew I had been upstream for a long time earlier in the year, as well as having been in hiding yet a third time before coming into the open. They saw I was greatly enfeebled as compared with six months previously, but their inability to tell time stood me in good stead, as they also believed I had been around longer by far than was the case. I had shown a tenacity unusual for a soldier, in their experience, and this impressed them, as did my language prowess and my happy laughing attitude to their children. By then I was surrounded by the kids almost all day long. I taught them all manner of different things, ranging from the three-card trick to dancing 'boomps-a-daisy' and from making funny faces to blowing through my hands to make bird and monkey noises. When I asked them anything, their invariable answer was, 'Why ask, you know everything.' Adults were equally friendly. Mrs

Helwood came to me one day and invited me to live in their house as their children took more notice of me than of their parents. Men sought advice on very intimate problems, one asking how he could influence a girl to marry him when he was so ugly and another how to make his wife cohabit with him. Yet a third approached me about his dreams. I, for my part, was so relieved not to be hiding, not to have to worry about sickness, hunger, falling trees, boredom, botched airdrops and my Gurkhas generally, that I was in love with life. I could look at the sky, drink water or even sing! I was washed out, drained of all normal emotion and I saw things in a completely different perspective then ever before. Much of this atmosphere Heelis could observe for himself.

So it came as a rude shock when Heelis showed me a report that Helwood had made to Herbolt when they had met during that 'timber contract' business. Part of which read: '... when asked why he hated Major Cross, Penghulu Helwood had said that the officer concerned was an angry man, always shouting and bullying and so he was very afraid...' I was asked to answer it, to refute it. My reply was very simple: I pointed out that Helwood had been among the group of Temiar who had come to welcome him at the landing point and the ensuing conversation that I had translated was so obviously friendly that I felt I could stand on that alone. This was accepted and no more was said.

But that was not the only matter that shocked me. Towards the end of the hour Heelis had with me, during which the helicopter flew to the nearest police fort to take on fuel for the return journey, I was given an envelope, containing that most important of military documents, my Annual Confidential Report. This I had to read and initial as having read, though not necessarily agreeing with, before handing it back.

It was not a good report, if only because it did not properly reflect the activities of the past twelve months. I read it and saw that some of my worries and fears – those I had confided to Heelis about conditions arising from having to go back into the jungle for a second and a third time – were treated as defects of character. Having read it through, I turned back to the page that contained my personal details to check that it was, in fact, mine and not another's. It was mine, but – in retrospect wrongly – I did not voice any qualms about it, nor ask for it to be deferred. I was still 'punch-drunk' with fatigue and had not the mental resilience to argue with Heelis when he wrote, in effect, that he could not make up his mind whether I was of commanding officer material, so could not recommend me for command of a battalion nor for promotion to lieutenant colonel. To help him decide, I had to attend a company commanders' course in England and, the better to give me a chance of a good grading, he would arrange to send me early, as a foreign student, to catch up with those military developments that had passed me by these last eighteen months. If I were to get a good grading, that would clinch an affirmative decision; if not, no.

Such vacillation, to my mind, was trivial pettiness when compared with the sheer joy of not having to hide away under the trees, with all that entailed, or to engage for much longer in unending, convoluted conversations with the Temiar, nor, as it transpired, to be a target for aggressive ghosts...

*   *   *

I had three weeks in which to deal with Ah Soo Chye. I doubted whether we would ever catch up with him, as did Goh Ah Hok, who was worried about security and wanted to start a rumour that we were not patrolling because we thought Ah Soo Chye wanted to surrender. We were clutching at any straw.

Then, on 7 December, the Brunei rebellion caught people unawares. How much master planning there had been is hard to say, but we knew that the rebellion was precipitated prematurely. Possibly it was never meant to erupt in isolation. Certainly around that time the Singapore government suddenly arrested over a hundred people to prevent trouble. The Malayan Railway staff also went on strike and postal services were disrupted. There was a rumour, where I was, of an incursion of guerrillas into Malaya from the Betong salient in Thailand. This last fact has never, to my knowledge, been substantiated, but we felt lonelier still on being informed that the battalion would soon be moving down from Ipoh to Singapore as a back-up for Brunei.

We rehearsed surrounding houses in our own ladang at night, just in case Ah Soo Chye visited. We cut clubs and formed four teams of ourselves and Temiar. Apart from that we lived quietly in our camp. Christmas, like the previous year, was another day. On the afternoon of the last day of 1962, we learned that a soldier, the third in D Company that year, though none of them with me, had been drowned while washing in the Puian. It was a beastly way to see the old year out. One way and another, I was glad to see the back of 1962.

*   *   *

I have recorded a number of times that I had conversations with the aborigines. I have made the dialogue appear easy, albeit simple. Often this was far from the case, as their vocabulary was limited. On New Year's Day, 1963, for example, Mudak came to tell me that the day before he had overheard one of Helwood's men telling Helwood that tapioca was being dug up near by. There were rumours in the ladang: was it by a mad aborigine or by guerrillas? Was it by a sane aborigine for hungry guerrillas? Or, as I privately thought possible, was Mudak trying to implicate Helwood or Alang because they were now more in the limelight?

I called all the 'penghulus' up into my camp for a talk. I would not let on who had told me, so, when I broached the subject, they speculated how I had heard. We started talking at 4 o'clock and went on for two and a half hours. The talk went round and round and round, frustrating in its elusiveness. My head swam by the end of it and I did not know what to think. After I had sat them down, I opened the conversation with one or other Temiar answering, and it went like this:

'With what news?'

'With no news.'

'I hear, I hear strong, I hear wind, tapioca it steals.'

'How you hear?'

'I hear wind. True or not?'

'Hear women talk. Talk tapioca it steals.'

'I hear,' I continued after that part of the conversation had been repeated and had taken five minutes, 'I hear mad Temiar he from that side of the river, he steals tapioca, true or not?'

'Tata, I say, and if I say good luck, good, and if I say bad luck, bad, if you are angry, what am I to do? But I say, yes.'

'Yes, what?'

Came the devastating answer, 'Yes, no.'

So I started again: 'Is there a mad man?'

'Yes.'

'Tell me about him.'

'He lives in the jungle. Sometimes he comes. He has long hair and we are afraid. He has no knife. He has no fire. He cannot eat.'

'Where is he now?' I asked.

'Dead.'

'When did he die?'

'One day in the past.'

'So he does not steal tapioca?'

'No.'

'Who does?'

'The mad man.'

'But you say he is dead.'

'No, he is not dead.'

This point, try hard though I might, was never satisfactorily resolved, despite twenty minutes solid cross examination. So I switched tack.

'If the dead man does not eat, does not steal tapioca, then inland man steals?'

'No.'

'But tapioca it steals, mad dead man not, inland man not, who?'

'It steals.'

'The bad men China, that Ah Soo, that Lo See, they steal?'

'They are in the high hills. What am I to do?'

'What do they eat?'

'Food.'

'If no food?'

'No food.'

'If no food they die?'

'They die.'

'How long they no food they die?'

'Long.'

'Dead now?'

'Yes.'

'Dead now?'

'No.'

I gradually brought them around to thinking that the guerrillas might be living off the land, lying up, stealing tapioca and here having to use the word 'river' (even where the existence of a river was notional rather than actual) in order to pinpoint the location.

'Ah Soo is near?' I asked.

'No.'

'Ah Soo is far?'

'No.'

'Where is Ah Soo?'

'If near, near, if far, far, if this side of the river, this side, if that side, that side, if upstream, upstream, if downstream, downstream. If you are angry what am I to do? I hope strongly.'

'What do you hope?'

'Yes.'

'Yes, what?'

'Yes, no.'

'Ah Soo is upstream?' I asked.

'Ah Soo is upstream.'

'Ah Soo is downstream?'

'Ah Soo is downstream.'

'How is he upstream and downstream?'

'Yes.'

'Yes, what?'

'Yes, no.'

'Where is Ah Soo?' I started again.

'In the high hills.'

'Is Ah Soo in the high hills?'

'No.'

'What is no?'

'Yes.'

'Yes, what?'

'Yes, in the high hills.'

'If he is hungry?'

'He gets food.'

'What does he eat?'

'What he can get.'

'What does he get?'

'Tapioca.'

'From here?'

'Yes.'

'Yes, new of it?'

'Yes.'

'Who, new of it, it steals?'

'The mad man.'

'But the mad man is dead?'

'No.'

'Not dead?'

'Yes.'

'Yes, what?'

'Dead.'

This went on for two and a half hours. It remains in my memory, typifying Temiar conversation. Most of it was in this vein, as hard to pin down as quicksilver, mercurial in its inconsistency, vague, ephemeral and often meaningless. At the end of any session I felt an acute sympathy for Job. I never lost my temper, although I was sometimes angered by their greed, but I expect they had just as much trouble understanding me as I them.

Senagit, later, was more sanguine. He told me that he would give me ample warning if anything drastic were likely to occur. I was not to worry. He would, he said, tell lies to everybody else on all possible occasions but never to me. Hearing this was like a breath of fresh air.

During the weeks I lived at Blaur, I had ample opportunity of talking with many Temiar. I was naturally very interested in their maintaining a friendly pro-government attitude after I left. I was visited by some Malay Special Branch officers to see how I worked and to learn my methods. I made a point of talking to the aborigines in front of these people, hoping that confidence would be instilled. They asked me if I thought what I had done could be described as a success. I thought deeply before answering them, considering that there had never been, since 1942, a period longer than three months without a physical communist guerrilla presence somewhere among the Temiar. So I replied that if, after my withdrawal from the jungle, the communists stayed away for more than a year, then I supposed that that could be described as a measure of success.

One question I often asked the Temiar: 'Will you go back to the Chinese after I have left you?' Their answer was always the same. 'If the Malays come and scare our women and call us jungle pigs, we will go back to the Chinese.'

On 7 January the drowned soldier's body was found. The next day half of my small force was helicoptered out on orders from Ipoh. I walked down to the platoon of the dead soldier to conduct an inquiry. I took one Temiar as escort. The Puian was very full and we rafted across both ways. I returned on 10 January.

I greeted the men left behind and learned all was well. I told them I was going down to the river, the Blaur, to wash as I was hot and uncomfortable. The washing place was twenty or so yards above a waterfall which fell some way into a deep pool. I stood on a small upraised stone soaping myself and suddenly heard maniacal laughter. I looked up and saw no one. I heard it again and, a moment later, was caught completely off balance as though I had been pushed in the chest. I was swept down towards the waterfall and arrested myself only feet from its edge. I waded back, determined not to pay attention to such things, and started soaping myself again, standing on the stone. More maniacal laughter, another push, repeated gasping and being swept to the very lip of the waterfall. I just managed to clamber out and went back to my stone, this time keeping my feet out of the water on the side. I had no false pride and I was sure one of my men had been playing a joke on me though why I could not imagine. I finished washing, returned to the camp and angrily demanded an explanation. 'Who was laughing at me and why?'

I was met by the most genuine of blank surprises. 'Not us, Saheb,' they chorused. Nor was it Temiar, nor Chinese. It was later explained to me by Alang; by living on their old burial ground, what else could we expect?

Accepting that explanation solved other curious happenings: lying in my hammock, tied between two stout trees and being pushed violently from side to side with no person present; men knocked off their bamboo seat platforms, with no other man in reach; candles blown out when it was windless. How else would these have happened? It was most eerie.

My time was running out. I had been spoken to so sincerely, so often and by so many different Temiar that not even the most hardened cynic could say it was all flattery. I was told by Senagit that his wife would cry when I left, that they were all fond of me, that they would never forget me.

And then, at long, long last, on the two hundredth day of my three-part special operation, on 12 January 1963, at 1026 hours precisely, I was given definite news from two independent sources, that Ah Soo Chye and three others were only 4000 yards away. A wave of relief flooded over me. I had been vindicated by events. I radioed the good news to battalion HQ. Arrangements had been made for me to hand over the military side of operations to a Queen's Gurkha officer and the personnel side to a Special Branch officer, on 14 January. Surely, though, I would now come into my own and be allowed to finish the job off?

The seventh veil had been lifted: I waited expectantly for the answer.

CHAPTER 11

... and Naked we Leave

It was not to be.

I received a curt reply to my message, stating that the battalion was off to Brunei and I had a 'very important task' to do, details of which would be disclosed on my arrival in Ipoh. Once more I was completely flabbergasted and could only think that the 'very important task' in store for me was of such overriding importance to the battalion that even being so close to success had to take second place; although for the life of me I could not imagine what it could be as I did not know anything about Brunei. As for the information of Ah Soo Chye, I was too weak to go and finish off the job and return to the ladang in time for the lift-out; and mentally I was beaten to the extent that I had not the courage to disobey the order.

On 14 January a helicopter came to take me away. I had a sincere and touching farewell from the ladang folk; the maidens danced their goodbyes and Senagit's wife did cry. I was not far off tears myself. I flew to Fort Chabai by helicopter, where I changed into a fixed-wing aircraft to go over the divide to Fort Kemar. There I met Ismail and we had half an hour's talk. He was very pleased with what I had to tell him. I flew on to Grik and motored to Ipoh, where I arrived shortly before dusk. All was quiet, with most of the battalion in Singapore. There was a dream-like quality of unreality to it all.

I walked over to the mess, taking my time. Alastair Rose waiting for me, with a look I did not understand on his normally kind face – it was set and hard. However, he greeted me pleasantly and, as I stepped inside the building, I heard the telephone ring. The orderly answered it, asked the caller to wait and came to fetch me. I walked over to talk into the black intruder, disquiet filling me. It was Heelis from Singapore: so I was back? Had I yet got the message that awaited me?

Wearily I told him that I had only just got in, that I had yet to take off my equipment, that I would, if he really wanted me to, go, there and then, to the office and look for it ... all right, but tomorrow first thing.

I spent a wakeful, hot-eyed night, scarcely sleeping in the comfortable bed, my first for more than eighty nights. I went over to the office next morning and Alastair handed me an envelope, looking away as he did. I took the letter out and the print danced in front of my eyes: 'Dear John, the battalion is going to Brunei and I have withdrawn you to be in charge of the rear party and the families ... you will also keep an eye on operations from Ipoh...'

135

My eyes blurred and my head swam. It simply was not possible. I read it again. After all that effort ... a 'very important task' ... in charge of the families ... I not even married. I felt utterly feeble and, for the next few days, I was not myself. But I understood why Alastair had looked at me as he did.

*   *   *

So the drama played itself out, 'not with a bang, but a whimper'. Ah Soo Chye was contacted near Gemala within the week. Shots were exchanged and he got away unscathed.

Before the battalion went to Brunei, I met Heelis. I said I presumed he wanted a report of my operation. Yes, came the answer, only a very short one was required. I wrote, on half a sheet of foolscap, that I had been so many days with the aborigines and found that work with them was possible. The only other piece of information I included was that the new pattern of army sock had not shrunk. Heelis thanked me for it and said it was all he needed.

After he had left for Brunei I wrote a much longer report, from an intelligence angle, and sent it to General Walker's headquarters and Special Branch. It caused much interest in both places, so I gathered, but there was never any 'political fallout' as regards the future of the Brigade of Gurkhas. I did not realise, nor could I ever have imagined, that the report would lead me into more difficult decisions, more dangerous and more important situations in the not too distant future – but not in Brunei.

I put in for home leave and had to wait six weeks, gradually returning to something like my normal self. I was asked to give a lecture, about Operation 'Bamboo' and the Temiar, to some Malay troops before they were deployed in that area. In the 'Bamboo' periodical report it was written, rather quaintly and pleasingly: 'Major Cross had hero welcome on his return to Ipoh'.

Two days before my leave, I managed to pay a fleeting visit to Blaur. I had heard rumours of unhappiness among the aborigines and Special Branch asked me to go to see what I could glean. It transpired that Malay soldiers had visited the ladang, had been frightening their womenfolk and had called the Temiar 'jungle pigs'.

On my return I told the police what I had found out: they were as concerned as I was.

I left for England in a daze.

Part Three

BORNEO, 1963–4
Border Scouts

CHAPTER 12

Genesis of the Border Scouts

The contrast between England and what I had left was too sudden for comfort. I would find myself staring at the sky as I marvelled at being in the open and my freedom of movement in the undulating Dorset landscape. I found it hard to settle down, hard to meet people, hard to get the events of the past year and a half out of the forefront of my mind. I was strained, tense and withdrawn.

I was thrilled to get a letter from the Office of the Prime Minister of Malaya asking me if I would accept the award of an Ali Menku Negara, a high Malayan decoration, for services to that country. Would I confirm my acceptance? This I did. However, for reasons I did not then understand, it never materialised. The Queen's Birthday Honours made me an MBE.

Within days of successfully completing the company commander's course with which I had been threatened in that aboriginal ladang – a lifetime before – I was telephoned by the War Office asking if I would forgo most of my leave and travel to Borneo. I asked why. No reason was given, but it was not to be with the battalion. That meant I would be shot of Heelis for a bit, which suited me fine. There was no need to spin the proverbial coin. On 23 July 1963, I left England.

Immediately I arrived I was whisked away to meet General Walker, now Director of Borneo Operations. Then started a series of briefings about the Brunei rebellion and the Borneo 'Confrontation' with Indonesia. I became more and more addled as more and more facts and figures, theories and thoughts, plans and projects were fed me by 'experts'. I was soon to find out that, while everybody thought they knew a lot about 'Borneo and its Natives', no one person in authority ever agreed with any other.

Apparently there was a grave emergency in Sarawak, one that was played down by the British government. Furthermore, Indonesia, confronted by communist subversion and outside aggression, was trying to prevent something to be called Malaysia becoming a reality.

Easier to comprehend was General Walker's blunt announcement that the British government were about to order two Gurkha battalions to be disbanded. So much for our efforts in north Malaya!

Before I could properly fathom the meaning of all I had heard and read, I had to find out more about Borneo and its background. I learned that the island of

MAP 4: THE BORNEO TERRITORIES OF BRUNEI, SARAWAK AND SABAH.

Borneo comprised four separate countries: the British territories of Brunei, North Borneo and Sarawak; and Indonesian (formerly Dutch) Borneo, known as Kalimantan. The first three covered about one quarter, the northern tier, of the island, the world's third largest. Until the Second World War Sarawak was ruled by the Brooke family – the White Rajahs – Brunei by its Sultan and North Borneo by a trading company of that name, based in Hong Kong. The border between British and Dutch Borneo had been so ill-defined as to be a cartographer's folly, not that it had mattered then. The island of Labuan was a Crown Colony.

For administrative purposes – and this intimately affected me in all that I would have to do – Sarawak was then divided into five Divisions, numbered, from west to east, First through Fifth. Each had a Resident as chief administrator and each was subdivided into Districts. The capital, Kuching, was in the First Division. North Borneo was divided into Residencies: Interior, Tawau, West Coast and Sandakan. It was only in the first two, which had a common border with Kalimantan, that fighting would take place. The capital was then known as Jesselton. When Malaysia became a reality, North Borneo reverted to its historical name of Sabah, and, much later, Jesselton was renamed Kota Kinabalu. The land frontier with Indonesia is 1200 miles long.

Much of Borneo is mountainous; most was then covered by dense, tropical rain forest, thicker in many places than the Malayan jungle. The one main road near the coast connected the largest and most developed centres of population. Apart from air services, hinterland travel was by river or foot. Many of the villages were built under one roof, in effect a very long house, hence the continual reference to 'longhouses'. The longest stretched for half a mile.

In the early 1960s Borneo painfully and unwillingly came into the limelight as colonialism receded. Apart from the British wanting to be rid of it, attention focused on three people whose aspirations merged, then clashed: the Malayan Prime Minister, Tunku Abdul Rahman, who wanted to preserve his mainland Malays' way of life by keeping the Chinese at bay, yet preferring to have Chinese-swamped Singapore allied with Malaya than to seek any alliance with communist China; the Sultan of Brunei's wish to preserve his old feudalistic order, yet give it the outward appearance of a parliamentary democracy; and the President of Indonesia, Sukarno, who dreamed of building a Greater Indonesia, stretching from the Indian Ocean to the Pacific, with Malaya and Borneo a part of this modern empire.

The proposal for Malaya, Singapore and the three Borneo Territories to become one new country to be called Malaysia was not only one method of achieving a population balance that gave non-Chinese an ascendancy over those of Chinese stock; it was also a neat way out for Britain to decolonise a large part of her remains of Asian empire without ruptures and traumas. The scheme, however, was frantically opposed by Indonesia which had already started military activity at the western end of Sarawak as early as the previous April.

It was a tricky time for Sarawak and North Borneo to face hostile acts. The only military force, the Sarawak Rangers, had no automatic weapons, so was of little value, except when its men had been used, individually, as trackers, by British battalions during the Malayan Emergency.

To add to the political confusion, it was feared that the December 1962 rebellion in Brunei, still simmering, might spread to Sarawak. There was perhaps only one man who could help here, the legendary Tom Harrisson, who had a real, long-term standing with the people of the Borneo Uplands as a result of his wartime escapades with them. He rallied them by sending a traditional red feather upriver. This was the catalyst, the mobilisation order and the supreme authority for action. Men came flocking to the aid of the government and prevented any spread of the rebellion. Such enthusiasm, loyalty and success provided the germ of the idea of expanding these qualities, tapping them nationwide.

General Walker realised that, over and above the conventional security forces, an indigenous force, associating the border peoples with the security and defence of their own territory, was essential. So an auxiliary police force, called 'Border Scouts' and already over a thousand strong, was in the process of being raised and trained, despite the opposition of the colonial administration of the two territories contiguous with Indonesian Borneo, namely Sarawak and North Borneo. Its badge was a hornbill, Borneo's national bird.

It was to command this outfit that I had been recalled from leave. The importance of the Border Scouts was made crystal clear to me later that first day by General Walker. It appeared that Confrontation would succeed if so much pressure was brought to bear on the border peoples that either they were absorbed by the Indonesians or forced to evacuate their border homelands. If the border peoples could stay put by being made to feel they were taking an active and positive part in their own defence and that government was behind them, Confrontation would probably fail. Border Scouts were, therefore, essential for victory. The converse was also true; unsuccessful Border Scouts could hasten defeat. I was told that it was up to me to make the organisation work. It was an enormous responsibility.

Extending over a thousand miles, involving different types of peoples and terrain, the job was a tremendous challenge, with the merit, in my eyes, of not having a 'school solution' tailor-made by text books nor postulated by pamphlets. It had the supreme virtue of being utterly unconventional, and the correct solutions, whatever these might be, could be based upon common sense and experience.

A major role of the Border Scouts was as gatherers of intelligence. Before this could happen, however, they were given basic training by 22 SAS and the

Gurkha Independent Parachute Company. After that, Gurkhas acted as section leaders until indigenous leaders had been trained.

It turned out to be the greatest pity that I had not been in on the initial policy sessions. The experience I had had with the Senoi Praaq and the Temiar, especially all the lessons learnt from Senagit, would have prevented many mistakes and abuses had they been applied to the Scouts from the very beginning. I soon discovered that the wrong sort of person had been enlisted, was being trained in wrong tactics, was under a wrong impression of what was wanted, and was being looked after by British and Gurkhas who used, for the most part, the wrong language! Even so, the Border Scouts would never have played the essential part they did in defeating Confrontation without Gurkha support, example, dedication and leadership. Luckily for my peace of mind, I was happily ignorant of all the many problems, mistakes, frustrations, decisions and dangers to come as I listened to the general briefing me that first full day in Brunei, 28 July.

* * *

My parish at first only covered Sarawak, but later, for a few months, included the two Residencies of Sabah that had a common border with Kalimantan. It would be tedious to go into details of the many administrative frustrations I encountered before I could even make an initial tour of my new domain. As there had never been such a post of Commandant, Border Scouts, I had many battles about such mundane but necessary matters as pay and accommodation before I was even accepted as being official. For instance, although Sarawak wanted me as a policeman, the country was due to be subsumed as part of Malaysia within a few weeks, so the Commissioner of Sarawak Constabulary, Mr Turnbull, was powerless to act on my behalf. As I had to go over to Malaya to get my kit from Ipoh, I thought it would be a good idea to call in on the Inspector-General of Police (Designate) of the Royal Malaysian Police, Claude Fenner, in Kuala Lumpur, where he was Commissioner of the Royal Malayan Police, to seek his advice.

I had learned that the difference in staying on in the army and becoming a policeman could lose me up to £30,000 (big money then) and a full pension. Therefore, as I had no intention of leaving the army, I asked Fenner his advice. He was quite uninterested in such details, although he was to be my boss, and replied that, as Malaysia had yet to exist, he could offer me nothing. 'In that case,' I said, 'I might as well start planning to go home and finish my interrupted leave.'

At that I did get some response, so I asked him what he would do were he in my shoes? 'Wouldn't look at it,' was his immediate reply.

'Yet you ask me to take it on?' A silence ensued but I had made my point. In the event I finished up by being a lieutenant colonel in two armies, the British and Malaysian, and a superintendent in three police forces, Malaysia, Sarawak and Sabah. None of them wanted to pay me in my new incarnation, nor did any, for ten months.

While in Kuala Lumpur I was informed that the Malayan award that I had been put in for and asked to accept had been cancelled 'on the telephoned instructions of a Gurkha battalion commander in Ipoh'.

I returned to my new base in Kuching to start learning my new job. The next year of my life was to be as peripatetic as the previous year had been static. At the end I was as exhausted as I had been after my time with the Temiar. Then I had been the hunter, mostly in hiding: now I was the hunted, always on the move. The Indonesians evidently wanted me and there were times when only the dhobi and myself knew how frightened I was.

*   *   *

My first task was to tour as much of my new command as I could on a ten-day visit that took me to nineteen different places, including a return to Brunei. Now that I had a background to the situation, I felt that the arranged tour would make a lot of sense. It did. It was all new and I enjoyed meeting so much diversity but, militarily, I became more and more unhappy at what I saw.

Everywhere I went I found that local languages, intonations, dialects, idioms varied considerably. There are twelve different languages, to my certain knowledge, along the border, and I eventually identified twenty-nine dialects where I had to operate. It was a linguist's paradise but an interpreter's nightmare. The population is a conglomeration of many ethnic groups: Land Dyaks, Ibans, Malays (a very small minority), Muruts, Kelabits, Kayans, Kenyahs, Punans and Dusuns, to name but some of the bewilderingly complex jumble of people, the raw material of the Scouts, and they were all splendidly different.

The First Division contains people called Land Dyaks and the Second Division Ibans. The first British settlers had asked them who they were. Being unsophisticated folk, they replied 'person' – in their languages 'dyak' and 'iban' respectively – so the names stuck. The First Division has no rivers of any noteworthy size and is near the sea, so the original settlers called them 'Land Dyaks' because they went overland to the coast. In the Second and Third Divisions, miles from the coast as regards the Iban homelands, but with many large rivers that allowed boat access to the coast, they were called 'Sea Dyaks'.

The Land Dyaks had never been regarded in the same romantic light as the more picturesque and ebullient peoples of the interior, story-book Borneo, and were seen as inferior stock. They seemed to have a built-in inferiority complex and a pathological dislike of taking the initiative. Unpromising material for resisting Confrontation, but I was to learn that they could be as good as if not better than the others despite, over the years, having been cowed by predatory Malay pirates, acquisitive Iban raiders and governmental inertia.

At the other extreme, I was to learn that the reputation of the mercurial Iban – the so-called 'Head Hunters of Borneo' – had been misrepresented. This habit of lopping heads off, dying out until it was rekindled during the Japanese occupation, was not necessarily confined to acts of derring-do in battle. Far from it: often it would be the result of a hen-pecked husband driven to distraction by a nagging wife or a young blood wanting to impress some deliciously nubile lass in order to wed her – a somewhat drastic method of clocking up enough points to redress an adverse balance in the 'manhood stakes'.

What usually happened was that a small child or an old woman might be waylaid after wandering away from the longhouse, perhaps to wash in a stream. After the unfortunate victim had been disposed of, the great thing was to get the head home before angry relatives caught the perpetrator and lopped off his own head in retaliation.

The target presented by Japanese stragglers proved too much for many Ibans who revived the practice that still lay close beneath the surface. Each time a head was topped, a joint of the fingers on the left hand, starting with the little finger and working down towards the thumb, was tattooed. A man's personal score could thus easily be counted.

There were some savagely cruel acts done to the Japanese stragglers. I came across one house where some had asked for shelter. Their wrists and ankles were broken and they were thrown under the longhouse to fend for themselves on the slops that were thrown between the bamboo slats of the kitchen above, fighting for them with the curs, until they died of starvation. I like to think that was an aberration, but doubt it was exaggerated.

Despite all that, the Iban community is open and democratic, as indeed is all Native society, with natural and acclaimed leaders but with no class system. Ibans acknowledge such men and treat everyone else as their equal. Their social behaviour cuts across society and there is no toadying. They are attractive people, with poise and immense natural dignity, so I was never conscious that they were almost naked. Men wear their hair long, fringe in front, bun at the back. Their skin is copper-coloured and copiously tattooed, with rosettes between neck and shoulders, and other patterns on their arms and legs. They wear scarlet loincloths, with long tassels in front and behind, and also silver arm and calf bracelets. The women, often bare-breasted, wear a short black skirt from waist to knee, are tattooed on their wrists and have as much say in affairs as have the men.

Men carry shotguns as naturally as city men carry umbrellas in London, so there was no problem in arming the Scouts. Based on their longhouses, it was natural for them to reconnoitre for strangers, either in the jungle or around their homestead, as they hunted, fished or farmed. No suspicions need be raised that they were, in fact, working as auxiliary policemen.

In theory, there were three great merits to the Border Scouts, apart from associating the border peoples with their own defence. They had local knowledge of terrain and personalities; they were always available; and they were simple and cheap to operate as a 'screen' or 'first trip wire' to enemy incursions. This last was to provide the 'eyes and ears' for the conventional security forces, early warning, and for Special Branch, long-term information. In addition, they were detailed to harass and shadow the enemy, only themselves dealing with small groups of stragglers and infiltrators; and to provide military support in the form of patrols, tracking, ambushes, guides, interpreters and watermanship — impossible though this was with only three weeks' training. Eventually I had fifteen hundred Scouts in Sarawak and another thousand in Sabah.

What was difficult, however, was getting the Scouts to achieve any results at all when they wore uniform and carried a service rifle. When footwear has never been worn, telling men to wear jungle boots is tantamount to crippling them on purpose.

As I made my initial rounds, visiting a Royal Marine commando, one British and two Gurkha battalions, I became more and more unhappy at what I saw and what was not to be seen. Each group of Border Scouts needed to be talked to: all expected a message from their new boss. Not normally tongue-tied, I did not then know whether the Malay I spoke, essentially of the mainland, was properly understood. I must have made some laughable mistakes, but I was determined not to show too much ignorance.

I learned from the Gurkha section commanders that many of those enlisted as Scouts were not jungle men but 'townies', quite unsuited to the rigours of what was expected of them and needing to be weeded out. Some individual sections, commanded by a lone Gurkha, lived satellite to a longhouse, while others would live with and operate from a military patrol base. The farther west, the less was there of the 'red feather' spirit. All were unhappy and hoped I could wave my magic wand and put things right: alas, it was all too new to change, and I was no magician.

*　　*　　*

During this time there was considerable military activity. On the one hand, the Indonesians came over the border to harass isolated posts, hoping to intimidate and capture arms and ammunition. On the other, as a counter, platoon-sized bases were established in villages, with defence works and helicopter landing pads. A curfew was also imposed. British and Commonwealth forces were entirely defensive.

The Indonesian strategy was twofold: one prong was to weaken civil resolve by mounting a series of raids on essentially civilian targets, tying down and weakening the security forces and, at a later stage, turning the civilians against Government as, by then, their position would be untenable. The other prong was to bolster the Chinese communists, who were chiefly on or near the coast, in their attempt to gain the ascendancy. This they did by infiltrating agents in small boats. In both cases, the Indonesians badly erred in their thinking that the locals were only too keen to get rid of the British and embrace their southern neighbours instead. In fact, it was quite the reverse: the Natives were so pro-British that they did not really want peaceful incorporation into Malaysia, let alone forced assimilation by Indonesia.

The story I now tell describes only a selected few of the many challenging and unusual incidents of many as I tackled the problem of rebuilding the Border Scouts into the type of unit for which they had originally been raised.

CHAPTER 13

A Policeman's Lot

The three Borneo Territories should have merged with Malaya and Singapore to form Malaysia on 31 August 1963, but that did not happen as planned. Brunei never did join and Singapore opted out after two years. So much opposition against the merger was raised by Indonesia and, to an extent, the Philippines, which laid claim to part of Sabah, that a United Nations' fact-finding team had to be organised at short notice to obtain the views of the people. This was in addition to an earlier inquiry, the Cobbold Commission, with British and Malay members, which had already visited Borneo in the fond hope of finding out the people's wishes.

The Malays had hoodwinked the British with verbal tricks they played on the Natives, many of whom said that they would be happy to see Malaysia as long as the British remained. A form, in English, was produced. Very few Natives could read English and they were told, by the Malays, that, if they were to put their 'cross' against that bit of writing, indeed the British would stay. The box, in fact, stated that the marker was happy to accept Malaysia without any preconditions, so the Natives had, in fact, 'welcomed' Malaysia!

British rule came to an end on 30 August when the Governors of Sarawak and North Borneo left and the Union Jack was furled for the last time, but Malaysia did not come into being until 16 September. During the hiatus the United Nations' fact-finding team was taken to some coastal towns where local leaders told them that Malaysia was a 'good thing'. What the team could not have realised was that the police had received orders to lock up those considerable many whose anti-Malaysia opinions were common knowledge.

For sixteen days there was no government. It is intriguing, therefore, to speculate who it was that gave the orders for the anti-Malaysians, chiefly Chinese, to be locked away during the United Nations' team's visit. If ever there had been a moment for Sukarno to have attacked, it was during those two 'empty' weeks. Luckily, nothing dramatic or untoward happened. In the past few months so many cases of indecision and bumbledom had occurred, with the civil administration almost totally ineffectual, that both colonies were virtually paralysed in any case, so no one noticed anything different.

A United Nations' observer team from Thailand went to the border village of Tebakang, near Tebedu, where the first overt Indonesian raid had taken place. Under the eyes of the team, a line of Indonesian soldiers walked out of the Sarawak jungle and, having been checked, moved across the border into their

149

own country. The observers were assured that they had been in Sarawak for some time and that, with their departure, there were no more troops trespassing. However, their uniforms were so clean and well pressed that they simply could not have been operating in the jungle. Special Branch knew that these troops had crossed from Indonesia only a very short time beforehand, but the observer team, having witnessed a nice little charade which they chose to believe, departed by helicopter for Kuching where a reception was held to celebrate their help in stabilising the situation. Meanwhile, those Indonesian troops who had previously infiltrated into Sarawak stayed there.

I had never been so close to international decisions before but my opinion of that august body, the United Nations, which I bitterly described as a High Level Platform for Low Level Propaganda, has never been the same since.

*   *   *

From the very early days I saw that the Border Scouts needed a new slant and I had pondered on how I could best retrain them, based on jungle lore, and produce indigenous leaders. The Gurkha Para soldiers were wanted elsewhere, so suitable Scouts had to be trained as junior leaders and all Scouts had to be retrained. I decided to make a modest start, within individual sections.

I was uncertain, in the first instance, as to whether Border Scouts was the best name for such an outfit. True, if compared with some of its prestigious counterparts in other lands – Tochi, South Waziristan, Gilgit and Somali – the name had romantic associations. Yet a hapless Land Dyak, cowering behind a tree, being addressed by a complete stranger in an utterly foreign language, Nepali or even mangled Malay, and with no clear idea of what to do, was a world removed from his famous namesake, renowned for being a hard man, crack shot and intrepid fighter. I also wanted another name because, when the Natives pronounced it, it nearly always sounded like 'Bodoh Sekat', which unhappily translates into Malay as 'Stupid Hindrance' – hardly conducive to generating esprit de corps!

Based on my own knowledge, and remembering that the majority of fatalities in the jungle occurred because humans left signs to be tracked rather than by sudden direct action, I set about producing guide lines on how to move, live and fight in jungle which the Gurkha instructors and the Scouts themselves could use. I covered essentials such as living undetected in a jungle camp, patrolling, shadowing and tracking. Since not many of them were good at reporting details, one of the more enterprising Gurkha instructors hit on the idea of lying up in places frequented by bare-breasted maidens, and, on return, the Scouts were asked to give particulars of the colours of their skirts, the contents of any back-basket and a description of their anatomy. This method stimulated considerable interest and amusement.

All that, and a lot more, had to find its way down to the trainees, using at least three languages, the most common being English, Nepali and Malay. I reckoned the potential leaders needed ten weeks' training to become minimally proficient at their task.

In my spare time I concentrated on learning Iban, an exercise complicated by a dearth of textbooks, a plethora of differing pronunciations and meanings, and a general lack of Iban speakers with whom to communicate.

*   *   *

The Inspector General of Police (IGP) paid his first official visit to Kuching in late September and, while there, news broke of a military reverse for Gurkha and Border Scouts alike. It was opportune to have the IGP in the country at the time. The incident centred on a remote village, called Long Jawi, in the Third Division. The terrain was sparsely populated, mountainous, jungle-covered, unmapped and intersected with innumerable fast-flowing and often unfordable rivers. Guarded by 1/2 GR, who were responsible for the 382-mile stretch of border, the small isolated military post was almost 300 miles by river from battalion HQ. Helicopters cut down travelling times from days to hours or even minutes, but for the foot-slogging natives all journeys were slow, uncomfortable and, when the rivers were in spate, dangerous.

The small settlement of Long Jawi was thirty miles inside Sarawak, with no other habitation between it and the border. Fifty miles farther north, downstream along the River Rejang, lay the administrative town of Belaga, where some Border Scouts had been trained. A post of twenty-one Scouts had been established in the village, strengthened by some Police Field Force radio operators and a few Gurkha soldiers from the company at Belaga.

A meeting was called and three British officers explained to the villagers how the small combined force was planning to defend them. A reconnaissance party from an Indonesian force that had penetrated to within a short distance of Long Jawi was also present, mingling with the villagers, sitting at the back of the crowd in the gloom of the longhouse.

Next day the British officers left by boat and the day after, 28 September, the Indonesians attacked. The Border Scout post was heavily outnumbered and the Gurkha and Police Field Force radio operators were killed very early on during the engagement. However, the determination and bravery of the remaining Gurkhas managed to keep the enemy away for a considerable time. Initially the Border Scouts remained firm but, as the tension and danger increased, they began to slip away from their posts. They had never expected anything like this, nor were they in any way militarily trained to withstand it. Eventually, the Gurkhas, having suffered casualties, were driven off the position and the enemy ransacked the settlement before making good their escape.

1/2 GR later exacted their vengeance upon the Indonesians, but not before most of the Scouts had been taken prisoner and massacred. Only a few managed to make their way back to safety and, although the news of the military victory over the enemy spread quickly from one longhouse to another, the morale of the local people, especially of the bereaved relatives, was badly dented. From that point of view, the basic aim and purpose of the Border Scouts had not been fulfilled. They had been unable to defend their village and the border people had lost trust.

According to General Walker's initial brief I had, somehow, to remedy the situation – but how?

*   *   *

The IGP went on to Brunei to confer with the Director of Operations. It was now obvious to all that not only had the initial ideas of Border Scouts deployment been suspect but that military thinking, tactically, had been too passive. Based on the Long Jawi incident and the increased enemy threat, I was ordered to reappraise the role of the Border Scouts. This was to go far beyond the training in jungle lore I had already instigated within sections. In virtually the same breath I was told to take command of the Border Scouts who were being raised in Sabah. This meant that the length of border for which I was 'responsible' had been increased to 1200 miles, and my charges to 2000 men.

So started a new phase of my Border Scout life. I flew to Jesselton with Brigadier Patterson, the commander of the brigade based on Brunei, with operational responsibility for that part of Sabah where the Border Scouts were being raised. It was fortunate, I felt, that I was able to be in at the beginning of the Sabah Border Scouts so that I could properly influence their initial training, even though I had been brought into it all so perfunctorily and everything was so rushed.

I was dressed as a Superintendent of Sarawak Constabulary, which was exactly the same as for Sabah, except for the cap badge. I felt that it was remiss not to wear a Sabah Police Force badge when in that country, for although Sarawak and Sabah were now officially part of Malaysia, relations between the two were still poles apart. The other problem was that my police writ ran only in Sarawak, not in Sabah, so I felt there was some urgency to swear me in as an Auxiliary Superintendent of the Sabah Police Force.

The brigadier and I went to Police Headquarters and were escorted into the office of the commissioner, Mr Matheson, a big, heavily built Scot. We sat in his office and he and the brigadier talked about matters of common interest. It was then my turn. I had the impression that he was irked by my appointment as commandant of the Sabah Border Scouts and the fact that I was to have a police warrant of his force without having vetted me. But he was civil enough and told me he wanted me to go and see the embryo Scouts due to join for training in three days' time. I was happy to learn that no uniforms were to be issued, but winced inwardly when it was announced that a 'hornbill' badge as a brassard was to be issued to each man. Moreover, the Natives would be issued with army rifles rather than shotguns, which would have been more suitable. This, he could see, made me unhappy. We talked about the mistakes that had been made in Sarawak and I expressed certain reservations about not having been in on the planning from the very start. I soon saw I would get nowhere by voicing such opinions, so I changed the subject.

I asked for a cap badge. When he asked why, I told him that the Sarawak badge meant nothing to any of the people of Sabah and that, as their Commandant, were I to wear the badge of a different force – which none of them would recognise – I would either be thought a phoney or have insufficient authority with the new Scouts and their police NCOs.

He called for the office runner and told him to go to the stores and buy a cap badge. Although it was the bewitching hour of lunch time on a Saturday, the man duly went away, only to return to say that everything had already closed and nothing could be done till the Monday. Had I been sure of returning to Jesselton before visiting the Scouts, this would not have mattered, but I knew that to be impossible, so it had to be there and then.

Matheson turned to me and asked if I really wanted a Sabah Police Force badge, to which I countered that I supposed he really wanted me to go as a representative member of his force.

On his large desk was an ash tray out of the base of an expended artillery shell onto which had been welded a North Borneo Police Force badge. The commissioner drew the heavy brass shell casing towards him and tried to pick the badge off with his fingernails, an effort that did his nails no good and made no impression on the securely fixed badge. The brigadier and I watched him, fascinated.

With a sigh he pushed it away and his eyes turned to his hat also lying on the desk. I could see the struggle going on in his head. At last he made his painful decision and, with a deeper sigh that spoke volumes against impetuous army officers, he picked up his hat, lifted the flap inside the brim and started to remove his new Sabah Police Force badge. I remonstrated but that had no effect on this slow-moving and very determined Scot. At last he dislodged it and laid it reverently on the desk. Then, scrutinising the empty patch on his hat, he saw that polish had dried on the blue cloth, turning it white. Angrily, he muttered something about his 'damned orderly' and, without another word, shoved the badge across to me. As I removed my Sarawak Constabulary badge and replaced it with his old one, I remarked with a flippancy that was well-meant but ill-received, 'Sir, this is probably an occasion that neither of us have previously witnessed.'

It was time to leave. We stood up and put on our hats. I wore a blue beret, the brigadier a green one; but neither was as majestic as the commissioner's peaked and braided silver and blue hat, now unhappily shorn of its identity.

Matheson stalked out of the room in front of us and opened the door. Outside the office runner jumped up off his chair and gave his boss a smart salute. Just as the commissioner was returning the compliment he realised his sartorial shame; in one deft movement he smartly brought his right arm up and saluted, then, as smartly, his left, to shield his badgeless embarrassment. For all the world he looked as though he were suffering from an appalling headache or saluting with both hands at once. The office runner gawped as the commissioner, half-blinded, stumbled on past him. Brigadier Patterson and I were not invited to lunch, so flew back to Brunei unfed.

I do not think Matheson ever forgave me: our relations were always cool after that. But I got my badge and, depending in which country I was, wore whichever badge was appropriate, keeping the other clipped to the little piece of stiffening that shielded the badge clasp from the forehead. Indeed, I had been told by Fenner that, when I went to Kuala Lumpur in uniform I would have to wear the Royal Malaysia Police badge – an item that was not, in fact, produced until after I had left Borneo.

If I had thought that Sarawak was run on a financial shoestring, then Sabah's shoes were stringless. The Commissioner of Police was also Head Customs Officer and Head Fireman, while the Chief Native Police Officer, a Panjabi, added a further touch of unreality to the scene by having, as his badge of rank, four crowns. Later on I would discover that the European expatriates in the Sabahan administration were even more suspicious of 'outsiders' than were their counterparts in Sarawak.

* * *

One of the results of the Long Jawi fiasco was that the Scouts who remained in the general area were unwilling to continue serving in the same way as before. Until I had made my report to the general about the Scouts' future, I could not change their tactics, and until the IGP had received that report, there would be no alteration in their terms of service. With the Scouts unhappy, so were the border people, something the general had told me to avoid. All very difficult!

Although the remaining Scouts had done nothing wrong (as opposed to doing nothing at all) the accompanying troops considered them as not 'worth their rations'. 1/2 GR had provided some high-calibre NCOs to be their section commanders and, naturally, no one wanted to waste such men on an unpro-ductive task especially when they were urgently needed to do their own jobs. Yet again I had been asked to go and 'sort out' a problem that had no ready solution nor any precedent. With no magic wand and precious few sanctions, I had no clear idea how to proceed.

The Scouts were concentrated at a place called Long Linau, between Long Jawi and Belaga. On my way there in a chopper I decided how to tackle my task. Some of the Scouts were Kenyahs, whom the charitable would call home-loving. Their training to date had been adversely influenced by a British soldier with an unpronounceable mid-European name who, apart from nurturing unacceptable political views, was also allergic to Asians. Apart from his detrimental effect, the Indonesians had managed to subvert much of the area and the Scouts were unwilling to risk any more trouble after the Long Jawi incident. Moreover, the Scouts had joined under the misapprehension that they would only be wanted to do their three weeks' training, after which they could return home. Had they known that they would be required on a permanent basis, they would never have volunteered in the first place. Finally, the tasks given them were beyond their capabilities. Until any higher directive was announced, the best solution for them would be to act as 'boatmen with a military bias', and, as they used longboats as a matter of course, this was calculated to suit all parties.

The temptation was to be easy with them, but I knew that being gentle would be counter-productive in the long run: I therefore determined to adopt a hard approach.

The helicopter circled around the area where the Border Scouts were drawn up, armed and uniformed, in three ranks, about forty men in all. I saw Gurkha NCOs with the Scouts trying to get their charges 'spot on' for me, with more Gurkhas to one side. We landed, the rotors came to a halt and I emerged. The parade was called to attention and a Queen's Gurkha Officer marched up and reported to me. I told him to stand the Scouts at ease.

I addressed the Scouts. I had heard, I said, that some of them were not willing to serve any more. Who were they? Up with their hands so I could see them! A dozen or so arms shot up. Any more? Eight or nine others were raised. Any more? Silence – no movement.

'All who put your hands up, come forward. Ground arms!'

A group came out in front of the others, laid their rifles down beside them and looked at me. After their initial show of bravado, I saw that they sensed they were going to 'have the edge' over me. They were deflated by the next order.

'Off with your uniforms!' Hats, shirts, boots, trousers, the lot, all came off. I ordered two Gurkha NCOs to collect the clothing and asked the Queen's Gurkha Officer there to arrange weapon collection and to send someone for their webbing equipment and any other item of military kit they might have from their camp.

The stripped Scouts stood nonplussed, dressed only in singlets and drawers. I ordered them to turn and face the others. Rather unkindly I declared that those wretched men in front were unwilling to fight for their country, were not better than a bunch of chickens and it was best for all that they went home as civilians. Shivering from discomfort and humiliation rather than the cold, the near-naked men made a sorry spectacle. Any more for that treatment? There were none.

'Will you all obey the orders I give through these Gurkha soldiers?'

Having got an affirmative, I told them they would be used as boatmen for a trial period and, at the end of that, they could reconsider their decision whether or not to stay on as Scouts.

It was then the turn of the men who were no longer Scouts. I told them they would get paid until that day, they were now no longer auxiliary policemen or Scouts and they were free to go home straight away. I sent them off with a wave of my arm, thanked those who had said they would stay, thanked the Gurkhas for what they were doing and told the Queen's Gurkha Officer to dismiss the parade.

From the look on the faces of the Scouts, dismissed or still serving, and the Gurkhas, my 'deus ex machina' performance had made an impression on them all. I flew away, leaving the Border Scouts now thirty fewer than they had been at the time of the Indonesian attack.

As I lay in bed that night I mulled over the way I had 'played' my visit to Long Linau. Wherever I went in Borneo I found that there were, in effect, two kinds of visit; one I called a 'skim visit' and the other a visit in depth. Both had their uses: only so much could be learned or achieved in a two- to three-hour visit. After that, nothing much would emerge for the next two or three days, by which time the strangeness of my being there had worn off, and the men, inclined by nature not to be taciturn, would talk among themselves as well as to me. By hint, allusion, intonation, facial expression, inference, gesture and sometimes silence, I could then pick up much that I never could have done during a 'skim visit' or through any amount of reading. It was more for effect than anything else that I 'played' the disarming and dismissal of the recalcitrant Scouts, however unfair it might have seemed to a dispassionate observer. For my reappraisal, however, I saw that only in-depth visits would provide me with the background if not the answers to the problems facing user and used.

CHAPTER 14

Quest for the Best

By now the pressure was on; I had to rewrite the basic concept of the Border Scouts, had to be present at the start of the training of indigenous leaders and was constantly called by police and military for consultations.

I finished my reappraisal and took it up to Brunei, where the IGP happened to be. General Walker pronounced it excellent, just what was wanted, and told me to produce yet another, a phased programme for the implementation of my scheme. This I had already done.

I had suggested lines of thought along which Border Scouts' potential could best be developed within the framework of certain fundamental tactics. I wrote:

> Basically the new concept is with the Scouts out in front roaming like a screen, being the eyes and ears of the Conventional Forces, with a sting. This entails getting them to merge in with the background, taking off their status-symbol jungle boots and going without their morale-raising rifle, so as to appear like a farmer, fisherman, trader, wood-cutter, etc. Not only that, but it is hopeless him forgetting what he has seen, so he must have memory training as well: Kim's game, treasure hunts, initiative tests, story telling, with questions, practise debriefing and briefing people, eavesdropping. With that must go a faculty of remembering places and faces, for descriptions, for alibis and cover stories against the day when one of the opposition is playing the same game.
>
> The second role of the Scouts is tracking an enemy, and using jitter tactics against him, fading into the background, shadowing him and picking off stragglers, leaving signs so that those following can readily understand what goes on: a bent branch with one meaning, three stones with another meaning and crossed twigs with yet a third meaning, or whatever secret signs they evolve. I merely give suggestions. What are they to do if pressed by the enemy? Fade and go to a chosen RV, moving as best they can. How best to ensure they give warning of their approach, or to signal asking for bearings without giving the game away? I have been teaching monkey calls and bird noises with my hands and a 'yodelling' whistle for close-in work. Recognition of enemy uniforms hiding up so tightly that no one knows where you are (planting living camouflage in your foot prints as you go — very slow but effective), hints on how to keep the pangs of hunger off when food is low: all these and many more have I been teaching...

I now felt confident that the general's stern briefing about the efficacy of the Border Scouts and the part they should play in defeating Confrontation, would

157

much the better be put into operation. It was some time before I realised my efforts were to founder on the seemingly intractable problem of not having enough money to pay for what the Police seemed to regard as a totem of mystical properties – the 'plain clothes' allowance.

What went on in the councils of the great I was never to know, though when operational common sense was so stupidly and blatantly overridden by departmental bumbledom, hierarchical blindness, or even pure pig-headed Fenner stubbornness, something 'had to give'. It seemed patent to me that such a wet reason for not putting the force on a better footing surely would not prevail. But it did – and eventually I 'gave'.

*   *   *

Towards the end of November I was ordered to accompany the Director of Operations and IGP Fenner on a tour. For five days I was satellite to the Very Important Party as we inspected the Border Scouts in twenty-five separate locations in the First, Second and Third Divisions.

On the third day we visited a place called Jambu and met as many of the sixty Scouts as were in camp. During a picnic lunch I was asked about the surrounding area, Ulu Ai. The folk there were a fractious lot, more mercurial than many and had been since time immemorial. Their particular branch of the Iban tribe straddled the border; when it suited them, they were Indonesians visiting their friends and relations in British territory, and when it did not suit them, they claimed the opposite.

Except for normal family feuds and quarrels about hunting rights, Iban had no quarrel with Iban. The larger political issues of the day were normally too remote for the longhouse population to be affected. When they were, however, parochial outlooks coloured opinion so much that most government edicts, orders, plans and ideas were greeted with mute disdain or, more likely, vociferous antipathy. Because there had been so much enemy activity in the Ulu Ai area, the administration felt that the lives of the farmers were in such danger that it could lead to crops not being tended properly, hence famine. Accordingly an order, singularly unpopular and bitterly resented, had been given for the main longhouses to be moved farther north, out of range of Indonesian harassment. One house so affected was at Nanga Sumpa, some distance downstream from Jambu, right in the heart of Ulu Ai territory.

Shortly before we were due to leave, an Iban sidled up and, through me, asked if he could talk to the Big White Chief. But which one? I asked him what it was about, remembering the Brooke tradition that anybody could, at any time, go and see the Resident on any matter. Fenner met him and asked me what he wanted: the man, Jimbuan, was asking the group to visit Nanga Sumpa and cancel the hated order to be resettled elsewhere.

Jimbuan had a colourful history; in the war he had been responsible for lopping off many Japanese heads, including an officer's, whose sword he kept as well as all the skulls. He had been decorated for bravery, promoted to the government-appointed position of headman and finally promoted to being the headman of a group of other headmen, a 'Pengara'. Nothing more militant than cockfighting and pig-hunting had occupied his time for rising twenty years. Now pensioned off, a younger man had taken over his responsibilities. He had basked in his former glory and had revelled in the respect all had paid him, then fretted at his lost authority. The order to move back from their familiar house and beloved hunting grounds had given Jimbuan an excuse to exert his personal influence to a degree which threatened to override the authority of the current, younger 'Pengara'. Feelings were running high and tempers were explosive. Not all that detail came out there and then, but part of his story was backed up when I counted nineteen tattoo marks on his left hand!

Fenner told him there was no time to go to the house but was sure I would visit him when next in the area. This Jimbuan reluctantly accepted. Apart from a vague feeling of disquiet at the old man's insistence, I forgot about the incident as we flew off.

The IGP then ordered me to go to Kuala Lumpur to talk Border Scouts with him, in the light of his tour and my reappraisal.

At his headquarters Fenner was very pleasant in his bluff, genial way. I think he was impressed with what I had managed to do and learn about the various places and people. He told me that no guerrillas had yet met up with my Temiar since the abortive contact with Ah Soo Chye eleven months previously. I found that particularly pleasing news.

I was ordered to carry out, as soon as was convenient, an in-depth reappraisal of the Border Scouts in the remaining part of Sarawak as well as in the Interior Residency of Sabah. We agreed I would try to start by latest mid-January 1964, as I wanted to see the trainees out from each of the training camps before I was committed on such a long project.

*   *   *

Four days later I was in Belaga to attend the enlistment of Border Scouts in place of those killed at Long Jawi and those I had sacked so ignominiously. The Resident, a pompous man allergic to common sense, had told me that he, not I, would publicise the requirement and that his putting it out over Radio Sarawak and by word of mouth would produce the desired results. I travelled to Belaga with two junior officers of the local administration to represent the Resident.

In the event no one turned up.

After the deadline had passed, I suggested going upstream by longboat to Long Linau, where the headman was an influential person who would probably help us. Certainly we could achieve nothing by staying where we were. Off we went, only having to leave the boats in one place where there were some particularly dangerous rapids, the river surging through a narrow gorge. We hired a towing party from a nearby longhouse and the men made a fine sight as they ran, jumping from one spray-covered rock to another, pulling our boat with a rattan rope against the strong current. Two and a half hours after starting out, we arrived. It was mid-afternoon.

At Long Linau we met the headman and the local councillor, who made us comfortable. That meant we were given a mat to sit on, which was just as hard as the wooden floor. They retired to one end of the longhouse and left us at the other, in splendid isolation. The two administrators decided to go fishing and left me on my own. On looking around I felt that there was a glass curtain between me and the inmates, distorting, clouding and colouring what they saw, so making normal contact difficult, if not impossible.

To pass the time I went to the river for a wash, but the water was muddy, so I did not bother and returned, feeling stale. I went back to my mat and sat down, completely ignored. Once more I was faced with a situation I did not know how to tackle.

I glanced up and saw the children, who had also been gathered with the others at the other end of the longhouse as far removed as possible from the government men who had so unexpectedly arrived to disturb their peace yet again. I wobbled my eyebrows independently of each other and was seen by one youngster. For the next hour I carried on a one-man cabaret show, by which time, face aching, I was festooned with children. Meanwhile, the women glowered balefully at me from the other end of the longhouse.

Another half hour passed and, as it was growing dark outside, the men moved up and joined the women who, by then, had gathered around me. They were a fine-looking lot, their hair grown long, right down their back, and with greatly developed pectoral muscles from rowing their boats.

The others returned. During the meal one of the officers choked over a fish bone, which was funnier by far than anything I had done with the kids. Serious talk started after that: what, exactly, did I want? Thirty men, I said. They conferred among themselves a distance off and returned to tell me it had all been wrong from the start. I then saw how to get these stubborn and frightened men to agree with what I wanted. It was a gamble. I told them, point by point, just how I wanted the Border Scouts to operate, which was, in fact, the exact opposite of what I had in mind. Point by point I was beaten back, forced to modify my requests with their counter-suggestions. Point by point I gave in, until I had my way, so could drop the remaining few in a show of conciliation and camaraderie. The old men were delighted. They had outbargained a man of the government, they had imposed their will on the man who had commanded those of their community who were now dead and now they had repaid him for sacking their relatives. They had got what they wanted — and so had I.

A particularly fine-looking savage, grinning from ear to ear, ceremoniously set the seal on our deliberations by rolling two cigarettes and offering me one. I am a non-smoker and the thought of smoking revolts me. But, were I to refuse, all my efforts might be to no avail. So I smoked it and gave him my glass to drink from, thus clinching the deal. We shook hands and I nominated him as my bodyguard should I ever require one in that area. I also promised the headman I would try to obtain a hearing aid for him.

*   *   *

After spending my third consecutive Christmas in the jungle, at Jambu, Jimbuan came to the Border Scout camp to take me to his house. I was skilfully navigated downstream by two Iban youths. I had two Border Scouts with me, more as status symbols than any deterrent against possible Indonesian nastiness on our way down to Nanga Sumpa and beyond.

Jimbuan's house, twenty doors long, lay between the strongly flowing Sumpa and Ai rivers. We climbed up a notched pole onto the long verandah.

I was shown some floor space opposite Jimbuan's private door. I put down my pack, took off my jungle boots and put on 'flip-flops'. I was invited into Jimbuan's room and sat down with him on the bamboo-slatted floor, between the main room and the kitchen. Rice beer was offered in two glasses, one small and one large. The smaller glass was raised first, brought up to the mouth as though to be drunk, and the contents then poured through the slats onto the ground below to appease some of Jimbuan's gods. The larger glasses were for ourselves and I was ordered to drink mine up. Although a strict teetotaller, I did so as not to cause offence. I refused to refill but ate the rice meal. Jimbuan was old enough not to worry about drinking more than a guest. I could not tell how much he could stomach, but I guessed an all-night session would cause him little discomfort.

Whether it was pique that riled him when I told him that I could in no way influence the unpopular decision about moving the longhouse, chagrin at my refusal of more drink, or aggressiveness as the result of his having been drinking all day, Jimbuan started to pick a quarrel with me. He took me back onto the verandah. Outside it was dark and raining. We sat with our backs to the outer wall. The two Border Scouts had eaten in another room and sat well away from us. Gradually the men of the longhouse came and squatted, in serried rows, facing us. They were a strong-looking bunch and, in the dim light of the open-wicked lamps, the flickering shadows made their unsmiling faces relentlessly stern and satanic. There were about forty-five of them, young and old. They sat, silent and staring, their eyes boring into mine whenever I looked up at them.

Jimbuan, no stickler for protocol, jumped up and started savagely to berate me. To him I embodied all that threatened his treasured lifestyle. Then, to my alarm, he produced a Japanese sword. Unsheathing it, he threatened to take my head off, as he had done to former enemies. I was told to look up at the rafters. I saw a hideous bunch of blackened skulls above me – nineteen of them, Jimbuan added. I took his word for it.

I turned my terrified gaze from them to Jimbuan, to the men who were still staring unwaveringly at me. Their expressions were set, without regard, without remorse, without regret. They were all at one with Jimbuan. I was horror-struck. The old man still had his sword over me, poised, ready.

Did I have a reason why my head shouldn't be the twentieth? I glanced at him and the implacably staring eyes of his men sitting in front of me. The atmosphere was unbearably tense. My throat was dry and the sweat of raw, animal fear had yet to break. Escape was impossible, argument out of the question. 'No reason at all, old man,' I managed to blurt out, desperately trying to appear calm. 'I am your guest, but tonight I am tired and you must be too from working all day. Also the light is dim. Put away your sword and use it tomorrow when it is light, after you have had a good night's rest. Your aim will be better then.'

There was an endless pause of a few seconds while Jimbuan considered what I had said. My soft answer must have turned away his anger, because he sheathed his sword, put it away behind the door and – improbably and ludicrously – sat down once more beside me.

After what seemed an age, a bard began to sing at the end of the house and Jimbuan got up and went over to him. 'Pantuns', rhyming couplets recounting glories of past deeds, now embellished with my present hapless situation, were being intoned about my fate on the morrow. Gradually the others rose and left to listen to the bard. I sat on alone and it was then that the sweat of fear broke out, running down my nose. I heard the drops hitting the mat on which I was sitting cross-legged.

My two escorts, understandably, were nowhere to be seen. After a few minutes of lonely introspection, I was approached by the headman's wife who directed me into an empty room, with a sleeping mat and nothing else. She locked the door behind me and, mentally worn out, I fell into a troubled sleep.

At dawn I was let out and was glad to see my two Border Scouts. They were as anxious as I was to get away from Nanga Sumpa, but I felt it wrong to leave without having the last word with Jimbuan. My fear had turned to anger by this time. When ready to leave, I sought him out and had a few terse words, my courage fortified by seeing that his anger had cooled since the previous evening's encounter.

That evening, as it was turning dark, the three of us stumbled into the nearest security force camp downstream, a Gurkha platoon base. We had walked all day to get there and I, for one, was tired out. Never did mug of tea taste better! I reached Kuching on New Year's Day, 1964.

*   *   *

Towards the end of 1963, Indonesian incursions had become more frequent and widespread, while the communists on the coastal fringe attempted to expand inland. The last few hours of 1963 were written in blood in Sabah when Indonesians overran a Malay Regiment position, the British later being blamed for not protecting it. So ended the year in Borneo, a year that began with the end of a rebellion and ended with the beginning of an undeclared war.

CHAPTER 15

Bumbledom in Bloom

I knew that my long walk to survey the Interior Residency would assuredly entail hardship and probably danger. I wanted a Gurkha with me, certainly a marksman, a Malay language speaker, a tight-corner man and, if possible, a friend. As 1/7 GR was in Borneo, I asked for and got Tanké Limbu for six weeks.

On the understanding that I might need help from one or other of the security forces along the border, I was given a code name, Black Prince. It was changed minutes later by an embarrassed staff officer who had inadvertently broken the rules by having chosen a colour in a nickname! This was militarily 'out', so Black was changed to Brave. It was not a name I would ever had chosen for myself, but it was much better than, say, Dirty Rat or Pin Head.

Our long journey was mostly on foot, carrying packs weighing 80 pounds, but we used rivers where possible and twice we hiked a lift by air. Nine days after we started, a cease-fire came into effect as a result of the Secretary General of the United Nations appealing, on 16 January 1964, for an end to hostilities. Sukarno agreed to a truce to allow the Foreign Ministers of his country and Malaysia to meet for talks in Bangkok. These peace talks were short-lived and, with their failure, the command of Indonesian troops engaged in Confrontation passed completely to the Indonesian regular army. This change resulted in the institution of cross-border operations by the security forces, code-named 'Claret', but for me this made no difference, except that it became even more dangerous to wander around the place.

Conditions were never easy. As an example, I spent one night at a house of Tagal Muruts, who thought that Confrontation was an extension of the Japanese War. One side housed the inmates in separate rooms; the remaining space was bamboo-slatted floor with, at either end, a raised platform. In the middle of the floor space was a crude table and bench: a continuous supply of the most gristly and putrefying mudfish and meat, probably monkey, was offered on chipped enamel plates. Between the bench and the table were large pottery jars, with dragon motifs, in which was liquid made from rice or tapioca. Two bamboo 'straws' protruded through a wooden lid that bunged up the contents of the jars and water was poured into the neck of them. The jars were big, knee-high, and the menfolk took turns at chewing the bits of smelly scrag and sucking the fermented liquid through the 'straws'. I, as guest, was invited to sit on the bench, along with the senior inmates, and have first pick and first suck. I found that, in the flickering light of the small lamps, I could go through the motions when my turn came round again. To see five of the locals sitting down, bending forward, sucking away, reminded me of so many pigs with their heads in the trough.

Throughout the evening, the noise never abated. Five large brass gongs were banged intermittently and very loudly. Voices were raised, rather sweetly, in part song; men asking riddles and exchanging quips; women talking and laughing; children, seemingly never tiring, playing and yelling; dogs yelping piercingly when they were thumped for being in the way; pigs, under the house, rooting, grunting and squealing; roosters, all round the house, crowing and clucking – in a word, bedlam.

Come the time for sleep, I was shown a patch of floor space, some six feet from the gongs. I managed to fall into a fitful doze, hoping they would pack it in. They did, at about 7 o'clock the next morning. I felt jaded.

Militarily, too, I found little to please me except the individual kindnesses shown to us by the British soldiers. Shoe-string apathy and the slow defeat of never doing anything properly over the years had sapped administrative zeal. This was exacerbated by the Police NCOs being inured to static duties throughout their previous service, so in no way cut out to be dashing leaders of a Border Scout section. One sergeant was so bad I had to sack him on the spot. Regrettably, the standard of soldier in the resident battalion was also deplorably low. I was particularly embarrassed when one headman told me that they had longed for the British to come and how sad they all were when they saw that 'the British are only brave when playing football'. I was glad that I had a chance to try to put the record in better perspective. I told my audience that the initial concept of the Border Scouts had not been wholly satisfactory, that the troops had misunderstood their role and thus it was that I was on a survey for that very reason.

One area for which this battalion was responsible was a place called Long Pa Sia. The Border Scouts came from Tanom, seventy crow miles to the north, and could neither speak the same language as the locals nor recognise any strangers who came their way. The last visit by an official had been seven years previously.

All the people were Christian, converted by the Borneo Evangelical Mission from a life, allegedly, of wanton and useless debauchery and drunkenness to one of complete sobriety. They had been forbidden all rice beer, their only source of vitamin B, and as the sole vegetables to replenish this source were cucumbers, their health had suffered. In many other ways their lot was not much bettered. In each longhouse they held religious services, daily for twenty minutes, and twice, for much longer, on Sundays. They said grace before meals. They were very pleasant people, but utterly colourless.

The mission had its own aircraft, two little Piper Cubs. I met someone who had flown in one when the pilot had a five-minute prayer session before he switched on, thanking the Almighty for past safety in the air and praying for continued assistance while flying. My informant wryly commented that he hoped that was not the aeroplane's only maintenance.

On the positive side, the missionaries had stamped out certain detrimental superstitions, including child sacrifices, and the painful practice of putting a very thin wooden skewer with protruding ends through the neck of the penis, which was designed to excite the partner during copulation but often caused terrible injury.

Sadly, there had been some stupid heavy-handedness in the way the British troops had been behaving with the local community. It started when the young platoon commander had found some Natives wandering around the longhouse that he was using as his base and had asked them to step inside. After tea and biscuits one of them asked a question about the enemy and the young platoon commander briefed them on the situation. It subsequently transpired that the most inquisitive of the group was an Indonesian sergeant on a reconnaissance of the area, and his friends, who had brought him to the camp in the first instance, were the local headman and the local schoolmaster.

There had then been an Indonesian probe, followed by a skirmish when a few enemy were killed, with the remaining forty-odd still somewhere around. By the time we got there we immediately sensed tension, with no love lost on either side, and villagers and troops alike counting the days before the soldiers were relieved. It was a pity that, after so much governmental neglect, their first contact with 'raw' Englishmen should result in so sour a taste in the mouths of everyone concerned. We stayed one night in the platoon base but did not like it at all, so went down to the village and spent the next two nights there, thus learning about the bad feelings that existed locally, having already heard the soldiers' version.

The villagers also felt deserted in that, before Confrontation, visits from the missionaries had been a regular feature of life. Now these visits had been discontinued, and the villagers derived scant comfort from their foreign-grafted, gloom-laden Christian God, let alone from the soldiers or the Border Scouts.

The platoon commander told me how he had punished the offending headman and the schoolmaster, by tying them to a stake in such a way that, if their arms slumped, the rope that bound them would throttle them as it also went round their necks. They had been left outside, tied to this stake all night, then put under house arrest, requiring permission from the platoon commander before being allowed anywhere.

The day following our arrival in the village, Tanké and I went to the harvest area to meet the two men under house arrest. It took us twenty minutes, through some jungle, to reach them. We climbed a small, stilt-raised platform and sat on the rickety bamboo floor. I noticed that the headman's wrists were scarred. It was general conversation until I began to be questioned closely about my future movements. I told them and the two locals immediately put their heads together and, for the first time, started conversing in their own language. Until then we had been talking in Malay. I felt uneasy, as did Tanké. The headman then turned to me and, once more using Malay, said he would like to talk with me further, on the morrow, and he would come to the longhouse that evening to fix the time and place. It was then ten in the morning.

On the way back Tanké asked me why I had needed to tell them so much. We had a long way to go, the enemy were still in the area, so why make life harder?

Privately I agreed with him, but told him to ask the villagers how they read the situation. Then I would decide what course of action to take. By the time the headman had arrived that evening I had heard from three sources that we would either be ambushed the following day, with the headman as decoy, or the day after that, if I stuck to my proclaimed programme of walking the twenty mountain miles to the next house to the west, past Ulu Trusan.

At 5 o'clock the headman came and we fixed an appointment for 11 o'clock next morning. He would not have time to come himself, but if I were to go down that jungle track – and he pointed in a direction that led away from the camp and the harvest area – he would meet me near a stream. Please would I go alone? Yes, I said, I would.

Had I been brave, had I not taken counsel of my fears, had I not listened to the advice of others, I would have gone, having first set up an ambush with the troops from the camp. But they were not my troops and there was no time for rehearsals, so I did not go. Instead, at 5 o'clock in the morning, while it was still dark, I told Tanké we were off, in the opposite direction from where I had been invited, across the mountain into Sarawak.

As we were packing up, a figure emerged from a room opposite us and joined us on the verandah, where we had slept. He was a middle-aged Murut, who claimed he had been awarded a gold medal for helping some American airmen who had been shot down over Borneo during the Pacific War. It was to this man that I had put my quandary, as a hypothetical question, the previous night. He told me my decision to move then was the correct one and he would guide me over the mountain.

'The man with whom you spoke yesterday is not to be trusted,' he told me. 'He is up to no good. You were to be ambushed.'

Two of the Border Scouts had been detailed to accompany us and away we went: eleven hours, twenty miles and a mountain later we were well out of the known danger and across at Ulu Trusan, in the Fifth Division of Sarawak. It had been a hard walk but uneventful. We had covered in one day what had taken the troops three and a half. Tired out, we went to the longhouse, dumped our kit, revelling in being able to sit down and take off our footwear and packs.

There was a refreshing chill in the air. Tanké and I went to wash in the nearby stream, which was cold and very refreshing. We put on dry clothes, our others being sweat-soaked.

Back in the longhouse, we sat on a wooden bench that ran the whole way along the outer edge of the communal verandah. The two Scouts and the 'gold medallist' were seated not far away. Tanké and I were hungry as we had not had much to eat that day. Being guests, albeit unbidden, it was against the laws of hospitality to do anything except wait to be invited to a meal.

It was a nine-door longhouse. The missionaries had been there and converted everybody. Waiting for something to happen, I reflected on how Anglican, Roman Catholic, Methodist and other missionaries had almost usurped the role of government in many spheres of activity all over the country.

The newer faiths stripped everything that the Borneans had held dear and tried to put down new roots in shallow soil. The lowest in the 'pecking order' of the community, with a peasant's eye to the main chance, had volunteered to be converted first, thereby, in the opinion of the missionaries, being the most important person there. This naturally upset the social balance and made many unhappy. Apart from banning rice beer, made of surplus stocks so that nobody went short of food, smoking had been forbidden, as it had been the habit for a boy to offer a girl a cigarette to gain her favours – if she accepted it, she would also accept something else, so the two of them could go off in a huddle. I grinned as I imagined how the first missionary discovered the custom. So that, too, had been stopped. The outcome was a non-drinking, non-smoking, funless group of people, out of sorts with themselves.

My thoughts were interrupted by an old crone who came from the end room and shyly invited us in for a meal. I was surprised that the headman had not appeared and that we had been relegated to socially the most inferior room for our meal, but was only too glad of a chance to assuage my hunger. We sat on the floor, around a simple meal of rice, wrapped in a banana leaf, and a spinach-like vegetable. Our hostess bade us close our eyes so she could say grace, after which she told us we could start. There was not much to eat and we were offered a second helping, which we accepted.

We thanked the woman and left. As we passed the second door, it opened and a smiling young man invited us in for a meal. I said that we had just eaten but he seemed to think that no reason for not eating again. So grace was said once more and rice was offered, as well as a sliver of meat in a watery soup, and vegetables. It was hard work but Tanké and I made a brave showing and flatulently patted our distended guts as we left him.

The third ... and the fourth ... and then the middle door opened and we were yet again invited in, this time by the headman, for our fifth meal. There it lay on the floor, lovingly put out by his wife, for the first European to visit them in seven years. Lord knows they were poor, but it was clear that they had gone to great pains to produce delicacies they could ill afford. It was a difficult situation: I knew that great store was set on proper appreciation of hospitality. I also knew that they were a proud people and it would do not good to offend them, as the headman would certainly have been had we not partaken of his offering when we had done so for those of inferior status.

I said to Tanké, 'Look, we must try! Let us go through the motions. Let him say his thank-you prayers. Let us join in. After all, eating ourselves to death is less frightening than being ambushed by the enemy.'

So as not to waste food, we shared a plate of rice. It was unusual, but so were the circumstances. As the headman and his wife looked on, we forlornly picked at what had been given us. I hope they both understood. The taut skin of my belly rebelled at being further punished.

'Headman,' I said, standing up, 'please eat slowly and in peace, we will go and wait outside.'

All the inhabitants of the longhouse had gathered where our kit was by the time I reappeared out of the darkness. I sat down, feeling uncomfortable and very weary. For four hours they questioned me concerning Confrontation and Malaysia, as well as such matters that normally only concerned the District Officer and about which I knew nothing. I forced myself to keep awake. By midnight, I could manage no more. Sleep overtook me in mid-sentence. Some kind person covered me with a blanket, as I did not carry one, for I had one over me when I awoke at dawn.

As the people left the house to continue with the harvest, we gave them our heartfelt thanks. The three from Ulu Trusan returned over the mountain and Tanké and I slowly set out on the next, thankfully short, leg of our long journey, regaled, refreshed, replete – and, for a while, safe.

In a report to General Walker I wrote:

... the Border Scouts are a dead letter. They are incapable of and unsuited to carrying out the tasks they were trained for and have yet to be trained for the role in which they were originally conceived ... The Borneo Evangelical Mission has made its influence felt for so long that it has by now pervaded all aspects of Murut life. Far be it from me to weigh the pros and cons of the situation; suffice it to say that where people have learnt to say grace three times a day before meals, but have yet to learn how to milk their cattle, their priorities ... may well militate against much basic thought or even basic initiative ... Many Muruts, especially the older ones, have big hearts; unfortunately, in this game, hearts are not trumps.

Having completed our survey of the Fifth Division, we crossed into the Fourth Division, over a range of mountains, by helicopter in a blinding rain storm. Refreshingly, at Bareo, the British soldiers got on extremely well with the

Natives – the Company Commander, Major Sidney Butterell of the Light Infantry, being a man of great sensitivity and sound common sense.

I was getting tired, not only of walking but of the continuous probing, trying to find out what was happening, trying to penetrate below the level of deception to the level of truth. I had concluded that two basic mistakes had been made: to believe that an impersonal hierarchy, although backed by cash, could produce results in any way similar to those produced by long-standing loyalties, and to assume that keenness shown during the initial training period could be sustained indefinitely without any proper organic command and control set-up.

We now knew what to look for and what to say. We made our way from longhouse to longhouse, normally spending eight hours each day walking. Everywhere we went my 'new look' concept was enthusiastically greeted. It was pleasant walking; the weather was fresh, the jungle paths easy to follow and, apart from the many leeches, our only discomfort was the threat of bumping into Indonesians. Once they missed us by half a mile, once by twenty minutes. Not a vain man, the only time I ever called myself 'soft and attractive' was when describing the sort of military target I made in the border areas!

*   *   *

We left the Uplands with their story-book Kelabits and, the bracing temperature now behind us, descended to 700 feet above sea level into the large bowl of country that constitutes the headwaters of the mighty River Baram and equally story-book Kenyahs. We found the heat oppressive. In one place we came across four longhouses, close together. Two were Christian and two were proudly pagan, the residents of the latter houses much the jollier. Outside one of them stood, and may yet stand, a totem pole, said to be a representation of the god of war. As the annual celebrations in honour of this god were in progress, an SAS patrol arrived. They were asked to join in and immediately a deer emerged from the jungle on the far bank of the river and swam across. As it climbed up the near bank, it was shot. The whole incident was regarded as a good omen and the four British soldiers were given the credit. They were invited in and stayed a week. On their last but one day Tanké and I turned up.

I introduced ourselves to the dignitaries of the houses and to the four soldiers. Sergeant Dearden, the patrol commander, and his medical orderly had done good work in fostering relations and tending to the sick. A large crowd sat round the patrol and I was most impressed that, when the soldiers spoke to each other, they did so in Malay so that the locals had a chance to understand what they were talking about.

Sergeant Dearden had a lot going for him, as I learned when we chatted that afternoon. It was he who, inadvertently but wisely, suggested how I could resolve some of the conflicting tensions inherent in such an amorphous body of men as the Border Scouts. He recommended two forces: one, a small élite nucleus in each area, whose enthusiasm could be sustained and on whom reliance could be placed; the other, a 'lower tier', consisting of men whose capabilities were more mundane in scope, yet who could provide a worthwhile service.

I thanked him: it was the catalyst I sought.

That night these four men gave a small party for the elders of the community. They had bought some chickens and had made an acceptable mess of pottage with them and their own tinned rations. Guests brought their own rice. A punch had been brewed, using rum, boiled sweets and sugar, all from the soldiers' resupply. It did not last long, but long enough to get the party started.

After the meal was over, hosts and guests moved out to the verandah. Liberal supplies of native hooch flowed and, to the accompaniment of flutes, mandolins and drums, the girls danced most gracefully. They pirouetted in flowing, easy movements, in honour of the hornbill, using much arm movement, with feathers of that bird draped over their shoulders. So much more graceful and pretty than the jabbing, stabbing, lunging, jerking version the Ibans preferred. The music was as enchanting as the dancing. Tanké and I sat on one side, slightly away from it all, for it was the sergeant's farewell party, not ours.

Later I noticed a commotion on the other side of the verandah. The headman was talking to Sergeant Dearden, who seemed to be expressing reluctance. The headman made a sudden movement with his hands and put a monkey-skin hat on the sergeant's head, the tail hanging rakishly over one ear. The sergeant pointed to himself, then at the hat, then all around, his face registering amazement and disbelief as the headman addressed him. Espying me, he came across. He leaned over and said, in an Irish brogue that sounded out of place, 'Sor, sor, do you see this monkey-skin hat on my head? Do you know what it means?'

Correctly assuming my ignorance, he carried on in a rush, 'This monkey-skin hat means that every virgin and every married woman in this house can be a mother to my children.' A graphic pause was followed by, 'There are over two hundred here but I cannot touch one of them.'

'Why not, sergeant?' I asked.

'Sorr, sorr,' he lapsed into purer brogue. 'Under other circumstances, possibly yes, but I'm away early tomorrow morning and I dare not discriminate,' a pause, 'and anyway, sorr, I'm still a soldier of the Queen!'

He returned to the other side of the verandah and I, feeling ready for bed, went to the corner I had been given. I was in no hurry the next morning, as I had to talk with the villagers, but I did notice the patrol set out later than had been intended, Sergeant Dearden having overslept.

Heavy rain in our fly-out caused a delay in our departure from the Fourth Division but, on 1 March, Tanké and I got back to Brunei. We flew back along the line we had so laboriously trudged, taking forty-five minutes to cover what had taken us a month on foot. In forty-three days we had covered 181 'map miles' on foot (easily equal to double that on the ground), 105 by boat and 54 by air.

I sincerely hoped all that effort had been worthwhile.

CHAPTER 16

At Cross Purposes

I reached General Walker's HQ but, before I could get cleaned up, was grabbed for two hours by the staff who wanted to know what I had for them. I was then allowed to get away for a shower and change.

Two days later Fenner took me on a helicopter tour of all Border Scout locations in the Uplands and to meet various headmen. Fenner was good with the locals: big, bluff, full of confidence, his chest ablaze with medal ribbons, he went down well with them and impressed them. He accepted rice-flour cakes, bananas and lukewarm cups of tea as though it was all his favourite fare, laughing and joking in Malay with everybody. I had briefed him on my ideas and findings and he asked the headmen for their views; they were all on my side. I also managed to put more points across to Fenner as we flew down to Kuching together. I was congratulating myself that I had won the Great Man over to the 'two-tier' concept of operations.

Fenner ordered me over to Kuala Lumpur on 8 March, so I had to work hard to complete my report, which took me fourteen hours' writing. My aim had been 'completely to reappraise all aspects of the Border Scouts' with the basic premise of 'whatever is done must be both within the capabilities of the force and the comprehension of the local people'. Everyone I spoke to liked my 'two-tier' solution. Feeling virtuous (always a mistake), I reached Kuala Lumpur as bidden and went to Police HQ to meet Fenner. I was told to return on the morrow. I left my report so that he could digest it before we met.

Next day I again reported to Police HQ and, instead of being alone with the IGP, found Dick Noone, a noted Asian expert, and, to my amazement, the odious Norman Herbolt. Bitter memories of lack of encouragement and slanderous reports surged up inside me, flooding through my mind and leaving me virtually breathless. To save my tongue, temper and reputation, I ignored him completely.

Talk centred on Noone and Herbolt being responsible for the Sabah Border Scouts. I suggested that they take it all on and leave me free to deal with Sarawak. This was refused.

Fenner called for my report but barely glanced at it. He said he would not pass judgement until I had 'tidied up' the other three divisions in like manner. He queried my premises, getting quite angry at the temerity, as he saw it, of my suggestion. When I had even more temerity to ask why he did not like it and what would he do to obviate the shortcomings of the force if he did not accept my proposals, I received no answer. I felt shocked and deflated, remembering how he had, in the aeroplane, accepted so much of what I had suggested.

Fenner had not wanted me to go straight back to Kuching but to travel to Jesselton to see Matheson beforehand. I could then continue retraining the force along the lines I had already started before his joint visit with General Walker, and continue to keep in touch with developments as well as complete my reappraisal. So that, as is said, was that.

At Jesselton, although my findings were later referred to by Matheson as 'verra logical', it was with marked coolness that we met. My report on the inadequacies of the Scouts had touched the European element involved with them on the raw, and the man I had sacked had been extolled as a paragon of police virtue and efficiency by the Interior Residency Superintendent of Police. Matheson pompously accused me of trying to run my own show and cause a rift in relations between those who knew what they were talking about and those who did not, I being in this latter category.

I felt I had to answer in his own coin and, equally pompously, replied, 'Mr Commissioner. You have put ideas into my head that were not there and drawn conclusions therefrom I would not have drawn.' Like it or leave it, warts and all, I thought bitterly.

So, a kind-hearted man in truth but clearly not liking to be out of his depth, he immediately became most apologetic. 'Oh dearr, dearr,' he said, in his broad Scots accent, 'I'm verra sorry, I'm verra sorry.'

This contrition was exacerbated later that afternoon when a senior officer, one ex-marine David Goodsir, reported about an inspection, undertaken for Fenner, of the Sabah Police Force. David had found himself at a police station in a remote place in Sandakan Residency, with nobody on duty. He waited a while, then went round to the back and eventually rounded up the one sergeant and ten policemen from their children and chickens, it being feeding time for both. They were as surprised to see him looking for them as he had been to find no one on duty. They went into the office and David demanded to see the 'two books'. These have almost biblical status and are the Monthly Inspection Book and the Visitors' Book. They were duly produced and, when opened, revealed that the last time they had been written in had been in 1957, seven years previously. Sensing something drastically wrong, David told them he would look into it, so not to worry unduly. It appeared that they received their pay from the local government office so, in the manner of those people, they were quite content to continue their unmonitored way.

David was told by both the Deputy and the Assistant Commissioner that there was no police station at that place, it having been closed down seven years before. Matheson, who confirmed this, was a resourceful man, as well as being determined. Having endured enough for one afternoon from me, this was something he could get to grips with. He got up and went into the clerks' office. He explained what he wanted. 'Check the files, check the files!' he commanded, clapping his hands in exhortation.

We waited as bundles of files were taken out of cubby holes, dusted and shorn of the red tape around them. At last the one being sought was found. Matheson took it, and pulling his spectacles down to the end of his nose, started to read in a sonorous voice, like a member of the Wee Frees, sure of his ground, proclaiming Hell and Damnation to those who do not go to kirk on Sundays.

'Closure of police station at Kuala X'. He looked up in glee: he was on firm ground. Back to the file, he read out the letter, which carefully explained the closure of this particular police station. He finished in triumph, then a startled look came over his face and there was a hush. Suddenly he burst out with, 'Oh dearr, oh dearr, we forgot to pass the order on.'

He went back to his office, humiliation written all over his back. The rest of us disappeared, I to the airport to return to Kuching.

* * *

I was concerned about having to pack up all my goods whenever I left my hotel in Kuching for more than one night, as I still had no permanent accommodation, nor yet had any terms of service been agreed. On the work side I was worried by the immensity of the terrain, the time-consuming travelling and the waiting that went with it, to say nothing of people not being where and when they said they would be. Then there was the sheer inability of so many of the expatriate Borneo community, along with their mirror-image staffs, to see that the Director of Operation's directive to me was a fundamental requirement for the very future of the territory. Had I not believed that, I might just as well have chucked up the whole job and happily returned to regimental soldiering, even though, while visiting 1/7 GR, Heelis had introduced me to a British army captain from England as 'This is John Cross, one of my company commanders really, but I don't know why he's dressed as a lieutenant colonel', which boded no good. He had previously told me how he had rung the appropriate 'desk' in Kuala Lumpur to stop the Malayan Award. How General Walker managed at the top was an object lesson and an inspiration. If he could do what he was doing at his level, then surely I could manage at mine?

Yet the strain of it all, added to the previous year's activities, was beginning to tell. The rebuff, as I saw it, from Fenner in not even discussing any fancied 'weakness of presentation' and all that effort taken for granted, had affected me more than I realised. But my chief difficulty was that I had at least two, if not four, masters. General Walker was one, but I was also a policeman in three forces, so I had my police oath and loyalties to consider and contend with. Turnbull was quiescent and hesitant, giving me the impression of being out of his depth. Similarly groping was Matheson who, like Turnbull, was clearly an exemplary colonial policeman in peacetime but lost regarding the problem of

Confrontation at the end of a placid career: he was dedicated, deliberate and inflexible and had the added misfortune of being ill served by his staff. Both these men were approachable. No, the 'personality problem' was with the IGP, Claude Fenner, King Claude, to his staff, a big man in every sense of the term. Full marks for his handling of Asians: none for his handling of Europeans. He was difficult to talk to as, so often, he would not listen. Moreover, his and Walker's aims never precisely coincided, thereby pulling me apart at my military and loyalty seams. Was I always to be at cross purposes with my bosses?

CHAPTER 17

The Flightless Hornbill

In the First Division I tried first to get to the village of Sapit, by way of Padawan. The Royal Marine Company Commander there, a very nice man called Tim Priest, invited me to spend the night but I said I had to press on. Tim gave me an old-fashioned look and away I went, through very hot secondary jungle, up a steep hill, which, embarrassingly, I found I lacked the strength to climb. I sat down, feeling wretched, my thoughts going back to that time last year near Blaur when a similar lack of staying power had overtaken me. I knew that my only sensible course was to return to Padawan and ask for a corner of a room.

Tim Priest showed only minimal concern at my reappearance and my request for a bed for the night. It was supper time and he asked me to join him.

I did not eat much and, rather to my surprise, Tim asked if my stomach was upset. It was easier to make this excuse than to have to admit I was too weak to carry out my assignment. He kindly volunteered to fetch me something to settle it. I tried to dissuade him but he insisted. He was away for longer than I expected. I sat still, too tired to bother myself, but remonstrated when he returned with a glass of medicine. He said it had taken time to find the Sick Bay Attendant.

I drank it up. Soon afterwards sleep overtook me. I vaguely recollect getting up to relieve nature, surprised to find it was light – I only had Tim's word for this later – and went back to sleep. When I did wake up, he smilingly asked if I knew the time. I had no idea as my watch had stopped, and was flabbergasted to learn that it was not the next morning but the one after that! I felt very ashamed but, as Tim explained, I had seemed so 'all in' that he had decided to give me a knockout brew.

Two nights later, near the village of Pang Ammo, I came across a company of the Royal Malay Regiment. Although cordially received, I was not invited to share their camp facilities for the night, so I made my way to the school and dossed down there on the floor.

Early next morning, as I was still asleep, I dreamed I heard a voice softly whispering in my ear. I awoke and the voice was still whispering. I looked up behind me and there was a villager urgently bidding me listen to him. He said that when the Malay patrols went to the border they would meet up with the Indonesians and talk, not fight. They wore a feather or flower in their hats to apprise the Indonesians of the situation. It made no sense to me, but I lay there trying to absorb what he was saying, not interrupting in case I broke his train of thought. Suddenly, without any warning and without changing the tone of his voice, he started talking about the crops, almost in mid-sentence. A moment later a figure appeared in the doorway and looked most suspiciously at us both. It was an officer from the Malay camp.

He invited me over to breakfast and, with another hard look at my unexpected visitor, left.

I got the gist of my informant's message; if there were no danger of being spotted by outsiders, the Malays would go to the border, their headgear bedecked with a feather or flower. On the other side of the border, the waiting Indonesians, by recognising the marker in the hat, could decide whether it was safe to cross over and have a chat.

I found this hard to swallow but reported it when I returned to Kuching. I learned that my information was not new and indeed confirmed. It transpired that the Indonesian unit over the border had been in the Congo, as part of the United Nations force, at the same time as the Malay battalion. On some occasions, parts of both battalions had even been put under command of the other. Now, thousands of miles to the east, instead of being allies, they were enemies. Recognising that fact, they had reached mutual accommodation. The man who told me about it had been one of a group of suspicious villagers who had shadowed the Malays to the border more than once and had seen for themselves what went on when both sides met.

*   *   *

All this time the war grumbled on, flickering into activity then dying away as incursions were met and countered. I did not keep close tabs on the situation, although I did try to find out if there was any untoward activity in areas I was about to visit.

Towards the end of March I received a letter from the Pay Authorities in Kuala Lumpur telling me they could not decide how much I was worth. On 10 April I was called in by Turnbull and, in a typically one-sided police manner, was informed that I was no longer in any way responsible for running the Sabah Border Scouts. I felt angry that I should have been told in such an off-hand way, but it was nothing to do with Turnbull. To my further surprise and chagrin, he went on to tell me that, after the receipt, though not the acceptance of, my complete recommendations, and following the arrival of the 'field workers' (gazetted officers and inspectors), there would be no further use for my services. So that was that.

I talked over my predicament with my friend of nearly twenty years, Brigadier Patterson who, with General Walker, was one of the few senior officers I held as a hero and really trusted. The thinking was, he suggested, that a commandant was no longer necessary and, even if one was, I was no longer the only man who could do it. That, he said, had been strongly refuted by the general, who reckoned I was doing a sterling job of work and needed me. It was conceded that some local leave, after I had finished my final report, was of prime importance. The brigadier said that in this game I was being used 'not as a pawn but a bishop' by both the IGP and the Director of Operations, in trying to convince the Malaysian political authorities that their own opinion and method of running things were correct. True or not, I felt the only thing to do was to finish off that which I had started, write my report, then have a long heart to heart with General Walker. 'If you go on like this for another year, you'll be dead,' was the brigadier's verdict.

I finished off in the First and Second Divisions, leaving three weeks for the Third Division and the writing of my final report before talking to the general. I passed through 1/7 GR and spoke to Heelis about my future. The upshot was that I was to rejoin as second-in-command to be in a position to earn a recommendation for command. To stay in the police for my whole tour would put me outside the age bracket for such a command.

It was on this trip that I made a strange discovery; in one of the longhouses I noticed one of the posters on the wall – a map of Malaysia. Between the two parts, Eastern and Peninsular, the flags of all the states had been tastefully depicted in the shape of a question mark. Since the whole concept of Malaysia was just that, it amused me to contemplate the reaction of its designer were this irony to be pointed out to him. Then my attention was drawn to something far more subtle and clearly purposefully printed. East Malaysia was the larger entity with a total of 76,458 square miles, but Peninsular Malaysia, with only 50,700 square miles, was shown as being the larger of the two by a considerable amount. The Borneo native, sensing the vastness of his country, would naturally be impressed by being ruled by a government in a country that was even bigger than British Borneo!

I called in on the police station at Sibu and mentioned what I had discovered. Somewhat naturally, I was not believed, so we found a copy of the poster and I pointed out the falsification, measuring it to prove my point. The Native policemen were angry at the subterfuge, and a Malay policeman from the mainland sulked and would not believe the evidence of his eyes.

I flew to Brunei to see the general. This time I felt the gravity of the situation more than I had since my arrival the previous July. I had the final report of the Border Survey sent round to his house and apparently he spent two hours going through it as with a fine-toothed comb. He liked it very much – 'fallen into our laps like a ripe plum'. And then we talked. I told him much that he did not know about police attitudes and I felt this made him unhappy. I asked him what he, as a friend, advised and we discussed it for a while. We decided that the best thing to do, in the circumstances, was for me to resign. I told him that the last thing I wanted was to let him down and he said, 'John, you haven't. I called you out to do this job as I knew of no one else who could have done it. My faith has not been misplaced. You have done what I expected of you, as I knew you would and I feel, as you do, that your job is over.'

That, coming from such a man, made up for all the hardships and difficulties over the past ten months. Later he told me that wherever he went, people expressed their satisfaction with the Border Scouts.

Before returning to Kuching, I visited the Borneo Evangelical Mission at Lawas, on the coast. Those Methodist missionaries ruled the land with a hand firmer than that of the established government. They were all starry-eyed enthusiasts whose sole answer to all queries was, 'It is God's wish'. I told them, in a friendly manner, that the Border Scouts were not a rival organisation but a very important part of the community. The missionaries rejoined that the Border Scouts were riff-raff and not 'proper' Christians. I merely pointed out that I had a bigger parish than they did and we were trying to help the Borneo people to help themselves.

I wrote my letter of resignation on my return to Kuching. Dated 14 May 1964, it was addressed both to the Inspector General of the Royal Malaysia Police and the Commissioner of Sarawak Constabulary. In essence I wrote that I had slotted the Border Scouts into the existing organisation of the Police, that I had written myself out of a job, and that I would stay until 11 July when I would feel free to go and how very grateful I was for the privilege I had had of working with the border people.

I gave in my final report to the commissioner, along with my letter of resignation. The copies for Fenner were also given to Turnbull as the IGP happened to be in Kuching the following day. Fenner sent for me and expressed surprise at my attitude. He tried to bully me, but I would not be bullied. I explained about having been told by Heelis why I was wanted back in my battalion, apart from the fact that I had 'written myself out of a job'. Fenner considered both points but only gave judgement on the first: he would let me go on the date I had recommended because 'you are at the crossroads of your career'.

He gave me no indication whether he had read my report, or if he had, whether he had given it his blessing. Thanks for the work I had done was something I had not expected, nor was any proffered.

Everything, from then on, seemed a bit of an anti-climax. I still had a lot to do in the visiting line, both at field and headquarter level.

On 4 June I was told that the Sarawak Constabulary had accepted my resignation. The commissioner said that I had done what I had set out to do and, although it was quicker than he had anticipated, he would put no obstacle in my way.

I paid my last visit to the Borneo Uplands of the Fourth Division. The new Minister of Defence, a Mr D.W. Healey, was on tour with the Director of

Operations and we coincided at Bareo on 14 May. I was called over to be introduced to him. He looked me up and down for a moment and said, very disdainfully, 'I suppose you are one of those office-wallahs who only come out into the open during such a visit as this.'

That struck me as unacceptably rude and the general, no doubt seeing the look on my face and certainly knowing what the true facts were, quietly corrected him before I could make any riposte.

'No, Minister, Cross is the one man you cannot say that about.'

I had to be content with the ghost of a huffy apology as he turned his back on me.

CHAPTER 18

A Borderline Case

On 20 June more summit talks about peace broke down and within twenty-four hours Borneo Confrontation resumed more fiercely. On that same day I received a shock. I learned that the IGP had turned down the results of my survey, despite the general's and even Mr Turnbull's wishes. Next morning the First Division Resident asked me if my scheme had been adopted and was horrified to learn it had not been.

'You're ten years ahead of us all,' was his comment.

I was now gladder than ever that I was not staying on.

*   *   *

I made my plans to leave Sarawak and return to my battalion as Fenner had promised, but he now ordered me to stay until the British Army sent my replacement. For the only time in my military career I saw red to the extent of refusing to obey an order. I sent a signal to Fenner saying that I would stay on after my due date only if I was physically restrained from leaving. Three days later I was called to the commissioner's office to hear Fenner's answer. Just before I left I was given a letter. It was in Heelis's writing so I read it first.

Short and to the point, he wrote and apologised for letting me believe I was command material as now, after reflection, he felt I did not 'have that indefinable quality of leadership which makes people do what is required of them in the complex organisation which is the infantry battalion of today', although I had 'many admirable characteristics, generosity, a flair for languages, application to work, dedication to a cause and physical fitness'. I read on, 'I know that up to a company of Gurkhas would follow you anywhere, but I personally cannot see you moulding the sort of team that is required to ensure that the battalion continues to be a happy and efficient fighting machine.' In short, I had been put in an untenable position with Fenner.

Further down the page I read, '... offer you command of the Gurkha Para Company. It would be another challenge for you as the company certainly needs a more dynamic leadership... I hope this isn't too much of a disappointment to you and I'm sorry I didn't warn you of it earlier... Please slip over for an interview if you want to...'

Dazed by my change in fortune, I made my way to see the commissioner. I was told that Fenner had, reluctantly, allowed me to leave because he saw I had a good chance of being given command of a Gurkha battalion. I thanked

Turnbull, too cowardly to tell him that I was, in fact, now acting under false pretences.

So that, as is said, was that.

A few days later Heelis and I were talking face to face in his office in Ipoh. Part of what I had to say to him made him admit that maybe he had made a mistake in his judgement of my abilities, to which I replied that that was the one remark of his in the past few years that I really believed and trusted, which put him in some confusion; part was that I had been allowed to leave the Police almost 'under false pretences' and, were there any repercussions, he would have to make my peace with Fenner. I also told him that, under the circumstances, life would be happier for both of us were I to volunteer to take command of the Gurkha Parachute Company.

* * *

With twelve days left, I was asked to go to a battalion of the Royal Malay Regiment, based on Serian in the First Division, where the CO, whom I knew well, had complained bitterly about the Border Scouts. Before I left Kuching to visit the Malays, I asked if a helicopter could pick me up from the last place I was planning to visit, Plaman Mapu, sometime on 16 July. I hoped I would live to see it as I had a pressing premonition of disaster or death.

The complaints levelled at the Scouts were that they did not cover the whole area, they were not representative of the area where they were operating, they worked too much in the rear, they worked too independently and they did not give any reports of what they had done. I suspected that this was not the unvarnished truth and promised I would try to solve his problems.

I ascertained, from the nearest Scouts in Balai Ringin, that they were anti-pathetic to the Malays, finding them arrogant, insensitive and disdainful to the customs and feelings of the locals, and less than enthusiastic about their own patrolling commitments. Indeed, it seemed that the soldiers were spending much time in camp or with the girls in the neighbouring villages, sending out the Scouts instead of going themselves, then writing up their daily situation reports, 'sitreps', as though they had in fact been in the field. So much, thought I, for not taking the Scouts out of uniform. The Scouts felt that the Malays were cowards and idlers who 'wanted to rut more than the animals in the forest'. Dispirited, I was back in Serian by mid-afternoon, unwilling to say anything until I had been to the other two places, the villages of Bunan Gagak and Plaman Mapu. A Malay platoon was based in both locations.

The CO asked for my findings so far. I took him to his office, looked into the adjoining rooms to ensure no eavesdroppers, then sat down opposite him. I looked him straight in the eyes and told him that what I had to say was painful and that he was not to take it personally.

He nodded. Steeling myself, I continued looking at him and started on my distressing litany: '... cowards ... liars ... boasters ... oversexed ... idle ... inefficient...' until I at last finished.

It was then his turn to be equally blunt. 'John, you have merely confirmed my worst suspicions. That is why I was sent at short notice to take over command of this battalion.'

I admired his frankness and we went over to the mess to have a cup of tea together.

*   *   *

My companion was a Dyak Probationary Inspector, George Young Siricord, who was under instruction. Three days later we reached Plaman Mapu around noon, having avoided two Malay ambushes in areas where the CO had said there were no troops. An agitated headman hustled us inside and upstairs, into the loft, where we were ordered to hide from approaching Indonesians. This was unexpected news; certainly no intelligence reports had suggested such a large force to be in the offing, although we had heard rumours of an intended incursion while at Bunan Gagak. I asked what the Indonesians expected to achieve and got the chilling response that they would exterminate Europeans – 'We hate them like dogs' – would ambush airdrops and had targeted the Border Scouts, security forces and government servants. Once more I was struck by the notion of being a 'soft and attractive military target in the border areas', since by representing each prong of that unholy trinity, the odds were heavily against us.

At dusk we were called down and offered some rice and vegetables. Neither of us had much of an appetite. Our equipment had been hidden and we only had our weapons with us. I had taken the precaution of extracting a towel from my pack, for use as a pillow-cum-head binder to keep as many nasties as possible from going down my ears. George and I were lying on the bamboo-slatted floor and I was on the verge of taking off my boots when, at 7.30, the dogs started barking, not merely baying at the moon but reacting to the presence of human beings. It was decided we had better be hidden.

Part of the bamboo slats was rolled back and we were told to jump down the six or so feet and hide in a narrow trench that had been dug for the headman, as a gesture of goodwill by the Marines who had been relieved by the Malays, in the event of the longhouse being shelled. This we did, with urgent whispers imploring us to hurry. Once we were under the floor, a man rolled the bamboo slats back in position and placed his sleeping mat over the 'trapdoor'. It was hoped he would act as a decoy if the Indonesians were to enter the house.

Underneath it stank of stale rubbish, pigs, curs and chickens. We squirmed down as comfortably as we could, arms pinioned to our sides. I managed to put the towel over my head and draped it over my face as we soon found ourselves beset with rats. George wriggled and moaned, bringing whispered curses and pleas for silence from above.

Dogs barked again at 10 o'clock. The rats continued to run over us and George's struggles to keep his face clear caused the earthen walls of the trench to start crumbling. More agonised whispers came from above.

I have to admit I heard nothing, apart from George's struggles and the whispers, sibilantly impassioned, imploring quiet. I knew I could do nothing about the danger and a strange calm overcame me. I now knew what danger I was up against, so could the better face it. Sleep was imperative, so I went to sleep.

What with George's squirming, the rats running over me and my moving my head from side to side, the towel slipped off. I was awoken by a large rat sitting on my nose. Instinctively, knowing that I could not get my hands to brush it off, I blew up, violently, through my mouth and it scuttled off. I managed to drape the towel more firmly and continued my sleep, albeit intermittently. It started to rain heavily.

At dawn we went up to the loft and, within half an hour, we heard that more than seventy Indonesians had moved north at 7 o'clock the night before. Later another man reported that there had been two groups, one consisting of six armed, hatless and bearded enemy a short distance away, at 6 o'clock. He had spoken to them. The second, and larger, group of 120 men had skirted the longhouse and had gone deeper into Sarawak. The reason why the Indonesians had not investigated our longhouse was thought to be because they had discovered that the Malay platoon was not there and had not suspected our presence.

I felt that I should try to get this news known as soon as possible but, probably just as well, my request was turned down.

By mid-morning the rain had stopped, so I once more asked the headman if I could leave, as I was certain there would be no helicopter that day. We had been given back our equipment and we could try to make a dash for it.

'Please do not go as long as the enemy are in the area. If they were to know that I had hidden you, they would punish me with my life. This is their threat.'

At 2 o'clock in the afternoon, twenty-six hours after we had arrived at the longhouse, we heard the sound of a helicopter. I hardly dared believe by ears. As soon as I was sure it was coming our way, George and I ran the 200 yards to where we had been told it would land if it came – and come it had!

It was an RAF Whirlwind, which meant we could hurl ourselves in and not wait to be strapped in. I had taken the precaution of writing down, on a scrap of paper, GO TO SERIAN. Having thrown in my kit and yelled to George to get in, I showed it to the pilot, who looked down, read it and shook his head. He had been briefed to go to another place so could not deviate without permission from Kuching; this was his first operational mission. I climbed up the outside and put my head into the cockpit. I pulled the pilot over to me, lifted his helmet and shouted, over the noise of the engine, 'There's an incursion and a hundred enemy are in the area. They've threatened to shoot down any helicopter they can. You're the first in.'

He needed no second bidding. I jumped down, clambered in and tapped his leg from behind, the sign that we inside were ready for take-off. I sat between the door and the front end and, as the helicopter took off, a deal faster than it had landed, there were tears in my eyes that could not have been caused by the slipstream. My only regret was that I had not thanked the villagers, and especially the headman, adequately for their help.

So we flew to Serian, where I got out. George had had enough and went on to Kuching. I told the CO about the situation but he seemed little interested. There was nothing on the 'sitrep' from his troops about any incursion so, as far as he was concerned, there was no incursion.

During the evening Brigadier Patterson rang through. George and the pilot had reported the incident. The Malay colonel gave the brigadier an evasive reply. Feeling unbearably tired, I excused myself and went to bed.

By then I had been on the move constantly for nearly a year and when I awoke of a morning I had always known exactly where I was. Next morning, however, on waking, I had not the faintest idea as to my surroundings. I was frightened: was I in hospital, jail, a lunatic asylum or where? I lay back, cowering at the implications of knowing nothing, and it was only some minutes later when someone came into my room to see what had happened to me that I learned what I so desperately wanted to know.

Later that morning the brigadier, suspicious of conflicting reports, flew up from Kuching to Serian. He wanted to get to the bottom of the inconsistency but the Malay CO and I differed so much that he decided to take us both in his helicopter to Plaman Mapu personally to debrief the platoon commander. The Malay CO was ordered not to open his mouth until I had finished talking to the young subaltern. It emerged that I had been accused of hiding from the Malays, thinking that they were Indonesians; the Malay platoon commander had reported a move out to the border to ambush the expected Indonesians to his company commander who, in turn, had falsified the 'sitrep' so that the commanding officer did not know the real situation. Now he had completely lost face in front of two Englishmen, his brigade commander and me. There was dirty washing being hung out where it was embarrassingly conspicuous.

There was not much more to be gained by staying there, so, thanking the platoon commander for his help, we clambered back into the helicopter. We landed at Serian, where the Malay colonel got out, saluted stiffly and went his own way. I flew on to Kuching but, before I was allowed to dismiss, Patterson took me to one side and delivered his verdict.

'As far as the outside world is concerned, you did hide from the Malays. We can't risk a row by publicly doubting their word. I'm sorry, but there it is. Keep your mouth shut!'

This I did, to my embarrassment. Folk were too polite to snigger in my presence, but they thought I had been pushing myself too hard and had taken counsel of my fears. The Malay battalion was redeployed in a less sensitive area; the brigadier got a ticking off, following a report the Malays had sent on their own net to Kuala Lumpur, giving their own version of the incident which reached the brigadier on the British net; and the Malay colonel received a bravery award in the next Malaysian honours list and promotion to brigadier.

*   *   *

I was invited, for the first time ever, to the Police Officers' Mess and, after (very) small eats and a drink, the commissioner made a short speech and presented me with a small ashtray bearing the Sarawak Constabulary badge. Knowing I was a confirmed non-smoker, he was either very unimaginative or had a more subtle sense of humour than I had credited him with.

For my part, I made a short speech of thanks and, remembering how I had been criticised for being out of the office so much, finished thus:

> He wanders here, he wanders there,
> That Hornbill wanders everywhere,
> So seldom in, so often out,
> That demned elusive Border Scout.

The day I left Kuching for Singapore, 23 July 1964, on the first leg of my journey back to England on leave, I received two communications. One was from the Commissioner of Sarawak Constabulary and it read:

Dear Colonel Cross,

As you are now relinquishing your command of the Border Scouts I wish to express my gratitude to you for your sterling work in the year you have been with us.

Your task has been a difficult one. Your brief to change the role of the Border Scouts, and at the same time to build up morale and a good appreciation of this role by the men, when all the time you were faced with an acute shortage of experienced staff, has been a challenge cheerfully accepted by you.

The Sarawak Constabulary and this country has good reason to be grateful to you. We wish you good fortune in the years ahead.

The second was a signal from General Walker and read:

Personal for Superintendent Cross from the Director of Operations. The Border Scouts as presently organised owe their all to the patience, understanding and diligence of the dedicated few whose business it has been to raise and train this extremely valuable indigenous force. As their first Commandant you may rightly take pride in what has been achieved, despite the odds. Your own personal efforts have been prodigious and these, I know, frequently have entailed your ploughing a lonely furrow, often against the grain. Yet your reward has been in your continuous contact with the peoples for whom you hold such affection and among whom you have become a legendary figure. On your handing over the Hornbill it behoves me to thank you and wish you a pleasant relaxing leave.

As I got into the vehicle to go to the airport, I was handed another signal from the general's headquarters. It read: FAREWELL BRAVE PRINCE.

*   *   *

From then on I remember little, until I reached England. I was told, five years later, that, while waiting to board the 'plane at Paya Lebar airport in Singapore, I was introduced to a brigadier from the School of Infantry, Warminster, who had concluded a three-week tour of Borneo, by his accompanying staff officer who knew me. Apparently I gave the brigadier a twenty-minute lecture. Suddenly I came to an abrupt halt, turned sharply away and left him, almost in mid-sentence.

I sat next to his staff officer on the way back in the aeroplane and he it was who told me, after all those years, about the talk with the brigadier. He also said he could see me unwinding as I talked ceaselessly all the way and that I was so obviously 'wound up', he wanted to 'pan me one' to quieten me.

But of all that I had no recollection whatsoever and, when he did tell me about it, I said I did not believe him.

I could see he thought I was a borderline case.

Part Four

MALAYSIA, 1965–71
Retreat from the Tropics

CHAPTER 19

Gurkha Independent Parachute Company

Once again, the contrast between England and what I had left behind was too sudden for comfort. Although I had only been away a year, I had not fully recovered from the privations suffered during my spell with the Temiar when I departed for Borneo. Once again, people found me difficult to get on with, just as I found it hard to relax, both bodily and mentally.

On the one hand I fully appreciated how lucky I was to be alive after a very narrow escape every month for the past year. On the other hand, I was smarting inwardly at how Fenner had ignored my work and Heelis had treated me. It was cold comfort to recall what the soldiers of 1/7 GR had told me when I went to Ipoh to 'have it out' with Heelis: they were sorry I was not to be with them once more, and wondered why the authorities felt I needed to be given a third consecutive job where I could easily lose my life. It were better for all if I went to command the Para Company as 'we would not have let you be bullied by Heelis and would have cut his head off'.

So, besides having such bitter-sweet thoughts haunting me as I regained my strength, I was wondering how I would cope by becoming a parachutist nearer forty than thirty-nine years of age. Even when an uncle suggested my changing my family motto to 'May all my droppings be soft ones', I could only respond with a wan smile.

I finished my leave and rejoined my battalion. I was made more unhappy to find that Heelis had warned his relief against me, and for the two months I had to fill in before starting parachute training, instead of helping the battalion out in Borneo (where I knew every headman in the area of their operations), I was held back in command of the rear party — looking after leave men and the families. On the other side of the coin, I was back in an organisation that I had grown to love over the years, I was no longer a unique embarrassment to two armies and three police forces, nor to the financiers of two governments puzzling how to pay me. I knew where I was, I appreciated all aspects of living, I was welcomed back by the soldiers — in short, I was home again.

I learned that the Indonesians had broadcast that they had killed Captain Cross, a theme echoed by the *Sarawak Gazette*. The battalion's pandit told me that anyone so announced was guaranteed to live until he was a hundred. My death being published twice meant a ten-year bonus. I said I did not want to live until I was 110 and was allowed a special dispensation to stay alive only till I was 105.

*   *   *

The Gurkha Independent Parachute Company, to give it its full name, had its genesis in the Brunei rebellion that started on 8 December 1962. Elements of a British battalion had to be airlanded on an unreconnoitred airstrip which was in enemy hands, something that no self-respecting air force likes to do. To clear such an obstacle is the role of parachute troops and it was the lack of them that showed up the need to have a parachute unit always on hand. Rather than denude the Home Base of such troops, it was decided to raise a small parachute force from theatre resources. This was provided by the Gurkhas and came into being on 1 January 1963.

Our fundamental objective was to be able to capture an airhead; our next and immediate task was to operate in small patrols in advance of conventional infantry; and thirdly, we had to be ready to act as an ordinary infantry company. For our first role we needed 128 Gurkhas, the basic minimum for all our three roles. Simple mathematics therefore meant we worked in five-man groups, unlike the SAS, the Guards Independent Parachute Company and later the Parachute Regiment itself, who worked in four-man groups.

Apart from being individually trained as medical orderlies, infantry pioneers, radio operators and linguists, we needed patrol training. This meant the men honing up their individual and collective infantry skills, supplemented by all the jungle lore I had acquired with the aborigines and the Border Scouts, in turn built on my own personal experience gained after being jilted in 1954.

As the maps in Borneo often showed no contours, we had maps of the Kluang area specially printed with no contours and certain conventional signs missing. We went on frequent jungle exercises and continued with our parachute drops. We even managed to give a demonstration jump to the Gurkha recruits in the training depot near Penang during the brigade annual conference. I jumped first, left my parachute as it was and ran over to where a public address system was ready to give the recruits a running commentary of what was happening and who were jumping. I had made a list of all those in the depot who were relatives to fellow villagers of my men taking part in the demonstration. Before I started talking I overheard one battalion commander say, 'Ah, a real saheb; he leaves his parachute for someone else to roll up.' On another occasion I arranged for the Gurkha families to watch an exercise jump near Kluang. Two gores of one man's parachute tore and he approached the ground very fast. Not knowing whose dearest was so rapidly becoming whose nearest, all the Gurkha ladies hid their faces and missed most of the demonstration!

I was engrossed by a problem: our different roles demanded different types of people. One reason, so I believe, why the SAS and Para men do not always hit it off together is that the former are introverts who do not like a crowd while the latter are extroverts who do. My men had to be both. Down in GHQ the chief 'trick-cyclist' had been medical officer during the war when Gurkhas were first trained for parachute duties in India, when there had been a fatality each week. I asked him his views on how to devise tests to help me choose men for such divergent tasks.

His answer intrigued me as much as my question had intrigued him: if all theatre resources were pooled and this problem worked on for a year, he doubted a suitable solution could be found. I had to establish a personality cult, I was told, and dispense with all except pure military testing. How refreshing to be told, in effect, to act naturally for a change and how different from the tasteless comments I had had to endure in the past two years, always behind my back.

*   *   *

In early September 1965 we were sent to Brunei and were billeted a short way out of the town in the so-called 'Haunted House'. Before I took over, men had been in the jungle from six to twelve weeks, but I cut that time down to two or three. We would not be sent on cross-border operations on our first tour, so we spent all four months operating inside Sabah and Sarawak. Easy tasks were gradually increased to harder ones and, although we did not have any contact with the enemy, we always did what was asked of us. We had no sickness so no elaborate air evacuations were needed, nor were aerial fixes ever a requirement for a lost patrol – the brigade staff later told me that our British peers were ever demanding in both requirements. The soldiers' line discipline in camp was as good as were their military techniques on operations, to the amazement of their British comrades-in-arms.

Before our second spell on operations, we were rebadged with the Parachute Regiment badge and allowed to wear the red beret. This was much more popular than the idea of wearing our own badge, parachute and crossed kukris, as the men now felt we had been accepted by the rest of the British Army as equals.

The company made a number of cross-border operations on our next tour. Being top secret, we all had to have security clearance beforehand. I recall opening an envelope addressed to me personally and reading the caveat which stated that on no account was the person named on the reverse ever to be told that he had been positively vetted. I turned the letter over and found my own name staring at me!

It was always a tense moment waiting for the evening situation reports to come in and I was ever relieved to learn that all was well. I had to obtain sanction for myself to go on such an operation and I remember the first time I went over the border in a way one remembers all one's firsts – the first day in the army, the first parachute jump, the first time one is shot at, the first time one shoots at and kills someone – it may be glorious to die for your country but it is far more glorious to make the other fellow die for his.

It was only a small reconnaissance to see if the Indonesians had been in a certain sector. There were ten of us and, once over the border, we were to split into two groups. We were not allowed more than 3000 yards into Indonesian territory, which was sufficient for the job in hand. It was, in the jargon, 'the last piece of blue sky in the jigsaw puzzle'.

The terrain was thick, matted jungle, ranging between 2000 and 4000 feet high, with swift mountain streams and deep rivers, beetling precipices and steep hills. If often rained and was rudimentarily uncomfortable.

Our destination was a track that ran parallel to and south of the border. It was thought that the Indons used it as a base line to mount attacks across the border and our task was to see if it was used sufficiently for a battalion ambush.

Moving down a narrow ridge well into the area, we reached a spot where the jungle was almost bare of foliage, except, at the limit of vision, where four thin saplings were growing on a piece of ground slightly flatter than the rest of the slope. It was then that we stopped for a breather, sheltering in a small rocky outcrop, a feature not uncommon in those high hills. We were ultra-cautious. I moved slowly to the edge of the outcrop, not exposing myself and, slowly raising my head, had a good look around. There was nothing untoward between me and where the ridge dipped again on the other side of the four saplings. All was peaceful, nothing was amiss. And yet, although I could not put my finger on it, I sensed danger. I went over to the saplings and tugged them one by one out of the ground. They were bivouac poles for the Indon ambush who had chosen to sleep on the flatter ground. At night, when the ambush was lifted, the saplings could have a covering draped between them and, by day, even when they had grown enough roots to regain their normal appearance, they constituted no impediment to the field of fire or vision. Having been recently cut, they looked fresh and natural. What gave them away (though we only realised it later) was that they were set in a rectangle, something not immediately apparent since I had not approached them face on. This disturbance of nature's pattern proved a lucky break for us as we then knew our area was occupied.

We arrived in our target area a little later than planned, but safely. The map was inaccurate so I was not perfectly satisfied that the track we had reached was the one we were meant to investigate. As I was probably beyond the limit of my permitted range over the border, I did not want to explore farther south. In any case I had taken a very heavy fall and bent the barrel of my rifle, so could only use the weapon as a club. As we were considering our next move, a civilian walked into us from the direction of the main Indon force of a few hundred soldiers to the south-west. I managed to talk to him in a garbled brand of Malay and he was obviously very upset by our presence. I did not want him with us and so I sent him on his way. Before we left he told us of a nearby longhouse sometimes used by the Indons. If we were to fulfil our mission and withdraw without too much fuss, we had to act more quickly, decisively and boldly than normal. Without further ado I took my patrol along the north-east axis of the track . . . which petered out after less than two hours. Obviously not the one used by Indon patrols!

Before we had reached the place where we had decided to meet the other group, I realised we were lost. As it was getting late I did not investigate the longhouse as we passed it but continued west, hoping to find them. The jungle fell away into open country. The track led us up a small hill before disappearing into a blanket of thick, matted fern. We would have been a perfect target had any troops been at the top of the slope in a small clump of trees. At the top of the knoll I turned round and saw that something had been carved at the base of the largest tree, just at the height of a man lying in ambush. It read, quite simply, RPKAD – the Indonesian Para Commandos – and had the previous day's date.

I knew we could go no farther forward nor, indeed, back to find the others as, by then, they would have set up an ambush facing our direction. We had to hide for the night. I made a stab at my position and sent it off before it was too dark. I also sent a radio message to the other five, telling them to try to find us by 8 o'clock next morning.

At dawn we saw that we had chosen the one clump of trees in a vast expanse of long grass, with hundreds of water buffalo grazing. By 10 o'clock they were still the only living creatures in sight as the other Gurkhas had not yet appeared. I grew anxious and one of my men suggested I made a monkey call with my hands which the others would hear if they were not very far away. Cuckoo noises were better and my mind flashed back eighteen years to 1948 when I had learned that there were no cuckoos in Malaya. Even though I was to be the biggest cuckoo in Kalimantan, I saw no other option of meeting up with the others, so I tried it – and twenty minutes later, to our intense relief, they turned up. They had been half a mile away and, not knowing where we were but anticipating what I would do, had sat down and waited for the call!

We investigated the longhouse and found a few old folk inside. They had no idea who we were. We spent a little time with them, eating bananas and warmed-up groundnuts. One old crone amused the Gurkhas by coming up to me and stroking my face.

We left to inspect an area where 1/2 GR had fought a battle. Since then the Indons had constructed a large, well-maintained helicopter landing pad which they used to good effect in a follow-up operation against us. I never knew whether they had fixed our position by my radio call or whether the man we met had returned along another path to tell them, but come they did, with a fighter escort. By that time we were too far for them to catch us – or we moved faster than they did and reached the border first. On being debriefed at Brigade HQ, I was told that that was the first recorded occasion that the Hook helicopter had been within 10,000 yards of the border for a very long time.

*   *   *

In early 1966 the company returned to Kluang for a spell of retraining. I toured all Gurkha units for reinforcements and, although I only needed a modest number, I could have had a thousand, so popular had the unit become with the rank and file. With daily 'para pay' and grade pay for medically trained men, a rifleman with me was earning the pay of a colour sergeant in a battalion. Even so, the Gurkhas were paid 22 new pence a day when their British counterparts were getting 35 new pence. The inevitable implication was that Gurkha lives were valued more cheaply than were British. Not true, in fact, although the explanation that in this case 'para pay' was not 'danger money' but an 'inducement to volunteer' to be a parachutist, was hardly convincing.

In June we were once more deployed in Borneo. It was the time of the Indonesian incursion into Sarawak in 1966 which came to be known as the 'Sumbi Saga'. Many rumours had reached the authorities about this Indonesian Lieutenant Sumbi who was believed to be about to undertake a dangerous mission for his country. Apart from any other training, he had apparently learned to parachute in Abingdon in England and had been taught his basic jungle tactics at the Jungle Warfare School. It was thought that the plot was for Sumbi to lead a band of some fifty guerrillas from Kalimantan Utara, as Malaysian Borneo was known, infiltrating through Sarawak to Brunei and then to sabotage the Shell Oil installations while Malaysia-Indonesia Peace Talks were being held in Bangkok.

The incursion eventually came from across the border in the mountainous area of the Fourth Division of Sarawak. It was Sumbi's bad luck that the border crossing was made through a sector that one of our patrols was guarding. A couple of ace operators, Corporal Singabahadur Gurung and Rifleman Dharmalal Rai, were patrolling when Dharmé noticed a tiny glint, unnaturally bright, among the leaves on the jungle floor. He examined it and found it was a piece of tinfoil which smelt of coffee. Gurkhas did not carry coffee in their rations and there were no British troops in the area so, he reasoned, it had to be Indons, yet there were no obvious traces of them.

Sumbi eventually lost the battle; some of his men were captured, some died of starvation and some were killed. He himself was eventually captured. Eventually all the group of would-be saboteurs, bar four, had been accounted for.

At noon on 11 August 1966 Confrontation ended, 'not with a bang but a whimper'. All troops in Malaysia were withdrawn from operations prior to a return to peacetime locations. We, in the Gurkha Para Company, were not in Malaysia but in Brunei where these cease-fire orders did not apply. The Brunei government wanted to know if the last four men of Sumbi's gang had infiltrated into Brunei or died in the Sarawak jungle. In an area of wild country that could have measured anything from 500 to 2500 square miles, the odds against finding four men were infinitely remote. Nevertheless a Gurkha patrol and a company of the Royal Brunei Malay Regiment (RBMR) were sent to the border of Brunei and Sarawak, a ridge of hilly country, to see if anything could be found.

It was by no means certain that the four wanted men were still alive and, if so, that they had got anywhere near, let alone reached, Brunei. The patrol had to evacuate a man and, having nothing better to do, I flew in as the relief.

The very next day, walking along a ridge a mile or so from the Brunei–Sarawak border, I was travelling end man and my eye was caught by just one leaf, lying on the ground, among the countless others – but with a straight crease across it. Nature does not work in straight lines so only a man could have folded it in half. None of the security forces had been in the area for a long time so who else could it be but one of the four men we were looking for? It had rained the night before and, by then, the men were superb at covering their tracks, so the leaf was the only clue. The search in the area was intensified and, a few days later, a patrol of the Royal Brunei Malay Regiment captured them. During the subsequent exhaustive interrogation, it transpired that one of them was a compulsive finger-twiddler or doodler, who was continually playing with a twig or a leaf. A tiny, but costly, idiosyncrasy, breaking the pattern of nature. So that was the end of the 'Sumbi Saga' and the end of the threat to the Brunei oil installations.

The original tracking foray was not considered of sufficient merit to warrant any recognition as it was all reckoned to be part of the day's work. But I did especially ask the Director of Operations, by now Major General George Lea, to visit us in our camp so that he could personally congratulate the two men who first spotted the suspicious marks. This he did in great style. It is strange to think that such a bold adventure should have been thwarted, initially, by a piece of tinfoil and that just one leaf should have ended it.

Shortly after that, Brigadier David House wrote my annual confidential report, one sentence of which read, 'The jungle is his home address.' He smiled as he confided that his original draft read, 'The jungle is his native habitat', but he had changed it as it might have been taken disparagingly.

*   *   *

Back in Kluang we received news that we had been affiliated with the Parachute Regiment. I paid a short visit to England and went to Aldershot where we exchanged presents: a ceremonial kukri to them and a statuette of a parachutist in full battle order to us. This I used as a four-monthly prize for the best soldier in the company during that period. The perks I included were to act as right marker on all ceremonial parades, to be excused all duties and fatigues, and not to have to pay any company subscriptions.

We were also tested to see if we were fit enough to become a permanent fixture in the Order of Battle. A tough exercise was thought up and we jumped from two Hercules aircraft in 'simultaneous twenties' at one minute's interval. This was the first time in the Far East that so many parachutists had ever had such large 'sticks'. From the first man out of the doors of the first 'plane to the last man off the Dropping Zone was about six minutes. Not only did we 'defeat the enemy' in less than an hour and a half (the deadline for this having been fixed at four hours), but the RAF parachute officer in charge, who himself had over thirty years' experience, reported that he had never seen such a high standard of drop. Furthermore, not one man of the eighty involved had to be put right when inspected on the ground nor in the air prior to exit. This, apparently, was a brilliant 'first ever'. I was tremendously proud of the men.

Our future ensured, we learned that we were to be visited by the Army Commander, himself a parachutist, on our next training jump. He duly came. It was my 84th descent and – yes – it was the only time I injured myself. Very near the ground I had to take evasive action and landed on the point of my right shoulder, badly dislocating it. I found I could not get up. Running my left hand up my right side, I was appalled to find no arm and no shoulder. I looked at my hand to see if there was any blood, presuming I had lost a limb. Terrible thoughts ran through my head. I looked over my shoulder – not an easy manoeuvre – saw my errant arm with the shoulder joint somewhere at the back of my neck, and managed to pull it forward to where the armpit normally is. I fainted three times as I was being X-rayed.

There were at least six of us in the company who had been hurt at one time or another, two when parachuting, the rest otherwise. Remedial treatment in conventional hands was slow, painful, time-consuming and not always successful. The threat of the surgeon's knife with the ensuing pins and cat-gut was never far away. Once things became drastic enough for these measures, the end was in sight: a medical board and inevitable down-grading. After a couple of months I was no better with the treatment at the local army hospital and my men told me they feared I would have to be boarded and compelled to leave the company prematurely.

When I was told that a local Malay not only had the power of healing but was also willing to try it on me, I was interested, albeit sceptical. Over the years I had heard of such men but had tended to disdain them. However, as in everything in life when a decision has to be made, it is the alternative that gives the impetus, and I asked to meet him. He was brought to my office the next Saturday morning. No man looked less like a healer than the small, gap-toothed, wizened little fellow who beamed his way chirpily in, clutching an old and very dirty trilby hat. Experience over the years has made me chary of judging by first appearances, so I just let matters develop naturally.

The man, Yasin, was of the fourth generation of healers. He bade me strip and sit down. He next asked for a glass of water, most of which he threw away. He then placed it on a table, closed his eyes and started muttering incantations over it and occasionally blowing into it.

I strained my ears to catch what he was saying but all I heard was a vague nickety, nickety, blow, blow, hamla, hamla, hamla. Any esoteric meaning was lost on me and on the group of interested spectators. This performance con-tinued for a couple of minutes and I was then ordered to drink the water and place the glass upside down on the table. Obediently I did so.

Yasin then set about prodding, pinching and gently exploring my shoulder. I was rebuked for not having seen him on the day of my accident as I would have been cured within a week. 'Now,' I remember him continuing, 'only if the gods so wish and you have a clean heart will I be able to help you get better.' Even so, it was quite possible he could do nothing for me. It was a gloomy outlook. His parting shot was that he would come round to the mess that evening for my first spell of treatment.

Thus began an exercise in therapy as well as dichotomy: Yasin came to my room as often as he remembered and I went to hospital as often as I was ordered. Yasin's home brew had a distinctively rural smell and had to be prayed over not only at the beginning of the session along with the water, but also at the end when he washed his hands. Each time I rewarded him with a packet of cigarettes or a soft drink; he wanted no money. As for my arm, I had been taken to the threshold of intolerable pain each time and both Yasin and myself would end up sweating. In sharp contrast, my conventional treatment was barren of action or drama.

Some four weeks after my secret treatment had begun, the senior hospital doctor threatened me with an operation, medical opinion being that it were better I had limited, though unnatural, movement than be 'frozen' for life, as seemed the probable outcome. Yasin was most disturbed. This prognosis was, he felt, mistaken. Twice he had been proven right in his diagnosis by a subsequent X-ray after his magical fingertips had found out why some areas were stubbornly not reacting to treatment. Now, in his opinion, eventual recovery was at stake. If Western medicine was to be drastic, Eastern medicine had to act quickly to forestall any irrevocable consequence. 'I will transfer your pain to a chicken,' he announced, 'and, if you have faith and a clean heart, you will get better.'

The threat of my being medically down-graded hung more heavily on me than did the fate of any innocent fowl.

Next Saturday evening Yasin asked me to provide, by early the next morning, six S$10 and seven S$1 notes, fifteen one-cent pieces, a betel nut and lime, a nutmeg, a new handkerchief, a clean plate, a healthy chicken and five rust-free nails. I forbore to ask him if a partridge in a pear tree was also on the menu, if only because I did not know the Malay for either commodity.

When all was ready, the glass with its inch of water, the chicken tied to the leg of a chair, Yasin, the high priest, opened proceedings. Incantations were loud and blowing intense, and I felt that only a roll of drums was needed to add just that touch of panache to a scene that otherwise was starkly informal. The muttering rose to a crescendo. The normal ritual was enhanced by Yasin eating the betel nut, lime and nutmeg, placing the handkerchief over the glass and pocketing the money. I noticed that the five rust-proof nails were untouched and wondered what part they had to play. The chicken was unwound from the chair, prayed over, blown over, forced to draw its claw down my injured shoulder three times, waved around my head three times and, likewise thrice, spat on by me – as precisely instructed by Yasin.

The bird's beady eyes held a tinge of reproach and I felt somehow that events were overtaking it too quickly for its natural composure. However, it only remonstrated once and that when it was banished to the mess lawn.

This marked the climax of the treatment. Yasin lay back in a chair, sweating profusely, obviously spent, and I was left contemplating one chicken looking for worms, one recumbent son of the soil getting over his exertions and five rust-free nails on the plate.

Yasin left, telling me that he would not see me for another three days. He would take the chicken home and feed it properly, 'for,' he added with a touch of peasant concern, 'it would be wrong not to look after one of God's creatures.'

The next three days saw my shoulder as stubbornly immobile as ever: there was no sudden freedom of movement, no welcome release from the irksome restrictions imposed by the injury. Maybe my heart was not clean enough for the treatment to be successful. The threat of being down-graded, thus having to leave the Para Company, loomed menacingly nearer.

Wednesday evening saw Yasin burst into my room, face aglow. The spell had started working: the chicken had until that morning behaved as any normal self-respecting chicken should behave but suddenly, around midday, it had mysteriously developed a stiff right shoulder which had prevented normal movement and had caused it to stagger round and round in circles. Two hours later it gave up the struggle that had obviously and unfairly been unequal all along: my pain had been transferred to it and it had proved unbearable. (That was well under par for the course; for badly bruised ribs a chicken normally took fifteen days to die, whereas for a broken leg its life expectancy was eight months.) Four days later my arm started moving more freely with much less pain, and before very long all was as it had been before the accident.

Meanwhile I had been called down to Singapore to be medically boarded. The night before I went I was asked by Yasin not to mention any help I had been given. I was to let the doctor think official army treatment had worked, which I thought either very broad-minded of him or else remarkably prescient. At the medical interview I was put through a number of contortions. The specialist burst out laughing when he saw the effortless ease of it all: 'Excuse my French,' he said, 'but this is bloody wonderful.' He had not expected that I would ever be fully fit again.

I still do not know what Yasin does with his mounting total of rust-free nails – nor what the Army Commander really thought of my poor performance.

*   *   *

With Confrontation over, we settled down to peacetime activities. There was a battlefield tour up in Malacca conducted by the Australian Lieutenant Colonel Anderson who had won his Victoria Cross against the Japanese during the retreat down the peninsula in 1942. We were at the scene of his award-winning action, near a new road, and the Great Man was describing the way he had led a bayonet attack against the Japanese. He had led another in the First World War against the Germans in South-west Africa and was comparing the two. He asked the assembled audience which of the two – a silent or a noisy bayonet attack – appealed to them the more? An embarrassed silence followed, as none of us had been in such situations. I heard a car approaching along the road and turned to see it go by, flying the Japanese flag as the first Japanese ambassador to be accredited to Kuala Lumpur since 1945 sped past. It added poignancy to the moment.

Exercises were held in Brunei and in New Zealand. I did not go on the latter as I was on trek in Nepal. Some time after my return I received a letter from GHQ saying that I was to go to Sarawak, to help, in the capacity of interpreter in Iban, in the case of the late Marine Collins, of 42 Commando. Apparently Collins had lost his life on a trans-border operation but his mother, a plucky Yorkshire lady, had had dreams which convinced her that her son was not dead, but in Indonesia, wounded and lonely, as a prisoner.

She had written to the President of Indonesia, Sukarno, about her convictions and her intention of using her life savings to visit the area where her son had been lost. It was a brave but forlorn gesture.

Somehow all this had reached the ears of Harold Wilson, the Prime Minister, and he had directed that the army take this case on as a welfare duty. Mrs Collins was to fly out, first to Singapore where her son's unit was stationed, and then to Sarawak to talk to the headman of the village where Marine Collins had been based and from which he had departed on his ill-fated mission. I was to travel with the party and be the interpreter between the headman and Mrs Collins.

Were it to be just a journey back to Sarawak I would have jumped at it. However, it was not nearly as simple as that. The fact that cross-border operations had been undertaken was still sensitively guarded. Whoever had drafted Harold Wilson's reply had been vaguely anodyne. Mrs Collins had been told that her son had been killed on the border, on steep ground, on a narrow path in a face-to-face contact with the enemy, his body rolling down into the river and not being recovered.

The facts of the case, however, were different. Collins's company had crossed the border on a flat piece of territory, there had been no river, no face-to-face contact. I gathered that it was my job to stick to the official line of the letter, whatever the headman said. I quailed at that and at the thought of what the mission-educated, English-speaking children, listening under the floor of the longhouse, would shout up when they heard that my 'translation' was utterly erroneous.

I also knew that the headman was strongly anti-British Army. Another British unit based in that village had suspected him of collaborating with the Indonesians, telling them about troop movements. The Indonesians had been successful in ambushing the British company there and inflicting casualties. Blaming the headman for this, they lobbed hand grenades into his house one night, a move not best calculated to win friends or to influence people.

In any case, as I had not spoken any Iban since my Border Scout days, I did not consider myself up to the job, so rang GHQ to tell the coordinating colonel that I declined to go on that mission. I was icily informed that it was the Prime Minister's personal order to the army commander that the best Iban speaker in the command had to go and so my name was put forward. Moodily and expressing grave reservations, I said I would obey orders.

I revised my Iban until I went to Singapore where I met Miss Jessie de Lotz, chief Red Cross lady in the command, the RSM of 42 Commando and Mrs Collins herself. We four were flown over to Kuching on the morrow and helicoptered out to the border village the following day. I had had some luck in Kuching. I met my one-time staff officer of Border Scout days, John Bagley, whose Iban ability was streets ahead of mine and he agreed to go with us and help out with the sensitive part of the conversation.

So we arrived at the village. All was as I had remembered it, only three years before. We went to the house of the headman and I introduced Mrs Collins to him. I told him that she had come to find out what he knew about her son, whom she thought was still very much alive. A genuine sadness crept into his eyes and he shook his head as he replied that her son was undoubtedly dead. Mrs Collins saw this, sensed the atmosphere, understood that there was no hope and crumpled into tears. In desperation she sobbed that she now saw no point in continuing with her quest. Jessie tried to comfort her. I was greatly relieved that neither John Bagley nor I had had to deceive her and, tinged by an even greater sadness, went out to talk with my ex-Scouts until it was time to return to Kuching.

That evening we were entertained by the senior British diplomat, Don Dunford, whom I had known when in India, in 1/1 GR. I managed to crack some jokes which greatly amused Mrs Collins. As we said our farewells in Singapore she thanked me, not only for helping her out in her sadness but for making her laugh at the end. A great lady.

*   *   *

I was called down to Singapore to meet someone from London. I would be met and escorted to the meeting place. I was to wear plain clothes and on no account was I to be late. I was vastly intrigued by the unknown quantity and peremptory tone of the message, so I left Kluang in very good time. Alas, a freak storm and a flash flood delayed me, and I was late. I met my escort who took me to a second who took me to a third who took me to a building that had no handle on the closed door.

A bell, a look through a Judas window, an invitation to step in and go upstairs. There, with his back to the light so that I could not see his face properly, was a large man – a civilian – sitting behind the desk. He introduced me to a man who sat in front of the desk. He was from the Ministry of Defence.

I was upbraided for being late. I apologised. 'We're behind time. I will be brief,' he began abruptly and continued. 'All our operatives are either dead or incapacitated. The colonel has come from London to enlist your help as it seems you are the only one who fits the requirement.' I kept my eyes on his shadowy face and listened, fascinated.

'To start with it will be for six months. There is an even chance that you would come back alive but you're needed.' He paused and I asked him about the job. He was vague, training people somewhere. Did I get promotion? No.

I told him I would have to ask General Patterson before I gave him an answer, after which he would provide me with more details. The two offered me lunch before I returned. That was the Friday and I managed to meet the general on the Monday. He was as intrigued as I was. He showed no surprise about the chance of survival but was sad that there was no promotion and only six definite months. He expressed doubts that I would ever be promoted and thought I was better off with the Para Company during the next few months as it transpired that the change of UK government foreign policy not to have permanent military connections east of Suez after 1971 had brought about a reduction in the Brigade of Gurkhas. No parachute role was envisaged in Hong Kong or Brunei and, were paratroops ever needed, they would come from the Home Base.

'Even so I can't stop you from going away for six months but you could not come back to the Para Company where I want you.' He looked at me quizzically but I did not answer. He went on, 'So my advice to you is not to take it.'

'General,' I grinned happily at the man I had known for over twenty years, 'I think that is the best advice you have ever given anybody.'

I rang the number I had been told with my answer. 'I understand your point of view,' my London contact replied, 'but you have made my task almost impossible.' We said our farewells and rang off. Back in Kluang I was asked by my Gurkhas why I had to go to Singapore and Seremban. I could truthfully say that I never, in fact, did find out.

In the spring of 1968 I got a posting order to go to the Jungle Warfare School as chief instructor for one year, with the temporary rank of lieutenant colonel, a footnote adding that I had no hope of becoming substantive. When the men heard of my promotion they rejoiced: when I told them of the caveat of the rank they could not understand how it was that, even when the Gurkha Para Company was an acknowledged success, Higher Authority seemed set on treating me in such an abnormal manner.

I learned that I was lucky to have been given even that; it was only because no British battalion officer of the required calibre was available. Major General Patterson said that 'justice had been done' and 'they would have to be shamed into making you substantive'. He also told me that I was too eccentric to command a battalion in peacetime or, as another very senior officer had put it so kindly, 'John, the army is too small an institution to offer a man with your particular talents a career over the rank of major.'

The time came to leave. Farewells were sincere. They gave me a party, garlanded me with petals and said nice things. I was very moved. At times I had felt more like a father or an elder brother to them than a 'saheb' at the top. Parachuting and small patrols in sensitive territory are great levellers. In a letter home I wrote:

In the beginning I was determined to be as clinical and objective in my approach as I could; but three and a half years of near-war and peace, of fear and fun, of stress and strain, of work and games, all as one and winning little feathers for caps . . . is bound to leave a mark, to rub off in some way or other. In fact, if there was nothing to rub off then I would, I believe, have failed in my job.

On 2 August 1968 I issued a Special Order of the Day, written in simple English:

Today I end my time with you. From now on you are mine no more, nor am I in charge of you. For me this is a most sad day. For three and a half years, in near-war and in peace, in the lines, in the field, at work and at play we have all been as one, worked as one, with one mind and with one heart. I doubt if I will serve with as good men as you in the years that are left to me. It is I who led you but it has been your guts, your skill and your hard work that have made us what we are, known by all as good and in whom men can put their trust. They know that we will not let them down nor fail in our due task. By now we have earned a high and good name. Let it stand thus.

At the start of my time here with you I warned you that there were those (not of us) who had doubts, who said we could not do our task and who feared we would fail when we had to take our place in the field to fight. Sure, we had much to learn and it took a long time to win through. But in the end win we did and now we have proved our worth on the ground and in the air, so men doubt us no more.

All you who stay here must make sure that our good name is not lost. I know it is hard to keep up such a high state of work for a long time but try you must. I know you will not fail, but it just needs one weak man in the wrong place at the wrong time to spoil things for the rest of us all and bring our name low. There are a few who find that they can not keep up with the rest. These must go back whence they came, as it is from such men that faith is lost and trust broken. Fate we can not fight: but men we can mould to our will. At all times we must do all we can to make sure our name stands as high as can be, that our work is good and true, that we are fit for all tasks.

We know the past, but none knows what is to come, yet what man has done man can do. I leave you in good and firm hands. Stay true to your oath, stand firm by the salt that is yours while you serve: give of your best at all times and in all places. Fight well, fare well, live well and, in the end, when go you must, go in peace.

*   *   *

I would only be sixty odd miles down the road so all contact need not be broken. As I had a month before I took over my new job, I was asked by the police, without the Malaysian or British armies knowing about it, to go back to see Kerinching up in Perak. They still thought I could get information from him that he would give to no one else. So bad was the feeling between the police and their army that I had to keep my presence a secret. If the British Army were to hear that I had gone into the operational area of another government without clearance, sparks would fly.

I was picked up by a police boat at exactly the same place on the Sungei Perak at Grik where it had all begun so many years before. It was almost unreal and I felt it acutely as, this time, I was returning, not starting out. Now I knew what to expect, understood what it was all about. I was still thrilled by the skill of the boatman as he steered his way up the rapids, happy to count over a hundred hornbills and to see the large monitor lizards sunning themselves on the sandy slopes. Next morning I walked half an hour to the dwelling where I was told I would find Kerinching. There he was, with five others. All showed the greatest joy at my unexpected appearance. I remembered the names of four of them. 'I knew you would come back one day,' said an ageing Kerinching. 'You are the only one who ever cared for us. You make your mouth look like a chicken's backside, but you have a kind heart.' He smiled the old smile and the others nodded their agreement.

Senagit had died a couple of years before, probably of tuberculosis. The rest of my gang were still alive. I was visited by Sutel and Rijed, both looking utterly savage, dressed only in a loin cloth, a proud almost disdainful look in their eyes. Sutel carried shotgun and cartridge belt. We were soon laughing as we talked of old times. They left after it was dark, their way lit by fire brands of split bamboo.

The information I brought back was of the greatest use to the police. What was also very rewarding was that, despite the hardships and setbacks, all my recommendations as how best to use the Temiar against the rump of the communist guerrillas had since been implemented, so that the area was now the quietest in all the 'hard' areas.

Some time after that, the Malaysian government flooded much of the area to make a new hydroelectric scheme; so that particular problem was solved for ever.

In my neck of the woods, however, there was yet another chapter to be written. Back in Kluang to collect my kit, I could not slip away the day I left for the Jungle Warfare School as the soldiers were lined in two ranks facing each other, some with garlands and others with petals to give me. I shook hands with them all in turn, receiving little squeezes of farewell from the inarticulates who found it hard to talk under such circumstances. I was nearly in tears but, albeit brittle, there was laughter as well. I thanked them for what they had done, in simple and sincere language and, as I climbed into my vehicle, they gave me three cheers.

So ended a wonderfully happy chapter in my life. I felt enriched by their loyalty and love, for, after twenty-four years with such men, there was a deep empathy between us. I felt very proud as I drove away down to my next job, the farewell garlands heavy on my neck, aware that I had just finished the best posting the British Army, wittingly or otherwise, could ever have given me. Life would never be quite the same again.

CHAPTER 20

Jungle Warfare School

The Jungle Warfare School (JWS) was then located sixteen miles up the coast road from Johore Bahru – where the causeway from Singapore Island joins the mainland – near the village of Kota Tinggi. There were two camps on two hills, with a superb range complex hard by and jungle, rubber plantations, mangrove swamps and rivers within easy striking distance. In one camp was the school itself. The other was empty until a battalion, out from England for jungle training, occupied it. Although I had visited JWS before, I had never been on a course there nor been on the staff.

The commandant was a Colonel Mike Dauncey, a charming man with much European experience, who had spent two nights in the jungle when his battalion was based in Singapore. I had a week to take over from the outgoing chief instructor, Derek Organ, who remarked how lucky it was that he had a name like that when he was in charge of a one-man band. A brilliant instructor, an ebullient man who never 'flapped' and always kept a bubbling sense of humour, he was a difficult man to follow and my British detractors felt that, as so many of the students and staff were British soldiers, my life with Gurkhas would make this task even harder, if not impossible. I knew that only by being myself would I ever have any hope of making a success of my new job.

The school had been a Battle School and Reinforcement Unit in Burma during the Second World War. After 1948 it adapted its teaching to cope with Communist Revolutionary Warfare, with lessons from Vietnam and Borneo included, if relevant. It taught individuals how to become instructors in basic techniques in their own units and, apart from British troops, seventeen other countries had also sent students, chiefly from South Vietnam and Thailand. All five continents had been represented at one time or another.

In brief, soldiers were taught the basic techniques of living, moving and fighting in jungle against an enemy at the Active Phase of CRW, in terrain and a climate that affected almost every aspect of normal operations. Apart from conventional phases of war modified for the jungle, much emphasis was placed on navigation, tracking, patrolling, ambush, survival (whether when being hunted or merely lost), flotation and watermanship, morale, health and hazards.

The school was divided into 'wings', the two main ones being allocated to jungle warfare, one of them reserved exclusively for the Vietnamese and Thais (known as STAP – Services Training Assistance Programme), and tracking, with or without dogs. Courses for the Vietnamese were an open secret in that the United Kingdom's official policy towards South Vietnam was one of non-intervention. This fiction had to be maintained even when politicians and senior officers visited us. Other wings were for small arms, trails and development, and signals. There was also a separate War Dog Training School in our grounds which we later took on as 'dog wing', and a helicopter troop. The school operated on the proverbial 'shoestring' and we were inundated by visitors from many countries and of many persuasions.

My initial impressions were unhappy: the whole place had an unprofessional atmosphere. I tried not to make comparisons with the unit I had so recently left and to make allowances for the staff being so mixed. The instructors were from Britain, Australia and New Zealand. A company of Gurkhas acted both as demonstration troops and 'exercise enemy'; I was delighted to learn that the Gurkha Para Company would be taking over in March 1970. Senior military administrative staff were British, and storemen, drivers and the like were, in the main, Malays, with a sprinkling of Chinese and southern Indian soldiers, with civilians of all three races. The Malays especially welcomed being spoken to in Malay but the Chinese were non-Cantonese speakers, while the southern Indians' language, Tamil, was beyond me.

I felt the place needed shaking up but I would be foolish to do anything for at least six months, by which time I would have a thorough knowledge of all the personalities involved, instruction, syllabuses, exercises, demonstrations and training aids. Changing an army school was slow work. Anything else I could ignore until June 1969, when I was also to be made the down-graded com-mandant. I had a letter from the army pensions office to tell me that the 311 days of paid rank I held when commandant of the Border Scouts did not count for pension purposes – an edict later rescinded when I reacted disbelievingly at this piece of military mindlessness – nor was there hope of substantive promotion.

I learned that there was to be a course solely for Thais the following May and I determined to give the opening address in Thai. While in the Gurkha Para Company I had started to learn that language as we had a role in the South East Asia Treaty Organisation (SEATO). Now I found I had both the time and the means to immerse myself in it, and planned to take an oral examination as soon as I could. I wanted to be able to read and write it and, as it is a most com-plicated script, with consonants both 'toned' and silent, I devised a system of colours so that I could read the script like music. Later I extended the system, using the same colour code format, into three other tonal languages – Can-tonese, Vietnamese and, eventually, Lao. My memory cards were of different colours, so I could think clearly in different languages yet not muddle up the tones when I had to use more than one at any one time.

The first strange days turned into weeks and I found myself accepting and being accepted. I had not realised how hard it would be to lecture in my own language to British soldiers and was delighted to be told that the style, format and content of my first attempt, on morale, was well thought of, even if the older sergeants found my theme of 'faith as a weapon' novel. Meanwhile I continued parachute descents with the Gurkha Para Company whose men still did not believe I had really left them.

There was a Filipino on one course who found that he was persona non grata when the Malaysian and Filipino governments broke off diplomatic relations. He should have left the country but we kept him on. He asked me to send a telegram to his wife to say that all was well. This I did by telephoning my old friend Alastair Rose in Singapore and asking him to do this for me – a Malaysian post office would have refused, and I never thought of sending the British attaché a signal. I heard a sharp intake of breath when I said: 'To Doris Romero' and gave a Manila address. He knew that I had staged there the previous April but I had not hinted at any hanky-panky! The text read: 'All well. Send my mail to [a Singapore address]', and I signed off, as I had been asked to, 'Daddy'. Alastair could not contain his mirth but never pressed me for an explanation.

In October we had a glimpse into the future when James Boyden MP, Parliamentary Under Secretary of State to the Ministry of Defence (Army), Mr Healey's number two, visited us. He was escorted by the Army Commander, Lieutenant General Sir Tom Pearson, who was present that time I hurt my shoulder jumping. We briefed them, showed them jungle survival, an attack on a fortified village and the war dogs. On his way back to his helicopter to leave, Boyden said to me that he now knew we were a good school and hoped he could influence his party to make the decision to go multi-national after 1971. 'I know,' he said, 'you soldiers do not like the decisions we make, but you are always very polite.'

From then on, for over two years, the Malaysian and British governments were locked in talks about the establishment of a five-power Commonwealth Jungle Warfare Centre (CJWC) after the British pulled out of Malaysia, within the Anglo-Malay Defence Treaty, and to involve Singapore, Australia and New Zealand. I was to have been the senior British army representative, as Chief Instructor/Second-In-Command. The wasted man-hours spent in trying to find agreement, the extra work put in to try to implement directives, the time-consuming shilly-shallying of the Malay hierarchy, both military and civilians, the acrimony engendered by prevarication, the heavy-handedness of some of the British representatives, the level of personalities involved – prime ministers, foreign ministers, high commissioners, secretary to the cabinet, chief of the army staff and all stations south – were worthy of a better cause. It was lucky that none of us knew at that time how it would all turn out, how much we would have to plan and replan when we could have been undertaking tasks of a more fruitful nature.

Defence Minister Healey had allowed us an arbitrary number of a hundred men of the British army to be used for the CJWC. A training colonel who visited me said he wanted to have British troops as a demonstration company. I remonstrated and said the Gurkhas were more suitable. Angrily he turned on me to ask me why I did not favour troops from my own country. I told him that the British troops training would most probably be out in the east only once in their service, and that 'red hair and freckles hiding behind a paddy bund' would not add any reality to the scene whereas slant eyes and brown faces would. 'You are a perfectionist,' he coldly and pointedly remarked. I replied that that was why I had been sent to the JWS.

I had a pretty compliment paid to me by the Vietnamese who said I was 'a senior officer in one thousand, in many thousands', because I 'ran in the morning, exercised in the evening and did not live with the girl friend mistress'. One can learn a lot by inference. Indeed the facilities for games at the JWS were extensive; football, squash, basketball and swimming. The same Vietnamese were around when we had another important visitor, John Morris MP, Minister of Defence for Equipment. As we showed him weapon developments, new radios, war dogs and soldiers on training he had to be pacified at our obviously circuitous itinerary, but I was not allowed to let on that there were Vietnamese exercising in that area as even a man as highly placed as he was not allowed to have knowledge of this. By the time we had finished a presentation on aids to night fighting, he reckoned that JWS was worth keeping on after pull-out in 1971 to train British soldiers.

As 1968 limped to a close, I had to give a demonstration of current weapons, developments, signals and radio equipment and seismic devices to the new commander of 99 Brigade, a Brigadier Heelis. He even shook my hand, evidently realising that Peaceful Coexistence was the name of the game. At Christmas I got a card from Mrs Dolly Romero thanking me for being kind to her husband, and from one of the Thai students, wishing me luck in my language studies.

*   *   *

I visited Thailand, with the assistance of the United States Army Special Forces, the 'Green Berets'. I was met at the airport by my sponsor, Captain Peter Crummy, at the airport, a veteran of Vietnam and a hero. We soon established a conversational breakthrough, I speaking slowly and distinctly enough to be a relief for him and his accent modest enough to be easily followed by me.

That first afternoon we were interviewed by an all-civilian research team, comprising three Americans, a Greek, a Frenchman and a Thai. Their mission was to write a thesis on how to conduct counter-insurgency in Thailand. High-powered men with high salaries and many educational qualifications, their words would carry great weight in the councils of those policy makers who influenced our lives, yet none had ever been into the jungle, done any fighting nor heard any shots in anger. I was asked a number of questions and what were considered as 'significant factors' were noted down. I should have asked them if they remembered what Mao Tse-tung had written about communist terrorists in Thailand: don't curse them, they have thick skins; don't fight them because when you move in they move out; don't kill them, they become heroes; improve the lot of the people.

On the morrow we first went to Special Forces HQ at Lopburi, where I was briefed on their assistance to the Royal Thai Army before watching training. I felt an air of tension. The colonel in charge seemed to take no decisions but left them all to the executive officer in a manner that seemed to reverse their ranks. It transpired that the former had, until very recently, been the sergeant-major in that very same unit but, being on the reserve of officers, had had his reserve promotion sanctioned, been made a lieutenant colonel and put in command of the same unit. Not the best recipe for smooth relations.

Everything was more flamboyant than our more modest British approach. I have never been convinced that trying to make a soldier spew three times before breakfast is the best way of training him, but I was diplomatic in my comments.

Next day we flew 400 miles to an air base used for operations against North Vietnam, an active service zone, and visited a Thai army HQ of one of the six areas where troops were engaged in operations against an enemy. The US were only involved in training missions, trying hard not to be sucked into any conflict, although many in command must have been tempted otherwise.

On our third day I was taken to a training camp where the Royal Thai Air Force was being trained in base protection and patrolling up to ten miles. The US army captain showing around had served in Israel, East Africa and Indo-China. He had lived a year with the Lao guerrillas and he showed me a typical Lao house: very like those of the Temiar. One thing stuck out like a sore thumb and, in the most tactful way possible, I told him. There was a wooden platform bed and a rough stool and table made out of local materials. I pointed out that if the guerrillas were to look into the hut they would probably booby-trap it as, first, the natives themselves never use tables and stools and, second, their size suggested use by an above-average height of person, hence probably American.

On my last full day I was driven to the training camp where Thai army reinforcements for Vietnam were trained. Finally I was debriefed by the Joint US Military Aid Group (JUSMAG) and met the Defence Attaché, Colonel Peter Body. Apart from the military side of it all being intensely interesting, it was good practice for my examination, which I managed to pass when I took it shortly afterwards.

*　　*　　*

Back at the JWS I started to introduce some of the changes I had envisaged.

Already a much 'sharper' approach was being made by all the wings. We ran courses for the South Korean army and the Nepalese police to track with dog teams, as well as for British troops in general tactics, as there were not enough vacancies in Warminster. Visitors included the Chief of the General Staff, General Sir Geoffrey Baker, and the Army Commander, Lieutenant General Sir Peter Hunt. Journalists Tom Pocock and Peter Chambers were also of good value and the *Evening Standard* published a glowing account saying that the JWS was the only unit in the Far East doing a worthwhile job. We passed the time of day with Dutch, French and Japanese television crews. I briefed the new Commander-in-Chief, a naval man. It was let known that a brigade of troops from Australia, New Zealand and United Kingdom, called ANZUK, was to be formed in Singapore towards the end of 1971; I gave a talk on my Temiar experiences to an interested group of Royal Air Force Regiment men; lectured men from my old company of 1/7 GR down from Hong Kong on ambushing, patrolling and tracking; entertained twenty-six of my staff to a meal and found it very expensive at S$40; and threw away my shaving brush that I had had since 1941.

I gave my opening address in Thai. I had practised this with my teacher, a Chinese born in Bangkok, down in Singapore, and had written it out with my five colours so that I could ensure the correct tones. My teacher suggested that I add a phrase at the end which would show if they had understood what I had said and bring a note of informality, if not of levity, to the proceedings. Initially I demurred but added it to my script.

My students assembled in our central lecture hall, one of the better buildings on the site. I was dressed in ceremonial fig. I began my talk, bringing in the odd Thai proverb, and told them what was expected of them. I glanced up from time to time. Not a flicker of interest, not a spark of a smile, not even a bored shifting greeted my efforts. At the end I decided casually to throw in my teacher's phrase. 'Oh, there is one more thing. The girls in Singapore are old and expensive.' Howls of mirth and much leg slapping of anticipation, or perhaps agreement, greeted this unmilitary sally but it did show that they had understood my meaning. My superficial knowledge of Thai enabled me to listen in and correct some mistakes of interpretation during the course. In one lecture on code of conduct when a prisoner-of-war, the phrase 'There will be a restriction of mail' was rendered as 'You will not be allowed to have any women', and 'mortar base plate' was misheard as 'motor car' and translated as 'garage'. On both occasions I managed to retrieve the situation during the break but shuddered to think of what went on at lectures I did not attend.

After that course was over and the closing address out of the way, I settled down to learn Vietnamese.

*   *   *

One of our duties was to take our STAP course students away for a beach picnic, paid for by Foreign Office funds. Half-way through a course we would go to a beach on the east coast, called Jason's Bay, where swimming and games, with a curry meal and drinks, helped us to pass the time.

On Saturday, 12 May 1969, I was sitting with a group of British wives on this same beach and one of them asked me if I thought there would be trouble in Malaya, by which name we all still referred to peninsular Malaysia. Indeed I did, and told them of tensions I had felt for quite some time. They scoffed at my answer and asked me when, if I knew so much, all this would happen. 'It could start tomorrow' – and it did. There was serious trouble in a number of places as Malays attacked Chinese. British Army Austers were unobtrusively sent to keep a check on events and to give warning if the base in Singapore seemed threatened by Federation Armed Forces driving down the main road. For the first time since I had left the 'Bamboo' area in 1963, six years before, guerrillas had come down from Yala province in Thailand to contact the Temiar.

Around this time plans were initiated for a large-scale five-nation exercise, 'Unity', but better known by its Malay name, Bersatu Padu, that was due to take place in 1970. This was to show how British troops, along with the other four nations, could come to the aid of Malaysia if it was attacked by a foreign power and was unable to look after itself. Much controversy was engendered by acclimatisation problems for the United Kingdom contingent. The argument raged between those who said six weeks was the minimum time required and those who thought otherwise. JWS would only be involved during the six-week training period before the exercise proper started.

The climax of the exercise came a year later, when troops of the host nation found themselves 10,000 yards away from their forming-up point minutes before the final assault was due. Not only that, they had climbed such a steep mountain that most of their tailored trousers had split. Not a pretty sight for the television cameras waiting expectantly with the 'enemy'! The exercise was halted while the Gurkha enemy were helicoptered forward to within striking distance – 'being struck' distance – of the attackers, and an airdrop of more than a hundred pairs of untailored trousers was arranged.

In June 1969 I took over as commandant when much of my time was to be taken up, if not exactly wasted, first with the CJWC project and, when that fell through, planning for a new JWS. That in turn foundered shortly before I finished in December 1971. Within the JWS itself, I could now turn my attention to all those points I felt had been neglected till then.

Major Jon Edwardes, commanding STAP wing, and I were invited to South Vietnam as guests of their army, ARVN. Senior officers and training establishment commanders were all listed: our brief from Saigon had also mentioned presentations, very important in any army modelled on the US forces – anything but plaques. The bayonet badge of the JWS on its green background was also considered too humdrum compared with the gorgeous gifts that protocol demanded the polite Vietnamese give their visitors, so we did not take any. Our main present was a painting, by the adjutant, Graham Buchanan-Dunlop.

By Day Five we had visited Central Training Command, given the commanding general the painting, and been taken around the Officers' and the NCOs' Training Schools, as well as a basic training unit for recruits. One day we flew to an island and watched US and ARVN special forces training for infiltration missions, using live ammunition. We had attended a joint US–ARVN day-long seminar on various aspects of operations, after which I spoke with American sergeants who had been on the JWS jungle warfare course before going on operations in Vietnam. I asked them what they thought of the training and, as I had not been at the school during their stay, that they were free to say what they liked.

After careful consideration, one said that he did not like the way we tied a knot in a rope around a tree as an aid to river crossing. I was delighted to tell him that that was one of the points I had changed. Everything else we taught was, so he opined, of life-saving importance and was valid.

By then we had finished our scheduled programme, dispensed with all our trophies and gathered a motley collection in our own right. Mid-morning that last day we were suddenly told that we were going to lunch with a unit not on our list. A disturbing thought struck me: would the British Army be found lacking in the 'plaque war'? I asked the liaison officer, Lieutenant Colonel Duc, if I should start worrying about how to react to any ceremony. He reassured me and I relaxed.

Half an hour later, just before we were due to sit down to our meal, Duc unobtrusively sidled over to me and whispered that I should start worrying. He then furtively put four small bayonet-embossed JWS brooches, of a type kept for when STAP students 'graduated', into my hand, instructing me to 'take them by surprise' and to give one each to the commanding officer, chief of staff and the staff officer, and the fourth to 'the American adviser'.

I caught Duc's eye just as the ARVN colonel was about to sit down to the meal and, as he nodded, I stentoriously bellowed 'Gentlemen!' I went on to say what a great honour it was to be with them . . . and as a mark of esteem I wished to present the graduation brooch of the Jungle Warfare School to the three officers. I fumbled a little with the pins and managed to fix the three brooches reasonably straight without impaling the victims.

Then I turned round to the American adviser. He was a giant: plug-ugly and just under seven feet tall. I stood on tip-toe and attacked the pocket of his fatigue dress shirt. His name plate glared at me, eye-level, Colonel Angel Torres. No one had yet sat down and when eventually I had finished, he spoke out loud and clear, 'Colonel, I'm motivated.' We sat down to mutual applause.

Midday on the morrow we made ready to leave. My room overlooked the small forecourt in front of the compound. I heard semi-martial noises and was intrigued when I saw American soldiers lined up in two ranks of three men each, with a subordinate officer in the act of saluting Angel Torres as though he were handing over the parade. I withdrew: nothing to do with me. I left my room soon after, carrying my overnight bag. The parade was still there standing at ease, with Angel Torres now facing his front. As I was espied, he called out to me to go and join him. On my approach he turned about and brought the group of seven to attention. I was nonplussed but, always hoping to please, went and stood beside him.

The American, taller and of even more imposing presence when measured against me alone, again made a complete turn and faced his front. He raised his hand in salute and announced, in a loud and commanding voice: 'Colonel, the -th Advisory Group. I hand them over to you. They're yours.' My hand immediately came up in answering salute, but, apart from that, the situation was temporarily beyond me.

We were standing side by side, I facing one way, he the other. I felt that Gilbert and Sullivan would have welcomed the chance of some free copy. With what appeared to me as lightning inspiration, I redressed the balance of power as best I could.

'Colonel,' I intoned, 'I hand them back. They're now yours again.'

I heard an audible sigh of relief some eighteen inches above my head, a scuffle of boots and Angel Torres swung around so that we faced the same direction once more, the long and the short of it. Then, turning to me, he gave me that which he had been clasping in his left hand the while, a brand-new, still tacky plaque of the -th American Advisory Group.

I accepted it, not knowing what best to say, but, as Angel Torres dismissed his parade, a happy thought struck me.

'Colonel, thanks,' I said. 'I'm motivated.'

It was a relief to get back to Malaysia, with both Jon and myself congratulating ourselves on having won the 'plaque war' on points.

Later that year I visited Australia and had a good look at their Jungle Training Centre, a much more lavish set-up than ours and one that concentrated on the conventional side of Vietnam operations out of jungle (despite its name) just as much as it did on jungle warfare. I listened to a series of lectures on CRW from another approach, which was stimulating. I met people on the staff at Canberra, where noises were made to see if I could serve in some capacity after pension, visited a unit that taught Vietnamese at soldier level and ran courses in interrogation techniques in Adelaide, and had a non-jungle-warfare day in Sydney meeting old friends, where I was guest of honour at a luncheon at the local military HQ in the heart of the local wine-growing area. I was offered red or white wine and when I said I was a non-wine drinker I was told to 'get your own drink of milk' and ignored in a pointedly rude fashion during the meal. Another guest, a Citizens' Military Force major, was sales manager at a local winery. A number of us were taken round the wine-processing place and at the end drinks were offered and I was once again ignored. When alone with the sales manager, with no one in earshot, he put his drink-raddled face close to mine and said, in a quiet voice, how much he envied my non-drinking habits and he wished he had the guts to do the same – 'but I daren't.'

Before I left, all those who had ignored me at lunch sidled up individually and softly told me that they admired the way I did not drink and wished they had the courage to do likewise.

Before the end of the year I had also been across to Brunei, to lecture the RBMR on jungle techniques. The knowledge gained from those visits, added to my own experiences over the years and what I now knew the JWS could pack into its syllabuses, set me thinking as to whether we knew enough about our Asian allies and enemies to ensure our approach to them was correct; and if not, how to modify that approach. 'Aspects of Asia' was a subject that also interested me in its own right.

*　　*　　*

During the first six months of 1970 we were busy helping to train troops sent out from England for Exercise Bersatu Padu. We also had sixty-nine members of the press who had to be briefed. Most of them were sceptical about Harold Wilson's promise of reinforcing Malaysia; many of them doubted our ability to manage the training requirements and all were prepared for the worst. For-tunately our presentation of 'the threat' was so slick and effective that most were converted that first morning. The *Yorkshire Post* man said it was the best he had seen in his thirty years as a journalist. During question time I was asked whether I thought Mr Wilson would honour his reinforcement promise. Whatever my private opinions about Mr Wilson or his political probity, that particular forum was not the place to divulge them.

A change of government in Britain did not alter our future, merely changed the personalities at the very top. Neither the Labour people nor the Tories ever properly grasped how the Malaysians 'played' with us in their negotiations. We on the ground found that the very threat of our closure brought us more applications for courses than before. The Gurkha Para Company had joined us in March; I managed to pass my Vietnamese exam in July. By September we were told that the future of CJWC would only be decided at the Common-wealth Prime Ministers' conference, to be held in Singapore at the end of January 1971. This did not leave much time for planning as JWS was due to finish on 31 March. On 21 September 1970 a new prime minister took over in Kuala Lumpur, Tun Abdul Razak.

Meanwhile the run-down continued unabated. British and Gurkha batta-lions moved out and local units had to prepare redundancy lists, affecting soldiers and civilians alike, based on the principle of 'first in last out'. We in JWS were the only people with any possible future in Malaysia after the magic date of 31 December 1971, so we had to be kept up to strength. Naturally everybody wanted to know his personal future as so much depended on it: schooling for children, looking for other jobs, selling the car and even moving house. Although I tried not to let it worry me, I was also concerned as to my own future. 31 December 1971 existed in my mind: 1 January 1972 did not.

I was allowed to bring my military staff up to date about the situation, but not my civilians. The reasoning seemed to be that, as the decision to postpone or cancel CJWC was a political one to be made by Kuala Lumpur, the British could not risk allowing the Malaysian government to capitalise on any public announcement that might hint at an impending change. None of our senior Chinese or Indian civilians wanted to work for Malaysia as not only would the pay be less but also they felt they would be doubly discriminated against – for having worked for the British and not being 'sons of the soil' – Malays.

By late October we had the long-awaited answer from Kuala Lumpur; there would be 'no CJWC ever and no JWS after 31 December 1971'. That meant that all the planning done since June 1969 was totally wasted. It also meant that, until the Prime Minister's Conference three months ahead, no planning for JWS from 1 April 1971 to the end of the year could be done with enough certainty to invite students, let alone take on staff and order stores. Many people were bitter and disgusted at being at the mercy of Malaysian prevarication. Foreign Secretary Lord Carrington agreed with Tun Razak's points but asked him, in the politest possible way, what the devil he did want. As the rest of the army could not be told about this abrupt cancellation of all our plans, we continued to get mountains of stores from home for the British element of the new unit that was now never to be formed.

We received a parliamentary visit. So old and fragile were some of the members of both houses that I was told not to use 'bulleted blank' in our presentation of the 'threat' as the noise reverberated loudly and it was not up to us to cause needless bye-elections. We gave the group lunch in the officers' mess and one of the noble lords asked why 'the lads' were not with us. We told him that 'the lads' had their own arrangements but he was not satisfied. I changed the conversation and asked him if he, too, had been in any of the services. Yes, he had been a submariner during the First World War but had missed a German boat when he had fired a torpedo at it. That had been the end of his naval interest because 'the boogers coot ma gradins', as he reminisced with melancholy, calling over an astonished Malay mess waiter to put a piece of meat back on the platter from his plate as it was too much for him.

Another submariner who visited us was an American admiral. He came under the esoteric rubric of CINCPAC and he had an Australian POLAD with him. Translated, that meant he was Commander-in-Chief of the Pacific and that all those in Vietnam were subsumed under his command. POLAD meant a political adviser. I took him to a lecture where I introduced him to the staff – a major of Gurkhas about to introduce an Australian major of gunnery – and to the students. These not only came from all five continents with America being represented by Guyana and Africa by Ghana, but also included representatives from the Royal Marines, Royal Air Force Regiment and Gurkhas from the Singapore Police.

The admiral was clearly dazed by this variety. He turned to me and asked, in a loud aside, whether there were no submariners here? I turned to him, and in a theatrical whisper said, 'Admiral, the fin-est sub-mariner in the U-nited States navy is standing right here beside me.'

A short pause, then, 'God damn it, son, you win.'

Another group of distinguished visitors included Professor Michael Howard, a man of great gallantry, charm and erudition. Part of a letter he wrote fourteen years later read:

I remember the day that I spent with you as one of the most interesting in my life. And I recall the deep sense of historical tragedy that I felt when I reflected that I was observing the last traces of centuries of dedicated service by Englishmen (and Scots!) at the other end of the earth, where they had brought, whatever Marxists may say, nothing but good. I wondered what on earth people like you would do with your lives after it was all over, and whether we would ever breed people like you again, and how sad it would be if we did not. I cannot tell you how much I respect people such as yourself and all that you have done for the world in so utterly inconspicuous, and dedicated a way...

I wrote back and told him that was one of the nicest letters I had ever received.

*   *   *

By the time for our STAP party in December, the news from Saigon was doom-laden. None of the Vietnamese students had any of their customary spark; morale was rock-bottom. At Jason's Bay men gathered in desultory groups, taking no interest in the programme of events prepared for them. I took my tape recorder and some taped Vietnamese songs. I also brought two songs I had written out on small cards and had, privately, practised. After lunch I sat down with the guiding officers and started playing a song. Some of the students gathered round. After a couple more I switched off the machine and, as I had expected, was asked by one of the interpreters, who knew I had one song, to sing it.

Squatting cross-legged on the ground, I took off my jungle hat in which I had hidden my cards, placed it nonchalantly in front of me, the cards shielded from my audience, and embarked on a very sad war refrain, a lament for loved ones lost, and, not that I knew it at the time, banned in Saigon. By then all the students had gathered around and were joining in and I sensed an uplift in the spirits of them all, rather wonderful and unexpected. Came the time to say goodbye, they all sang a personal thankyou. A golden moment that made worthwhile all those silent hours spent in study. And was it coincidence that that course turned out to be the best in all the years I was there?

So my approach had been correct. In my lecture on 'Aspects of Asia' I had quoted two cases of approach that, albeit correct, were inappropriate. One, most curiously, was written in a Thai military vocabulary, jumping out of the page as it was the only piece written in Roman script. When a diplomat says yes, he means perhaps; when he says perhaps, he means no; and when he says no, he is no diplomat. When a lady says no, she means perhaps; when she says perhaps, she means yes; and when she says yes, she is no lady.

The other was a true story of an incident that took place in the dining hall of the transit camp in Cairo during the Second World War. A haughty subaltern was doing the rounds and came across a soldier who had not eaten his meal. When asked why not, the soldier replied that not even a dog would eat it. It so chanced that the officer had his dog with him and, taking the plate with the uneaten food on it from the table, put it on the floor. The dog gulped it up. The subaltern turned to the soldier, telling him he was wrong as the dog had eaten it, so the food had been unnecessarily wasted. Unfortunately, the officer did not see that his dog had been overcome by an itch, just under the base of its tail and was busy nibbling at it with his teeth. Yes indeed, the soldier agreed, the dog had eaten it but 'look what it has to do to take the taste out of its mouth, sir.'

'Approach, gentlemen, approach is all.'

I went on to say that any generalisations on such a vast subject had inherent dangers but, set against twenty-five years of CRW, and with Saki's maxim of 'a little inaccuracy saving a wealth of detailed explanation', I would examine Mao's thoughts on protracted guerrilla warfare, modified by his experiences gained in Korea. Western armies were established for conventional operations of holding territory, hence having to 'find' such units as Civil Action Teams, Rural Reconstruction Teams and Psychological Warfare Teams for Vietnam.

We knew that the seminal thought behind Mao's philosophy was that bases and main force units should be in terrain normally inaccessible, politically or geographically, to his enemies and that ground was not to be held until the communists were politically strong enough not to be dislodged. So it was that people, and the approach to be adopted towards them, leading to the 'hearts and minds', were vital considerations.

One example I gave of language and communication was the story of the Dutchman looking lost in the milling throng of passengers just off the boat train at Victoria station. A zealous Salvation Army captain, sensing a convert, went up to him and asked him if he 'loved our Jesus', at which the Dutchman turned to him and said that indeed he did but he preferred 'the big, red, round Dutch cheeses much better'.

Then there was the English colonial police officer who when invoking a Hainanese not to break the law, addressed him in fluent Cantonese. The man desisted and the police officer snapped at his English junior that, really, he had to learn the language to get these people to obey. After he had gone, the younger man turned to the Chinese and asked him what the elder had said to make him change his mind. He had not understood a word but 'the other man was obviously so angry' that it seemed wiser to obey the law!

I tried to explain how it was that one day it was possible to understand a Chinese educated in Britain but not the next day. It depended whether his thoughts were in Chinese when he spoke English or in English when he spoke Chinese. I mentioned how hard the Chinese found it to send Morse, to whisper, to sing in tune and to do crossword puzzles in their tonal languages. And what made Malays say on one day, 'Life and death on the border' and on the next 'All quiet on the border' when the situation had not altered? Their language was as difficult to parse as it was to put one's thumb on quicksilver or as unpredictable as looking at colours in a kaleidoscope. No wonder so much of what we heard either did not make sense or could not be taken at face value.

I tried to define some of the fundamental differences between Asia and Europe that brought their own military problems: the Asian versus the European mentality; unorthodoxy versus orthodoxy; a guerrilla army integrated with the civilian population versus an army on a conventional war establishment operating unconventionally as best it could. Fighting with a conventionally based army was even harder when there was no front line, no fixed channel of communication, no confirmed direction of enemy approach, no set numbers. The enemy had infinite patience, moved more quickly and efficiently at night, possessed better camouflage, ate and slept less, was more ruthless and zealously determined; and he was numbered in millions.

Both the enemy and we British troops were products of our time, and we were called upon to react to such conditions. Yet the enemy was not 'six foot tall', and I saw the main requirements for all soldiers, after the obvious ones of being well trained and physically fit, as intelligence, integrity and self-discipline; motivation and high morale; constructive and personal leadership; and ingenuity when tackling a problem. I never hinted to my audience that I was asking too much of them. I finished by asking whether we defeat ourselves by not realising our weaknesses, weaken ourselves by not knowing our strengths or were we eroding our standards, so eroding trust? Were we living on borrowed time?

*   *   *

As 1970 ended, we were most certainly living on borrowed time. I had never known so much turbulence generated around such apparent triviality but which mirrored so accurately the difficulty of current international relations. As Jon Edwardes put it, 'At least we survived.' I had done three years as a paid lieutenant colonel so I had earned the pension of the rank but had no idea as to my future. I was getting tired.

On Christmas Eve we were officially told that JWS could stay until the end of 1971, an answer we had requested by 1 June or at the very latest 15 July. Even then it was only a military decision; the political confirmation of this edict was still awaited. Only now could we invite students from Bangkok and Saigon, only now could we go firm with our British nominations, only now could we start properly to plan how to close the place down on time. We still hoped to have a share of vacancies on jungle courses the Malaysians planned to run. Brunei had been mentioned as a possibility for establishing another JWS type of training centre, but that too blew hot and cold. The GHQ staff also had to plan the appallingly complicated make-up of the ANZUK brigade to be based in Singapore.

We were reminded of human problems when the mother of a serviceman living in Johore Bahru died very shortly after she arrived from England to spend Christmas with her son and his family. Her body could not be taken over the causeway to the hospital in Singapore until a Meat Import Licence was produced to the authorities.

In early January 1971 Lord Carrington sent his very high-powered and sharp right-hand man, together with HE the High Commissioner to Singapore and the Deputy High Commissioner to Malaysia, on a visit to see what the JWS was all about. They were very pleased with all we told them and showed them. I was rung up by Colonel John Fielding, my staff boss, within two hours of their departure to be informed that they were highly delighted, that the visit had given them exactly what they had wanted, and that a number of illusions had been corrected. 'I will tell the Chief of Staff all about it, but I thought you'd be pleased to hear about it first', which was correct.

Soon after that I was one of many invited down to Singapore to meet Mr Edward Heath, the British Prime Minister, and the Foreign Secretary, Sir Alec Douglas-Home. The former was late, having had a row with other prime ministers about his intention of sending military supplies to South Africa. A New Zealand brigadier said, 'We were beginning to wonder if they were going to let you out', at which Mr Heath raised his eyes to the heavens and said that Lee Kwan Yew had wanted to keep them until midnight – on one occasion they had talked till 4 am. Jungle Warfare School meant nothing to either man.

I was called over by a Mr Hibbert, Political Adviser to the Commander-in-Chief, and was introduced to Sir Burke Trend, the secretary to the cabinet, who was very interested in JWS and asked me if the 1972 version, the Malaysian

Army Jungle Warfare Centre, would work out. I said that if the small print satisfied the demands of both sides, especially in the euphoria recently engendered, there was a good chance of success. But when he enquired whether I was happy with the small·print, my answer was a negative one and I gave reasons. He paused and remarked, 'We [the cabinet] were probably too weak . . . we shall have to be harder on them, if our terms are not met.' Later I told the Commander-in-Chief that nothing about our requests to share the Malaysian facilities would be decided until at least the following September. Although laughed out of court by everyone from that distinguished gentleman down several rungs of the ladder, I was proved correct.

The Vietnamese military attaché based in Kuala Lumpur visited me and we had a long talk in my office. I was frank with him about our programme difficulties and he bluntly told me that, whatever the Malays told the British to their faces about there being a British presence, none would eventuate. When visited soon after by the outgoing Chief of the Army Staff, General Sir Geoffrey Baker, I left him in no doubt as to the real situation and how very diffused and watered-down our standards would become if matters were allowed to jog on as already planned. His reactions to his visit and my briefing are best in his own words:

> Perhaps the most valuable part of my visit was the brief you gave in your office. The message which was put across to me was crystal clear, and will help me greatly to be able the better to cope with the future talks which will come up in London on this subject...

It was very nice of such a great man to have bothered to write.

*   *   *

At soldier level I still managed to get out into the jungle from time to time. I surprised one lot of British troops by appearing 'out of the blue' on the Saturday afternoon of a ten-day exercise. On a long patrol course, men of the Gurkha Para Company outshone any previous students in their ability to move through the jungle, make a reconnaissance of an 'enemy' camp, retire without any geophones picking up their movement and avoid capture.

We found that guerrillas involved in the upsurge of activity in the north of the country were actually using our training facilities. One weekend they activated our 'booby trap lane' and nearly blew a hole in a British sergeant's side. Indeed, walking back to the spot where students had spent a night in a fortified platoon base, I came across a pair of them sketching the layout. They ran away as soon as they saw me.

I went to England on a meeting and, while away, there was a diplomatic crisis of such severity I was almost called back. There had been a party for a STAP course in a private house in Johore Bahru and someone had stolen a bauble from the bedroom. An international incident blew up when all the Vietnamese students were ordered to have their kit searched and bitterly resented the implied slur. They called down their attaché who demanded that the officer who had ordered the search be suspended. Eventually the thief was identified as the Chinese wife of one of the British instructors, who had posted her spoil to herself in a Singapore post office. No Malaysian citizen was involved, yet the incident had spread to two countries and the nationals of two more.

The situation had been resolved by the time I returned but, as no civil action could be taken, the woman had to be disciplined under the Manual of Military Law, Part II, as a camp follower. On being ushered into my office she proceeded to sit on the edge of my table, simpering at me. Mr Tuggey, the RSM, and the lady's husband were clearly out of their depth – that made three of us!

Meanwhile planning conferences between the Malaysians and the British rumbled on in such a bad-tempered atmosphere that the Malaysians were forbidden to have lunch with us in the mess. The head of the delegation was a Colonel Lai, personally chosen by General Templer in the 1950s as being outstanding, a future Malayan 'Superman'. On one visit he and I went away into the jungle, and he asked whether I had liked the idea of serving in the CJWC. Atypically, I replied that had he been the commandant, indeed I would have welcomed it.

He said he was flattered as, in fact, he had been chosen to be just that but the decision had been changed as a Malay, not a Chinese, had to be seen in the job. However, he said the reason the Malaysian authorities had reneged on the original concept was because of me. Apparently they had no one in their army as knowledgeable or as diplomatic. Lai had been warned against me as being difficult, but deciding this was untrue, he now let me into the secret.

On 30 June 1971 I was promoted to substantive lieutenant colonel, having been paid as one for three years and eight months, and losing nearly six years' seniority. A brigadier from the Military Secretary's branch, responsible for such promotions, out on a visit from England, told me how the group selecting the candidates had applauded when my name was announced – they were not against me, the system was. I recalled what General Walker had told me in 1965: 'The army is too small an organisation to offer you, with your particular talents, a career over the rank of major.'

I had an interesting talk with the Malayan Director of Infantry, Lieutenant Colonel Raja Shah, who rang me to ask if he could come down to pick my brains. He claimed to have known me in Sarawak but although I knew he was wrong, as the place he mentioned was one of the very few I had never visited, I agreed to receive him. He was a son-in-law of the Sultan of Kelantan, a cousin of the Chief Armed Forces Staff and a brother-in-law of the Chief of the General Staff. For two and a half hours we sat and talked. I had never had such a frank conversation with a Malay officer. Apparently the training of their army was being revitalised to meet the new threat and the new policy of operations to be based on it would not be implemented until he, the director, had returned to Kuala Lumpur and informed his superiors that I agreed with it. Officially nothing would ever be mentioned but unofficially it was my 'school solution' they were after. I was strangely touched and deeply honoured. I was vindicated in my belief that guerrilla reinforcements were using our training facilities prior to being sent north to the seat of the main trouble.

Twice during the next month the *Straits Times* newspaper trumpeted a new idea purporting to come from a particular general as to how to finish off the communist terrorist rump. I had never thought that confirmation of what I had told Raja Shah would be in that form.

*   *   *

The last-ever course run for the Vietnamese almost ended in a fatality on the very last morning of the final exercise when one of the students went up to a Gurkha 'enemy' lying doggo feigning death and kicked him sharply and painfully in the teeth. The Gurkha went berserk. By the time I had sorted it out I felt drained, but the crisis had passed. The students, impressed by a calm ending and their first ever – and also, I suspected, their last ever – mess night, left us on a note of appreciation, if not of happiness, as the war was going very badly back home.

The next day I paid another visit to Thailand, if only to try to recruit a better type of student than we had been getting: a clerk from a Thai naval store and a military policeman from the military HQ in Bangkok were a waste of course vacancies. Apart from that, I learned that I was to go, with the defence attaché, Colonel Victor Smith, to inspect a Royal Thai Army training camp and report back with my findings to the Thai Chief of Staff.

I had already visited this camp in January 1969. We were welcomed by the Thais and their US counterparts, given a briefing and taken around part of the area, being shown a number of booby traps, an 'extraction-from-enemy-fire' demonstration and firing on two types of jungle range. The standard was high as those taking part were all NCOs of the school dressed as private soldiers and not trainee soldiers.

All such camps are built on the same lines: all ranks share facilities and join the self-service queue. Walls are plastered with 'pin-ups' and everything is very 'tinselly'. The US thought the Thais were useless, the Thais thought the US uncultured and brash, and each could read the other's thoughts; but as it was never mentioned, both sides lived in superficial harmony. The Thais are taught from birth not to offend other people's feelings. They are also very colour conscious and the fact that the commanding officer was black was an additional source of irritation.

On our way back to Bangkok we were involved in an accident. In all I saw ten accidents, including a couple of stiffs, during the first day and a half of my visit.

We went to Army HQ, were met by a major, escorted up to the top floor in a lift where we were met by a colonel, and taken into a large room where we awaited General Sariket, the Chief of Staff. In the middle of one wall was an altar with burning incense and a huge photograph of the King of Thailand set on an easel. Our side was arranged like a royal drawing room, divans with green cushions, chairs, tables and carpets. Very extravagant and very oriental. A woman captain came in and stood by the door, glass-plated with a green veil over it, waiting to admit the general. In he came, all four feet ten inches of him, and 'all there'. I had half an hour with him. He had heard all about me, knew I spoke Thai, and asked what I thought of the training. It was a difficult question to answer as I had seen so little of it but I did my best and he listened patiently, asking some pertinent questions.

I also told the general that although JWS as such was closing, HBMG was most keen to help friendly Asian countries, including Thailand, and was considering how 'in country' training could be arranged if and when invited by the Royal Thai government. This I knew as I had seen a signal to that effect but it was still confidential.

Back in JWS we were visited by Anglia Television to make a documentary. It took three weeks and I had to answer many questions throughout the shooting. I suggested it be called *The Lion's Last Lair* but that was turned down in favour of *The Jungle Warriors*. I was delighted to be given a copy of the result.

By September the British presence had diminished appreciably. I was urgently called down to Singapore where offices were less than half full and informed that, in a single day, three firm jobs had been offered me. One was by the Singaporeans to raise, train and command a unit of commandos; the second was an attaché post in an unspecified Asian country, of which I was advised to await details; and the third was in a new FCO post, based in Singapore, to be the official British Army adviser on jungle warfare in Thailand and South Vietnam, followed by long-term employment when that came to an end.

By then I was beginning to react to the frenetic pace of life over the past ten years. Saturation point had been reached and I was told that my eyes had lost their sparkle. I felt I could just last out my time. When I left JWS I had taken seven weeks leave in seven and a half years. I expected little thanks for seeing my present jobs through to the end but it was a matter of personal pride in standards set and standards maintained. Two causes of particular strain were the uncertainty of the future, both general and personal, and the intransigence of the Malays at the top, in Kuala Lumpur.

By late October the world as I had so long known it had come to an end. 'East of Suez' had held an allure for government policy makers and Treasury officials, although many soldiers mourned the passing of what had been the scene of one of the British Army's more remarkable triumphs. Far East Command held a disbandment parade at which I thanked the senior officers for all their help during the difficult times we had been through. The last time I visited the main offices I walked down the corridor where photographs of all top men of the command were hung, from Slim in 1945 to the last of them in 1971. I had served under them all. The Gurkha Para Company, for which I had clocked up 124 jumps, was disbanded. Just before the last Thai course finished, we were visited by the Commanding General of the Communist Suppression Operations Command. I was taken to one side and offered a job in the Royal Thai Army as a major general, to take charge of all jungle training. Have three weeks leave, then join us, I was told.

There were many farewell parties. One I felt was the accolade of success was when the Chinese cooks of the officers' mess took me out to a Chinese meal in the town. Never had I eaten better.

At the end of the month I was asked to go, as the only officer, to the sergeants' mess farewell party. It was held in a hotel in Johore Bahru and I was driven there in my staff car and told not to ask why I could not travel in my own vehicle. After a very good buffet, a magician performed, and the master of ceremonies – an ex-RAF officer –informed the guests that the JWS was about to do something special for someone very special.

The President of the mess committee then announced that I was the guest of honour and invited the RSM to speak. This he did briefly and, from behind me, a trolley was wheeled in. There, on a red cloth stood a silver-coloured model of one of our training areas, the Jungle Village, made by the REME sergeant out of lead from the stop butts on the ranges. The lead had been dug up and flown off by helicopter from Singapore to be fashioned without my knowledge. For the first time in years, I was without words. Eventually I made a short speech saying that, after more than three years working with dedicated British senior ranks, I was more than ever convinced that the warrant officers and sergeants were the backbone of the British Army, whatever we officers thought of ourselves! This was widely acclaimed, many photographs were taken and my sergeants gathered round to shake hands and say how they had enjoyed serving under me. After another midnight floor show I took my leave. Four senior warrant officers put me on a chair on an open palanquin and carried me to my car, through the lines of sergeants, their wives and hotel guests. Furthermore, bless them, they had arranged an escort of four lance-bearing, uniformed Gurkhas from the Para Company and produced two Gurkha pipers from the Singapore police who played Auld Lang Syne as the whole procession slow-marched out of the hotel, down the steps and across the grass to the staff car. I had a big lump in my throat and almost wept.

*   *   *

The end was not far off. We had one more visitor, even as we were packing up, Major General James Lunt, the Vice-Adjutant General. I was asked which of the four jobs dangling in front of me I would choose: attaché in an Asian country, battalion commander in Singapore, FCO adviser in Thailand and Vietnam, or major general in the Royal Thai Army. All had pros and cons, so I asked him to choose for me. His advice was that I should remain in my own army – which is what I did.

The day after the Jungle Warfare School, Far East Land Forces (FARELF), ceased to be operational I had a Special Order of the Day published:

JUNGLE WARFARE SCHOOL
FARELF

SPECIAL ORDER OF THE DAY
1 Nov 1971

From today, 1 November 1971, the Jungle Warfare School as we all knew it, is already history. For rising a quarter of a century the School, under two names and operating in two places, has trained men for war against communists and bandits in jungle terrain. Those of you who served to the end of this phase should glow with pride not so much at what happened before you were here, but more at what you have done to enhance the reputation of the School up to the very end, especially at a time when life has been unsettled, abrasive and demanding to a pitch not normally met with the Army of a Monarchy. The value of your efforts has spread to five continents, eighteen countries, influencing many hundreds of students and untold thousands of servicemen. The School, highly regarded by many Asian countries threatened by communism, as well as being a source of inspiration and a pattern to be copied by a significant number of Free World countries everywhere, has engendered benefits that go beyond military victory in the Malayan Emergency, the campaign in the Troodos hills of Cyprus, the Kenya Mau-Mau rebellion and the Borneo Confrontation. It has been a constant and visible example of the retention of those high standards that are the hall-mark of the true professional British Army, the envy of some less well endowed, and which we would have been unable to sustain without our Commonwealth instructors and our Gurkha Demonstration troops: all this during a period when change has never been quicker nor the old values more threatened. Despite gnawing and bedevilling uncertainties you have all, painstakingly, played your part in ensuring that the reputation of the Jungle Warfare School has stood supreme. Those who have remained until the bitter end have withstood the stresses in an admirable way, properly reflecting one definition of high morale, namely the willingness and ability to give of your best when the audience is of the smallest.

So I am proud of you all, in the field and in camp, soldiers and civilians alike, whom I thank humbly and sincerely for all that you, individually, have done to enable us, collectively, to achieve.

And finally a word for the future: the question marks still remain and many problems are as yet unidentified. But this I know with a deep and biding instinct, that the nucleus that remains will continue somehow, somewhere, sometime and, by being true to yourselves and your salt, will prevail as well as, if not better than, before.

Good luck to you all.

*   *   *

After transferring for a while to Singapore, the remnant of the Jungle Warfare School moved to Brunei as a far distant appendage of the School of Infantry in England.

I took leave and was then posted to Laos as Defence Attaché. It was a bitter irony that, having spent most of my military life fighting against and training others to fight against Communist Revolutionary Warfare, I should serve in a country where the communists were the winners and the royal forces the losers. I lent my JWS precis to the best general in the Royal Lao Army but we both decided it was, by now, thirty years too late!

Conclusion

Communist Revolutionary Warfare

In Malaya, as in Indo-China, unconventional and unsophisticated communist guerrillas were opposed by a conventional army, sophisticated, cumbersome and 'tail-heavy', and thus geared neither militarily nor mentally to fight a low-intensity war. It took much blood and treasure to react properly to guerrillas who lived off the land, had no front line and were politically motivated. There was no clear-cut distinction between soldier and civilian, military response and political dogma. Above all there was Belief in a Cause, with Fear as a Weapon. Those brought up on pamphlets and promotion prospects floundered against such chameleon, non-regimental characteristics.

Even though the ending of the Cold War has rendered obsolete the concept of low-intensity wars in tropical rain-forest terrain, 'variations on a theme', such as drug running, illegal immigration and sectarian feuding, suggest that there will always be situations when conventional armies will be used in small-scale operations.

As long as such armies have men who can fight and live below the level of normally accepted standards of soldier comfort, retain the old disciplines, absorb new skills and remain faithful to themselves, there should always be a successful counter to 'non-state' guerrillas. It is the very paucity of *matériel* and resources that induces the unconventional. One only has to see the state of the economy in the one victorious country that used unconventional means, Vietnam, to understand that, militarily, their victory was infinitely more hollow than they could ever have expected.

The British Army is, I believe, more flexible than its much larger American counterpart. Realistic training, adaptability, strict personal discipline, high morale and personal example all allow junior commanders to exercise more command in the jungle than on the hills of Hong Kong or the plains of Germany.

Nor must it be forgotten that Britain had another advantage over the USA in Vietnam; the former had held positions of power, legal, administrative and financial, before the fighting erupted. Their heirs, the Malay/si/ans, continued in the same mould; in Vietnam the Americans had no such built-in advantage. In other words, they did not have a strong enough political base for victory. No matter how well the armed forces performed, victory could never have been theirs.

Nor, for that very reason, could the British have had any positive effect on the final outcome in Vietnam. The war might have lasted longer, more of the opposing forces might have been killed and fewer 'own casualties' taken but the result would have been just the same.

In essence the unconventional and even the eccentric have a better chance than others to do well in Counter Revolutionary Warfare. Perhaps this was what Balbahadur was trying to tell me as he lay dying.

Index

Notes: 1. Place names are in italics. 2. Place names are also included for seats and departments of governments; e.g. British Government will be found under *United Kingdom* and a police headquarters from a town's name; the context will determine the reference. 3. Page numbers are given for people whose names do not appear when they are referred to by, for instance, rank. 4. A country's national is indicated by that country's name. 5. * indicates full initials not established at time of printing.